The Travel Writer's Handbook

THE TRAVEL WRITER'S HANDBOOK

Louise Purwin Zobel

Writer's Digest Books

Excerpt from "Storybook Prague" by Ronald Schiller, *Reader's Digest*, May 1976, copyright 1976 by *Reader's Digest*; excerpts from "When It's Still Fair Whaling" by Theodore Vogel, *Realities*, January 1979, copyright 1979 by Theodore Vogel; excerpt from "Recipe for Cooked Film" by George Zimbel, *Travel and Camera*, August 1969, copyright 1969 by *Travel & Leisure*; excerpts from "The City that Died to Live," by Donald and Louise Peattie, *Reader's Digest*, February 1954, copyright 1954 by *Reader's Digest*; excerpts from "Los Angeles," by Herbert Gold, *Geo*, Number One, copyright 1979 by *Geo*, were used with permission.

First paperback printing, 1984
Second printing, 1985

Library of Congress Cataloging in Publication Data
Zobel, Louise Purwin
 The travel writer's handbook.

 Includes index.
 1. Travel—Authorship. I. Title.
G151.Z62   808'.025   79-27428
ISBN 0-89879-140-5

Design by Barron Krody

Frontispiece: *Sunset at Tumon Bay, Guam*

To Jerry

Acknowledgments

No venture ever succeeds alone, but is always reinforced and strengthened by the contributions of many people. I have been especially fortunate in the planning and writing of this book to find so many helpful allies who have enriched it, and in this modest way I wish to thank them.

I want to express my sincere appreciation to:

Carol Cartaino, as well as Howard Wells, John Brady, Barbara O'Brien, and others of the publishing staff, for their editorial direction and encouragement.

Dr. William Rivers, Professor Lyle Nelson, Professor Emeritus Clifford Weigle, and many other faculty members of the Stanford University Communication Department, who have contributed through their generous permission to quote from their works, as well as their generous sharing of wisdom and knowledge.

Dr. Richard Henning, Darlene Culbertson, and other Community Services staff members at Foothill College, Los Altos Hills, California; and Vicky Katz-O'Brien, Julie Nixon, and the Short Course staff members at De Anza College, Cupertino, California, for their assistance in arranging the travel writing classes and travel lectures that led to the nucleus of this book; and to Dr. Dennis Brown and faculty colleagues at San Jose State University, who provided new insights.

My many students, whose successes have proved the value of these ideas, and whose ongoing quest for learning keeps me searching for better and better answers.

The Scribblers, a group of professional writers with whom I have met for many years, whose criticism and advice have contributed greatly to my growth and development as a writer.

The referenece librarians, too numerous to name, at Palo Alto's main library and the Stanford University libraries, whose answers to my questions and assistance in tracing elusive details have always proved invaluable.

The Palo Alto branch of the American Association of University Women, as well as the California Writers' Club and the National League of American Pen Women, whose members have lent special professional support.

Humorist Art Buchwald and editors Jim Shaw and Thomas Lucey of *Off Duty*, Lilian Fine of *Medical Economics*, Ted Bredt of *California Today*, and Travel Editors Jerry Hulse of the *Los Angeles Times*, and his assistant Bill Peeples, Al Stahl of the *San Jose Mercury News*, Georgia Hesse of the *San Francisco Examiner*, and Carolyn Snyder of the *Peninsula Times-Tribune*, whose astute assistance and gracious permission to quote have provided enrichment.

The many people named in the body of the book, who are allowing me to share their ideas and experiences with my readers. The many friends, relatives, and colleagues who have contributed in so many ways, as well as all the people whose typing and filing skills have provided behind-the-scenes assistance. It would be impossible to name them all; but I believe they all know the sincerity of my gratitude. I do want to say a special word of thanks to Gerard Wagstaffe, for all his help and encouragement, to John Endres for the information he supplied, and to Newton Zobel, whose tireless efforts so often made the journey a joy.

And far from least, I'm grateful to my children, Lenore Zobel Harris, Jan Zobel, Robert Zobel, and Audrey Zobel Dollinger, my erstwhile traveling companions, whose stimulating company enhanced the trips, and to my other children, Thomas Harris, Todd Dollinger, and Karen Zobel, all of whom provide new insights and inspiration.

Finally and most especially, I want to thank my husband, Dr. Jerome Zobel, for his many contributions, his encouragement, and his support.

Louise Purwin Zobel
March 1980

Contents

Introduction   1

Part One

1. What Is a Travel Writer and Why Be One? 5
You can go anyplace, at any time/It's more like play than work/Learning new customs and new concepts/Asking questions/Finding yourself/You'll never be lonely or bored/Delving deeply, observing carefully, focusing clearly/Fringe benefits/You use all your senses, and everything you've known and felt, thought, and experienced/ Many kinds of travel writers, full time and part time/What qualities do you need?/ Finding the plus value/The patina of excellence/There is a market out there/Paving the way for future travelers/A great responsibility/Research you didn't know was research/Travel industry growing every day/Leisure time's expanding/Technology improving/What's down home to you is glamorous to others/Celebrate the differences/Learn about lifestyles/Inform, entertain, and motivate your readers/Your attitude is important.

2. Learn All You Can Before You Leave   13
Research is a subtle skill/It helps you decide where to travel/It saves time/It makes you familiar with sights and ready to write/Use the iceberg theory/Research becomes easier the more you do/Live research and library research/Much of it is informal/Talk to everybody/Attend

classes and lectures/Do your library work first/Books on writing and photography/Guidebooks/Specialty publications/Coffee table books/ Classic favorites/Touring maps and brochures/Periodicals/Government publications/Miscellaneous freebies/How do you find these sources?/How do you evaluate them?

3. Your First Trip Is to the Library   33
"Being there" is never enough/Investigate the opinions of others to supplement your own/Make friends with the reference librarian/Find the vertical file/Check interlibrary loan/How to find what you need/ City directories and phone books/Special books for special people/ Special books for special projects/Special libraries for special needs/ Making readers' guides work for you/You may find more than you expect/Easy ways to look it up.

4. Study the Marketplace Before You Start   43
Professionals talk about marketing/Where will you send it first? Where will you send it next?/No such thing as "writing generally"/The marketing manuals/What does the reader want?/How to get sample copies/ "Old boys"/Your target markets/Plan your article's itinerary/A trick to cure rejection blues/What do you want the most—money, prestige, or livelihood?/Plan your markets when you plan your trip/Study the ads in your target publication/Your market determines how you'll write it/ Payment on acceptance vs. on publication/Take a mythical trip/Find hundreds of "customers" for your stories/Consider every section in the marketing manual—from "Alternatives" to "Women's"/Use every facet—from your dog's kennel to your mother-in-law's health/Look for the special angle/Who is your potential buyer?

5. Getting Ready to Go   63
Do your homework carefully/Even the experts make mistakes/Your choices as a traveler/The sights you see and how you see them/Why are you traveling?/Why are your readers traveling?/Who are you?/ What do you really like to do?/Must you see the "musts"?/There's something for everybody/Don't choose the offbeat if you can't take discomfort/Sometimes "expensive" is a bargain/When you need a guide/What sight-seeing insights will you find on-scene?/Follow your special interests/Find friends through group membership/Know before you go/How to get a discount/Who do you need to talk to?/Set the wheels in motion early/Avoid holidays or embrace them/Research the possibilities/Consider the seasons, the months, the weeks/What day is the sabbath?/Submit your references/An audience with the Pope?/ Use your telephone internationally/How will you get your mail?/ Preplanned postcards/Travel documents/Identifying yourself/Find out the clothing customs/Blend into the local environment/Try out everything at home first/Will you have to pay duty?/Arranging money

matters/Can you learn the language?/Get in shape/Plan for comfort and pleasure/But be prepared.

6. What to Take Along with You 85

Put half of it back!/The four tools every travel writer *must* take/ Special writers have special needs/Don't forget assignment sheets, address list, travel documents, reminders of home, writing surface, alarm clock, flashlight, magnifying glass, batteries, glasses, Swiss army knife/Your "yellow card," photocopies of vital information, extra photos, currency converter, phrase book, extra supplies/Do you need a typewriter?/Avoid paying overweight/Luggage: how many and how big?/Use your pockets/Send stuff home/Let wheels save your back/ Register your valuables/Check the regulations.

7. What to Look for While You're Traveling 97

Looking for specific information/Do you have an open mind?/The travel writer never relaxes/Always searching for a story/Sometimes you recognize the plus value, sometimes you create the plus value/ Search for the special angle/But don't neglect the ordinary/Stay alert/ Additional stories/What "falls between the cracks" is best/Take an orientation tour/Ask questions/Use public transportation/Ride on the water/Take exotic conveyances/Shoe leather is best/See the sites at different times/Find the universal/Discover how the people live/Eat where they eat/Play where they play/Seek out old-timers/Visit the food markets/Explore the department stores/Who's at the laundromat? the beauty shop?/Shopping's not frivolous—you learn about lifestyles/Join the congregation/Observe the audience/How to count the house/Welcome chance meetings/Get lost/Person-to-person encounters/Buying food on the ferryboat/Wear a hat, win a trip/Ask the concierge/Buy the local paper, visit the bookstore and the library/ Depend on the kindness of strangers/You're on your own when it comes to alcohol/Take advantage of your presence on-scene.

8. Put Yourself in Your Readers' Place 111

You're the advance man/Let them in on the secret/Get the details/ Sample the unusual/Warn against the bad/Praise the good with caution/Can you write an exposé?/Be sure you're right, then go ahead/ Never use your typewriter to "get even"/Consider the circumstances/ Write amusingly/Investigate thoroughly/To "mention"—yes or no?/ You won't recall it if you don't record it/If you know the details you can write the rest/Organize your field notes/Remember your reader/ Update your facts/Be specific/What goes in a sidebar?/How to send it home/Sampling different travel styles.

9. Wrap It Up When You Return 121

Staging the many-pronged assault/Gather all you'll need on-scene/But if you didn't, you can still write the story/How to become an expert on the New Zealand sheep dog/How to become an expert on Chinese opera/You need everything and everybody/Find the expert/Use your files/Use your phone/Sometimes people tell you more than they mean to/How to update your files/How to compile your notes/How to judge your information/Your reader is quick to point out errors—even if they aren't errors/Asking questions by mail/Interviews by cassette/Eliciting anecdotes/Don't frighten the subject/Ask for information for the future.

10. Getting Ready to Sell   133

Sell the editor the unexpected/Assembly-line your market research/Forty ideas at a time/Reread the marketing information/Select target markets/Mileage: selling it more than once/One-time rights/Reprints, syndication/Mileage from negative editorial decisions/Plans for many markets/Change the emphasis; change the slant/Use the overflow/Mileage from spinoffs/Changing and updating years hence/Other ways to use your travel background/The "back of the book": a good market/Other marketing possibilities; newsletters, hotel reports/Trip sharing, contests/*Guest Informant*/Special publications/Stay-at-home travel writing.

Part Two

11. Sell Your Story Before You Write It   151

Be sure somebody's interested before you start your story/Querying saves time, postage/A query lets you shape according to editor's preferences/Sometimes an editor suggests something you hadn't thought of/It makes a reservation for your story/Give you a chance to get organized/Do you want to write that story, after all?/State your idea and qualifications briefly/Make your showcase sparkle/Summarize, or startle/This is no time for modesty/Don't talk yourself out of the assignment/Defend your originality/Explain the controversial/Send photos with the query/Don't promise *too* much more than you can deliver/But reach beyond your best.

12. Make Your Query Work for You   163

Address your query to somebody on the staff/How well do you know your editor?/One-sentence queries/Some publications say "Send the entire article"/Hurry if it's hot news/Research your subject enough to sound sensible/The editor is afraid to trust you—convince him that he can/Don't research *too* much/Think far ahead/When to query by phone/Should you send one idea or many?/Tying the disparate together/You can even sell the postscript/Using the checklist/Will word processing help?/Quick query forms/Can you make it look like a press release?/There are outlines and there are outlines/How to eclipse a good idea/Set yourself up for success/What kind of reply will your query elicit?/Save the rejections for the IRS/Learn to read between the lines/Turn rejection into acceptance/Who knows better—you or the editor?/How long dare you dally?/Send progress reports/Let the editor help you shape the story/What do your statistics look like?/What do they mean? How can you improve them?/On speculation or on assignment/Don't take no for a *final* answer.

13. Writing for Others to Read 181

What is talent?/Can you learn to write?/Your reader is asking a question/*Slant* is not a dirty word/What is your message?/Change the length of your piece by changing the capsule sentence/Select the identity from which you'll be telling the story/Maintain a consistent viewpoint/Hone your hook/Entice the reader—and the editor/Contrast and conflict are crucial/Don't begin at the beginning: begin at the *mattering moment*/Create a plot from facts/Emphasis and order do the job/Flash back and flash forward/Learn from the fiction writer/Show, don't tell/Expect to rewrite/Cutting is usually improving/Read aloud for new insights/A transition is a road sign/Leave the reader thinking/Avoid crashing conclusions/Titles to titillate/Play fair with your reader.

14. Asking Questions—The Interview 197

Finding the person who has the information/Interview for statistics and for anecdotes/Know your objectives/Keep your focus in mind/How to arrange an interview/Homework helps/Phrase your questions carefully/To tape or not to tape?/Avoid yes and no answers/Keep subject on the track/If the editor suggests the questions/Take notes without looking/Transcribe the same day/Don't violate confidence/Warming up the subject/Ask for layman's language/Recognize the value of silence/Give a wrong quote to get a right one/Where to put the hard questions?/Guidelines for "off the record" and "not for attribution"/Refining quotes/Avoiding libel/Never submit for approval—only for accuracy/Always send a thank-you/Telephone tactics/Interviewing many people for one story/Treating an important tool with care.

15. Bring Back Your Story in Pictures 209

You can get lost, soaked, shaken up, or arrested while absorbed in taking a picture/Photos are important/Illustrations help sell the story/Shoot the planned and the unplanned/Look for themes/Film is cheap, so shoot a lot/Seek variety/Try for the timeless/Use signs to enhance, not to detract/How will your picture be used?/The picture story/The sequence/The juxtaposition/The stopper/The drop-in/Can you make it look real?/Composing in the viewfinder/Framing your subject/Try silhouettes/Let the action carry the story/Playing tick-tack-toe in the viewfinder/Learn to shoot on the move/When you need an expert/Can you picture the people?/Watch for what the signs say/Pay subjects for posing if you have to/Do you need a model release?/What the release may say/Are you invading privacy?/Use your head before you take your picture/Protect your rights before it's published/Necessary equipment/Be sure a bargain is a bargain/Care for your equipment/ "Available light" and how to use it/Never forget your notebook/The low-profile camera bag/Black and white or color?/How to have it processed/A recipe for "cooked film"/Can you transcend the weather?/Special precautions/Selling your photographs/Showcases and contests/How to send photos/Don't tell the editor too much or too little/What goes in the captions?/Get the 5 Ws/Hope for the nonphotographer: sources of free and inexpensive photographs/Other ways to obtain pictures.

16. Freebies and Tax Deductions— Yes or No?   235

Is it free?/Is it deductible?/It all depends/Hospitality may come your way, but—will you be obligated?/Your responsibility to your readers/ Press junkets provide fun and freedom/Honesty means telling the bad as well as the good/The advantages of being invited *after* the story runs/Travel-related jobs/Hospitality that's a waste of time/"There's no such thing as a free lunch"/Enjoy behind-the-scenes hospitality/ Responsibility to the attraction/Don't let yourself be used/Freebies can be wonderful/Find a tax expert/Keep the receipts for expenses/ Keep an expenditure diary/Hard-to-answer questions/What can you take off?;Is it "directly related"?/Is writing your business or your hobby?/Can you show a loss?/Enjoying fringe benefits.

17. Around the World or Around the Corner: Your Role as a Travel Writer   245

Travel writers as inspiration for "creative use of leisure"/Will your readers follow your advice?/It's gratifying/It's frightening/What does the traveling public want to read?/People are interested in people/ Accurate facts and detailed advice will win you readers/Prepare in advance/What does your reader want to know?/Read for plus value/ Anticipate constant change/Travel writer needs self-discipline/The enticements are many, but so are the hurdles/Become a pro, or at least think like a pro/The real journey is within/Opportunity abounds/Not a profession for the thin-skinned/You can learn to be a travel writer/ Compare yourself to yourself/Have faith in yourself/Stretch to the best that's in you/You can do it.

Appendix—The Twelve Most Popular Article Patterns   251

Index   271

Photo Credits   274

Introduction

Some of you reading this book may already be travel writers, hoping to discover useful tips and shortcuts. You will discover them. Some of you are probably successful writers in other fields, yearning to move in a different direction, trying to find the tools that will help you. You will find them. Doubtless some of you are writing-relatives—English teachers, advertising copywriters, newsletter editors, and others who feel you can become successful travel writers when you learn how to move in the right direction. You will learn how. Certainly some of you are travelers, writers of exciting letters, tellers of inviting tales. You want to professionalize your product. You can do it. And some of you, with no background at all in writing or traveling, are reading this book because you think it sounds like fun to be a travel writer. It is.

This book is for each of you. While not a book on basic writing techniques (it assumes you already know how to write grammatical English sentences, and that what you don't know about punctuation, you'll look up), it does offer helpful approaches to organizing and writing travel articles. It explains the importance of market research and subject research before, during, and after your travels. It tells you how to write the most popular types of travel articles and gives you an in-depth look at the business of being a travel writer, including such diverse subjects as how to use the query as a sales tool, where to obtain illustrations and what to take off your income tax.

While not exactly a book on travel, either (it assumes a basic familiarity with traveling, whether around the corner or around the world), the advice you will find here on preparing for the trip, as well as profiting from it, should prove helpful to any traveler.

Street of the Knights, Rhodes, Greece

I have taught writing to college and university students of all ages, as well as to cruise ship passengers. I have participated in many writers' conferences and published in many kinds of periodicals. I've traveled from the Cape of Good Hope and the Straits of Magellan to the midnight sun and the Inland Sea, crisscrossing the equator and the international date line too many times to count. Much of my travel has been by plane, train, bus, streetcar, automobile, ship, subway, gondola, launch, taxicab, rowboat, cable car, and safari bus; much of it has been by shoe leather. I have enjoyed sharing my travels with my readers, and I hope you will enjoy sharing your travels with your readers. That is what this book is about—writing good travel copy that other people will want to read. Though writing of itself should please and satisfy the writer, and may even have some therapeutic value, here we are talking about writing as a public profession—writing about your travel experiences for the enjoyment and edification of your readers. Professionalism leads to pleasure *and* profit for the travel writer.

But being a member of the travel writing profession involves a tremendous responsibility—the writer's responsibility to the reader. Later travelers see what you have seen, not only in the setting of your words, but also within the framework of the emotional responses you transfer. The need for truth and accuracy in both hard facts and intangibles can never be emphasized enough.

While successful travel writers never forget the importance of accurate detail, they also know that even more important is how the writer—and the reader—feel about that detail. For no matter how literal your piece may be—counting the miles to every turnoff and the dollars for every dinner—in travel writing, as in most kinds of writing, it is the people and the emotions that count. Otherwise your reader might as well look up "Paris" in the encyclopedia.

Emotions are awakened by the travel itself; and the desire to write is stimulated by new faces and new places. Travel and writing complement each other, and the travel writer finds that thinking about the reader and trying to increase the reader's enjoyment enhances his own excitement in an adventure.

The travel writer's success is determined by how precisely he defines his audience. All good writers know that the reader is not only a partner in the writing, but is the ultimate boss. The travel writer has to *care* about the reader enough to break through the barrier of paper and ink to the magic of shared feeling.

PART ONE

1

What Is a Travel Writer and Why Be One?

 ars skidded on the damp street and pedestrians huddled in their overcoats as I scooted into the drugstore. I grabbed some Coppertone and a swim cap and thrust them at the clerk: "Please hurry. I'm catching a plane."

"Where to?" she asked.

"Hawaii. I have an assignment. . . ."

"Ha-wa-ii!" She fairly breathed the word. "Lucky you! Ha-wa-ii—instead of shivering here!"

"Well, I have this job. . . ."

"*Job!*" she gulped. "A job that takes you to Hawaii in February—you must have been a saint in a previous life!"

I don't know much about sainthood. But I do know that a travel writer's job can take you to Hawaii in February, to New Orleans in August, to India in time for the monsoon. If you like to write and you like to travel, if you're the kind of person who's continually captivated by new places, new ideas, new faces, you may find that this job sometimes seems less like work than play. But it's always more work than it seems.

Depending on how you look at it, the travel writer never takes a vacation—or lives in the vacuum of perpetual vacation. The hours are flexible, so you end up working most of them. I was amused by a letter from a program chairman thanking me for accepting a Saturday speaking engagement. "Such a nice day for relaxing," she wrote. "Appreciate your giving up your Saturday for this talk." To me, Saturday is a working day. So is Sunday. So is every day, 365 or 366 days a year. The travel writer's job is ongoing and demanding. It's also intriguing and rewarding.

Small Japanese girl dressed for ceremony

Anybody can be a Tourist. A Travel Writer needs instinct, insight, imagination, and enthusiasm. As a travel writer, you not only see and hear, you investigate and interpret and try to understand. You meet people of different colors and different backgrounds. You learn new customs, embrace new thoughts, absorb new knowledge.

Not satisfied only to ask *what*, the travel writer wants to know *who* and *how* and, more important, *why*. He or she recreates the travel experience, lending it relevance and perspective. In his desire to enhance his reader's enjoyment, he draws on his own spirit of adventure, rousing senses that tend to lie dormant and discovering that, as Herman Hesse says, "The true profession of man is finding his way to himself."

New places and new faces stimulate perception, encouraging you to delve more deeply, observe more carefully, and focus more clearly.

As a travel writer, you will never be lonely, never be bored, as you share with your readers the people and places, adventures and activities of your trips.

You'll find yourself behind the scenes in search of stories, and you'll come across areas and information the average person has no access to. Tell people you're a travel writer, and nothing's too much trouble for them to show you or take you to. Again and again, you'll be led to a front seat instead of a back one; picked up and chauffeured by someone assigned to show you around; or provided with a meal, a briefing, and a ticket to an event you didn't even know existed. It's always more fun to be on the inside looking out.

While travel writing, of itself, is not a notably lucrative field—not in the same ballpark as, say, ditchdigging or garbage collecting—its fringe benefits are irresistible. As we'll see later in this book, the travel writer can sometimes accept exotic hospitality, sometimes deduct expenses from his income tax, and often arrange lecture engagements and other related professional activities. You'll know the gratification of seeing your name in print, and your byline may lead to professional advancement in other fields. You'll appreciate comments of friends and colleagues; enjoy letters and phone calls from strangers.

For many of us, a special advantage of being a travel writer is the feeling of doing meaningful work, even on vacation. Raised in the puritan ethic of "keep busy," we sometimes feel uncomfortable in a state of complete relaxation for more than a few days. It seems as though we *should be* learning, absorbing, listening, taking notes, becoming expert. Being a travel writer gives you a legitimate motive for listening and learning. You know that later you'll use this information in some meaningful manner.

One prolific writer replies to questions about how long it took him to write this article or that book with, "How long did it take me? All my life." He goes on to explain, "Everything I've ever been or done or thought or known or experienced somehow went into the writing of this particular piece. I couldn't have written it exactly this way a year ago, and if I were to write it a year from now, it would be still different." The most successful travel writers use everything they've ever been and done, thought and known and experienced, as their jumping-off point.

Many Kinds of Travel Writers

The term "travel writer" encompasses newspaper and magazine travel editors, staff writers, columnists, and freelancers, as well as public relations and advertising practitioners, writers of radio and television scripts, art reviewers, compilers of cookbooks, producers of armchair travel books and audiovisual materials, and photographers who write on the side. It includes, also, the guidebook writers, whether nuts and bolts or literary and mystical, and writers who need an exotic background for other work—anything from juvenile stories and whodunits to historical novels and musical comedies.

This book will speak to all types of travel writers, but will focus on the free lancer who provides travel material for newspapers and magazines.

For some of you, travel writing will be a full-time occupation, for others a part-time profession. Some of you part-timers may also write other types of material, and much of the information in this book applies, of course, to other types of writing as well.

If you can't be a full-time freelance travel writer, is it better to work at a writing-related job, so you're primed to sit down at your home typewriter, or to work at a task completely unrelated to writing, so all your creative energy is hoarded for your freelancing? That debate probably goes back to Caesar and Cicero, and has no "right" resolution.

Because readers vary—in their needs and desires, age and financial position, level of education and travel experience, temperament and lifestyle—a varied group of travel writers will succeed with them. It's hard to draw a profile of the successful travel writer, but there are certain qualities every travel writer needs.

In addition to instinct, that spontaneous impulse that moves you to the right place at the right time, and insight, that quality of discernment that apprehends the inner nature of things, the travel writer also needs imagination, the creative ability to visualize something not currently present. Add to this great quantities of enthusiasm, the force that propels the writer forward and carries the reader along.

A travel writer should also cultivate the characteristic of curiosity (nosiness, if you wish), the readiness to observe, to eavesdrop, to look figuratively through the keyhole, always wondering what's waiting around the bend in the road. You have to be active, eager to see new places, and alert to simple pleasures.

You need to be energetic and willing to work hard, and you need to be healthy, as well as a good sport, ready to accept inconvenience. You should be a good listener, sensitive and perceptive, good at drawing people out, and interested in and knowledgeable about a variety of matters. If you know another language, that's super, but even if you don't, you should learn the basic words and mores of your target area. You have to be good at understanding unfamiliar accents and prepared to make conversation through pantomime, crudely drawn pictures, and fingers pointing to words in the dictionary.

To be a travel writer you need faith in yourself and in your opinions. You won't be the passive tourist who eats at the name restaurant because "everybody goes there." You'll seek out your own adventures and feel confident that what you have to say about them will prove valuable to others. One of my favorite cartoons shows a couple standing on the rim of the Grand Canyon, with the wife saying to the husband, "This can't be so very attractive. We're the only ones here." No travel writer ever says that.

You must be observant, conscious of small details, accurate in recording them, and prepared to undertake any amount of work to verify existing particulars or to uncover new ones.

Because both traveling and writing are things everybody would do "if I ever found the time," the travel writer must make the time. If you want to be successful you must learn to use your "thinking time" to best advantage, so that your writing time is used for writing. Thinking about what you'll write while you're standing in line, stopped at the signal, or waiting in the departure lounge means your time at the typewriter will be spent writing. You need self-discipline and the conviction that waiting for ideal working conditions will never put a word on paper.

You also need to be an aggressive salesman, knowledgeable about markets, confident of your own abilities, and aware that a manuscript in the desk drawer has no chance of selling.

You Need "Plus Value" for Success

To make your work salable in today's competitive world, the most important characteristic you need is "plus value," that special something that makes your piece better than the next fellow's. It exists, but it's hard to define. Yet all successful manuscripts have it.

Plus value, that patina of excellence that triggers a positive response in the editor and, later, the reader, may result from any of several advantages: a universality that communicates clearly; a strong connection with a topic of current interest; a personal background that lends depth to the experience; a theme so true we can't fail to recognize it; a conviction so firm it's only logical to listen; research so extensive it's impossible to discredit; information so relevant we can't ignore it; or writing so polished that reading is effortless.

Of all the characteristics a travel writer should have, this is the most essential. To be a successful travel writer today you must produce stories of higher quality than the editor specifies or than the reader anticipates. You need plus value.

When I speak of "success" I'm equating it with publication, preferably publication with pay. While you never want to be caught in the trap of writing only for money, money is the yardstick of professionalism. When somebody's willing to pay for what you write, you have, in a sense, succeeded.

On the other hand, the principles of effective travel writing applied to the standard trip postcard or Christmas newsletter can only improve them. What the traditional "Having a wonderful time—wish you were here" is really saying is, "*I'm* having a wonderful time. Don't *you* wish you were here? I'll bet you're jealous. I sure hope so." Whether it's a postcard or a bestseller, the writer's concern for the reader is the difference between failure and success. When you write on your postcard:

> I thought of you when the outboard refused to catch this morning—how many balky outboards have we coped with! I can hardly wait for you to see this place—you'll love the sandy beach and the gentle waves and the fishing—well, I'll tell you all about it when we get home. . . .

your reader's jealousy is mitigated by the fact that you wrote to *him*, specifically and concernedly.

This creative relationship to the reader, this feeling of kinship with him, should always predominate in the travel writer's mind.

I used to wonder about that reader. With so many people on wheels, waves, and wings these days, could there possibly be enough stay-at-homes to provide a reading audience for all the travel material being published? And when I came across a slim booklet, "The Moon on $5 a Day," I began to think of the time when earthbound travel writing would be obsolete. But since then I have sold, and my students have sold, so many travel pieces that I *know* there is a market for the travel writer.

Do You Know Your Reader?

Do you know your reader and what interests him? You should.

There is no such thing as writing "generally." Good travel writing is always addressed to a specific reader, and it's essential to visualize that reader. Market research tells us who our reader is; the travel writer tries to anticipate and answer his questions. For some articles and some destinations the questions may be: What is it like to take that trip? Where are the best places to stay, eat, shop? What sights should I see? What time of year is best? What shall I wear? How much will it cost? Under other circumstances, they may be: What kind of people live there? What are they like? How can I meet them? What and where are the flora and fauna? How can I see it? For still other pieces, the reader's questions might be: How can I get there? What special training do I need? How long should I stay? And in some cases some readers may be saying to some writers, "Just tell me about your trip."

Whether your reader is an active or an armchair traveler, whether he's planning a similar trip or reminiscing about one he's taken, or simply enjoying a vicarious view of the world, it's up to you, the writer, to give him the kind of story he wants. You bring to life reminiscence, and breathe possibility into planning. You pave the way for later travelers by telling them what it's like so they see it in the setting of your words, and within the framework of the emotional responses you have developed.

This saddles the writer with tremendous responsibility. Your opinion has great influence on others. A bad word from you, and the restaurant will lose customers. Recommend a delightful, out-of-the-way Paris hotel full of charming French customers, and a year later it's so full of American tourists there's no room for the French.

Whether you're going around the world or around the corner, you must take this responsibility seriously. You must know what you're saying and be sure you're telling it exactly like it is. You may be surprised at how much this book emphasizes research. But don't let it frighten you. Many activities you've never thought of as *research* are continually adding to your store of knowledge. Research, remember, is an exchange of ideas. Often it's done on the ski slopes or at the theater or at a sidewalk cafe. *Research!* Of course! So sit down and order some refreshment. Look around you. Listen. Ask questions. Take notes. Record how it feels, tastes, and smells. If you've already gone on the trip you plan to write about, and you didn't take all the steps this book advises, don't despair. You can still write a travel article. But it will be harder to develop the plus value without the preliminaries.

Your Reader Has Great Expectations

Today's readers expect a lot of plus value in a travel story, because they're sophisticated. They've probably traveled a good deal themselves, and, with late-twentieth-century communication systems, they're as familiar with an opera at the Baths of Caracalla as they are with a song in the shower. Travel is one of the most important facts of modern life. And today it's big business. Travel is now one of the largest industries in the United States, and seers predict that in twenty years it will become the major industry of the world.

As the gross world product multiplies and we find ourselves with more and more leisure, travel will take up the slack. At the same time, as scientific advances in travel technology uncover new energy sources, increase the speed and comfort of travel, and decrease its cost, the travel industry must grow.

Travel has a long history. Remains of caravansaries and entertainment centers that catered to visitors have been discovered at the most ancient archaeological sites. Over two thousand years ago the goddess Artemis/Diana lured pilgrims to her new temple at Ephesus, one of the ancient world's Seven Wonders. The goddess had a very efficient public relations organization, with branches on three continents. They used every inducement to encourage tourists to visit Ephesus, sign up for the temple sight-seeing tour, and take home a silver souvenir. (Some scholars think they probably offered charter rates on the express galleys, but so far no advertisements for this have been uncovered!)

Are people today interested in travel? A national magazine offering a free brochure on an upcoming festival had five thousand requests in the first twenty-four hours. Each travel article published finds new readers, thus building an ever-increasing audience for future travel articles, by that author or by others.

You don't have to travel to exotic places to be a travel writer. What's "down home" to you may be glamorously distant to others. It may not seem like *travel writing* when you tell about the haunted house that's a big attraction in your neighborhood, the new lodge at a nearby ski slope, or the local farmer's market. But that's what travel writing *is*— telling readers about something interesting beyond *their* own backyards.

If it's in *your* backyard, celebrate. If your own milieu is in the backwater, you can be first to tout its attractions. But even well-traveled areas can provide new angles of interpretation. How about inspiration from the homes of all the writers who've lived on Long Island? Backyard barbecues in Las Vegas? Touring California's wine country with a teetotaling relative?

Wherever you live, wherever you travel, there's a story somebody wants to read. Whether you go around the world or around the corner, when you discover the plus values of the travel experience, you'll be ready to share your pleasure with your readers.

Some people, of course, travel around the world but never leave home. They follow Michelin's advice for weeks, but don't find anything they like as well as Sally's Creamery at First and Main. The Black Forest isn't as pretty as Turner's Woods at home, Arlington Cemetery is only a larger version of their own church graveyard, and Saks Fifth Avenue doesn't have a thing better than the Emporium at Second and Elm does. Listen to them talk a minute and you're likely to hear somebody say, "We went around the world last year—but didn't like it."

The travel writer *celebrates* the differences in manners and customs. While he's interested in seeing temples and museums, he's more interested in learning lifestyles.

Travel should have an important purpose. It should result in meaningful experience. As Thoreau says, "It's not worthwhile to go around the world to count the cats in Zanzibar." The travel writer needs to be excited about his trips, so plan destinations and activities that intrigue you. Expand your horizons. Cultivate the urge to see, know, enjoy, so you can inform, entertain, and motivate your reader.

As a travel writer you'll find that your own attitude is intrinsic to the value of the trip. In the words of Emerson, "Though we travel the world over to find the beautiful, we must carry it with us or we find it not." Travel writing encourages deeper insights and a gratifying sense of belonging. While we welcome the travel experience, we realize that we have to take something to the experience as well as bring something away from it.

If you're already a vital, sparkling, worthwhile person, travel writing becomes you.

2
Learn All You Can Before You Leave

ravel research is a subtle skill. You *may* consciously say to yourself, "Today I'm going to the library and read up on Yellowstone," or "I'm going to call the Tollivers and ask about their trip to Yellowstone." But more likely you'll research Yellowstone when you run into Binky Tolliver at the drugstore, or pick up a consumer magazine that's running an in-depth issue on national parks.

Research is done in libraries, yes. It's also done in face-to-face interviews, on the telephone, and through the mail. Still more often it's done on the golf course, at parties, during coffee breaks, or while eavesdropping on the bus. Many informal encounters you never thought of as research turn out to be more help at parties, during eavesdropping on the bus. Many informal encounters you never thought of as research turn out to be more helpful than the fattest guidebook.

Research helps you decide where to travel in the first place. You may be wondering about that—how the travel writer decides on a destination. People often ask which comes first, the assignment or the desire to visit a particular place. Does an editor ever suggest you go to Blanketyville and do a story? The answer is, sometimes. Or, do you indulge a lifelong dream of seeing Blanketyville—and then decide to write about it later? Again, the answer is, sometimes. Most often, though, the impetus for exploring a particular place begins with the research that makes that place seem an attractive one to write about. And the research usually starts with an informal encounter or casual reading—things we'll be talking about in this chapter.

Research not only helps you decide where to go, it tells you how to

Fort Mackinac, Mackinac Island, Michigan

get there, where to stay, where to eat, what to see, what to do, what to buy, and what's likely to prove valuable to the travel writer. Pretrip research saves you time, because you're sure to see the things that most interest you, and you'll know what you're seeing when you arrive at your destination. You'll be familiar with the lifestyle you'll find; you'll be able to add to your store of knowledge without beginning at the beginning. You've probably already discovered some of the aspects you want to write about, and you're already thinking about a fresh approach to some of the others. Your theme and your angle are defined. With pretrip research you're in a good position to ask the right questions, and you're more likely to find yourself behind the scenes, where you want to be.

Samuel Johnson quotes an old Spanish proverb that says, "He who would bring home the wealth of the Indies must carry the wealth of the Indies with him." "So it is with travel," says Johnson. "A man must carry knowledge with him if he would bring knowledge home." The travel writer with preresearched knowledge will bring home the stories with plus value.

The successful travel writer subscribes to the iceberg theory—know ten times as much as you're telling. The part that's unseen, beneath the surface, gives you the voice of authority that makes your readers sit up and take notice. An information overload enables you to choose which materials to use, rather than simply using whatever you happen to have; and doing lots of research helps you to assimilate, understand, and enhance the parts you do use. When you produce a well-researched travel article, editors respect you. Readers respect you. You respect yourself.

Also, as we'll discover in Chapters 11 and 12, the travel writer has to do enough preliminary research to write a descriptive query letter.

Research always becomes easier the more you do of it. Some push-button mechanism in the brain starts sending out signals: "Yes, this goes with and enriches something I'm now beginning to understand," or "No, I already know all about that—I won't bother with this piece of research."

Subject research can be divided into *live* and *library*, and for most stories we're going to need both kinds. Actually, they're so intertwined it's hard to separate them. Your friend Jim tells you Pennsylvania is the most fascinating place he's ever seen. He shows you the pictures he took on his last vacation at the national recreation area in the Poconos. You ask questions and he answers them. That's live research. If he also brings over a book on Pennsylvania he wants you to read, and you read it, that's library research.

You then scan your own bookshelves and go to your public library to find materials to guide you in deciding which parts of Pennsylvania to see and how you'll get to your gateway city and what kind of transportation you'll use from there. Then you visit a travel agent and ask questions. Next you write to the Philadelphia Convention and Visitors Bureau, the National Park Service, the Gettysburg Travel Council, and the Pennsylvania Dutch Visitors Bureau. You study the brochures, booklets, and maps they send you. You write a letter to the Pennsylvania Bureau of Travel Development, asking specific questions. Then you call cousin Susie, who honeymooned in the Poconos and lived in Pittsburgh the first three years of her marriage.

You call the local reference librarian with a quick question, and go down to the automobile club to pick up the *Pennsylvania Camping Book*. You attend a film on "The Beautiful Keystone State." By now you've decided which facets of Pennsylvania are likely to have the most plus value for articles you will write. Back to the library you go for specific information on Valley Forge, the Amish Farm Home, the U.S.S. *Olympia* at Penn's Landing, and the Philadelphia Zoo.

You can see how pretrip research is a combination of writer and written word, and writer and other human beings.

Live research includes observation and interviews, both of which we'll discuss in more detail in Chapters 7 and 14. Less formal than interviews are encounters—your conversation with Jim and your visit to the travel agent, for instance. The encounter is less structured than the interview—often it's just the kind of casual give-and-take the travel writer needs. You absorb easily what the other person has to offer, using the information to fill up the chinks in your own knowledge. Somehow this comes through in your finished story, making you sound less didactic, because it isn't only you speaking to the reader—it's you along with your reference sources.

As soon as you've done enough preliminary research to ask sensible questions, talk to everybody you think can help you—airline representatives, steamship company representatives, government officials, other travel writers and editors, college students from far away, friends and friends of friends, and anybody else who has already been where you plan to go. Attend community college courses and illustrated lectures, as well as films about the area you plan to visit. Don't hesitate to ask questions.

Prepare yourself in advance, for instance, for visiting a town in a developing country. What will you look for? Does that country claim free, compulsory education? But will you see school-age children playing in the street during school hours? Do the houses have electricity? Plumbing? Privacy? What are the residents like? Do they have radios, books, mirrors, ice, newspapers? If you've done your homework you'll know what you're looking at and what it means.

If it's a ruin you'll be visiting, do enough homework to people it—with those who lived there; worked and played; made love, made war. Picture them relaxing in their atrium, fountains playing on a warm summer evening, or poring over their clay tablets as they discuss the inflationary spiral of household expenses. If you get to know the *people*, a ruin is more than a pile of old stones.

Travel agents are usually generous with information, but don't impose on them. When I gave a travel-related assignment to my class of university students, I soon discovered that every travel agent in the area was furious with me. It turned out that all my students, instead of using the university library to research the information I required, were calling local travel agents for quick and easy answers.

It's almost impossible to conduct live research until you've laid a foundation of library research. You have to know the right questions to ask—you have to already be familiar with the subject before composing a questionnaire or conducting an interview or even taking advantage of an encounter. So let's consider, in addition to informal live research, some of the less formal research you can conduct in your home library.

Again, some of your best sources will be those you really don't think of as research. Your home bookshelves doubtless already contain an up-to-date dictionary, a thesaurus of some sort—probably several—a style manual, Strunk and White's *The Elements of Style*, as well as a recent edition of *Writer's Market* or some other marketing manual. You probably subscribe to at least a Sunday newspaper and at least one travel-oriented periodical, like *National Geographic*, in addition to at least one writing-oriented periodical, like *Writer's Digest*.

What else does the travel writer need at home? That depends on how close you live to a public library, how good the library is, how often you go there, and how much it means to you to *own* the book or magazine and to be able to mark it up, cut it out, put it aside to read next week, or take it along on your trip. Don't forget to begin your *futures* files early—stockpiling information you may need at some future time. When you *do* get ready to visit the places described in your files, you'll find the clippings and bibliographic notes invaluable.

The Travel Writer's Home Library

A quick sampling of my own overstuffed travel shelves reveals a diversity of books, ranging from *The First London Catalogue* (interesting things to do in London) and *Get Everything Your Government Has to Give* (advice on freebies) to *Woodalls Campground Directory* and *Retirement in Spain*. Money is given its proper place with *The New Give* (advice on freebies) to *Woodall's Campground Directory* and *Retirement in Spain*. Money is given its proper place with *The New Attractions*. Quality is served by the *Warner Digest of Distinguished Resorts* and the *Directory of Unique Museums*, with its alluring descriptions of entire museums devoted to antique toys, watches and clocks, toy trains, candy, and Wedgwood china. Special interests are represented by *World Study and Travel for Teachers*, *Historic Ships Afloat*, *Celebrations in Asia and the Pacific*, *Temporary Military Lodging Around the World*, *Where to Go Boating in California*, and *The Traveling Woman's Guide to Beauty Salons*.

Other valuable additions to the travel writer's home library include:

Books on Writing and Photography

Although *this* book is, as far as I know, the first book ever written on *travel writing,* there are many excellent books that provide insights into nonfiction writing in general.

Rudolf Flesch, Henry Fowler, Jacques Barzun, and Theodore Bernstein stand ready to advise on the niceties of the writing process itself. Such books as Bartlett's *Familiar Quotations,* the *Home Book of Quotations,* or the *Oxford Dictionary of Quotations* belong on the travel writer's bookshelves. The *Oxford English Dictionary* (OED) contains nearly half a million words and two million quotations. The *American Thesaurus of Slang* and the *Acronyms and Initialisms Dictionary* help keep your language up to date, and *The Travellers' Dictionary of Quotation,* edited by Peter Yapp, is sometimes just what you need.

The wonderful three-volume *Traveler's Reading Guides* lead you to the most significant literature about a country—from newspaper articles to novels.

Do you have a question about usage, origins, pronunciation, shades of meaning, or new words? The G. & C. Merriam Company, publishers of *Webster's New Collegiate Dictionary,* will answer your question without charge. Write to:

Living Language Service
Merriam-Webster Dictionaries
Box 1424
Springfield MA 01101

and enclose a self-addressed stamped envelope (SASE).

Searching for nonsexist words and phrases? Write to:

McGraw-Hill Book Company
1221 Avenue of the Americas
New York NY 10020

They'll send you a copy of *Guidelines for Equal Treatment of the Sexes.*

Around the World with the Experts is a compendium of professional travel writing selected by professionals. Members of the Society of American Travel Writers produced this anthology of articles written by their members, and the would-be travel writer can study the stories with profit.

Since awareness of photographic techniques, sources, prices, and markets is part of the travel writer's essential knowledge, you'll want to read several books on photography.

Photographer's Market, published annually, not only gives advice on setting up a business, preparing a portfolio, and "How to Package and Mail Your Work," but also provides a comprehensive, up-to-date list of photography buyers. Buyers range from advertising agencies to audiovisual firms, and include consumer magazines, trade journals, and company publications. The listings tell you the name of the buyer, what each publication needs in the way of photographs, and what it will pay for them.

Petersen's *How-To Photographic Library* includes a helpful booklet on freelancing. Kodak produces many kinds of books and booklets. Its fourteen-volume *Encyclopedia of Practical Photography* covers everything from acetate filters and astrophotography to traffic accidents and photography in the tropics.

Other good books on technique include *Photography* by Barbara and John Upton, which has a lot of darkroom information, *Introduction to Photography* by Robert B. Rhode and Floyd H. McCall, and the *Art and Techniques of Journalistic Photography* by Otha C. Spencer.

Guidebooks

You'll surely want to read at least one guidebook on where you want to go—or several guidebooks while you're deciding what your destination will be. But consider the different types of guidebooks so you can make a sensible selection. You often can purchase guidebooks for less than half of their marked price at bookstores' end-of-the-year sales. You can buy used guidebooks for a few cents from Friends of the Library sales or rummage sales or thrift shops. If you're using a previous year's guidebook, be sure to update it from the public library's current copy. Restaurant and hotel information becomes obsolete quickly. And while sight-seeing information on Old Faithful or Pike's Peak doesn't change much with the years, still we all know that Niagara Falls was turned off for a while and that currently you can't enter the Parthenon or the stone circle at Stonehenge.

When buying guidebooks for your home library, select those most appropriate for your own writing. Just as you have in mind your reader as you research and write, so do guidebook writers visualize *their* readers. Ask yourself what kind of traveler your guidebook is written for—the shaggy teenager in blue jeans or the little old lady with blue hair?

Temple Fielding said he originally wrote his guides for the small-town real-estate agent or dentist who is afraid he'll be in a situation he can't control when he gets to Europe. If the small-town real-estate agent or dentist can stand Fielding's baroque prose, he'll be able to easily select a hotel and restaurant. Fielding emphasizes creature comforts—if you want culture, look elsewhere—and he's supercandid about these creature comforts. Brief tips inserted randomly tell the reader how to avoid unpleasantness and warn of "local rackets."

Kate Simon's *London, Places and Pleasures: An Uncommon Guidebook* emphasizes creature comforts, too. She describes in detail the restrooms of the London Tube and spends numerous chapters on hotels, theaters, pubs, restaurants, and shopping; but she completely ignores the British Museum's exhibits.

Baedeker, the doyen of guidebooks, on the other hand, devotes twenty-five pages of its *London* guide to the British Museum, while covering hotels and restaurants in a page or two. Even long-out-of-date

Baedekers are superior resources for finding out how things once were, and libraries keep them around for that purpose.

The *Blue Guides*, Hachette's *World Guides*, and Nagel's *Travel Guides* are nearly as detailed as Baedeker's and cover the same ground—a plethora of historical background and not much for the nightclub hopper.

Much less scholarly, and much more opinionated, are Robert S. Kane's *A to Z* books:

> Tangier is exciting for those to whom it is the first North African point of call. But . . . a few days there are quite sufficient—unless one's chief interests are bistros and beaches. . . .

Sydney Clark's *All the Best* books are equally personal, peppered with boyhood anecdotes, adult conclusions, and random historical notes. Instead of the entire book being revised, each of Clark's books is updated with five to ten pages of "revision supplements" at the end of each chapter, delineating the changes since the book was published.

More matter-of-fact, the gigantic (over seven hundred pages) *Texas: A Guide to the Lone Star State* covers the history, government, agriculture, folklore, and social life of the state. Then it describes the fifteen largest cities, giving brief information about the accommodations, airlines, and annual events. Then comes specific information about the history of the city and its points of interest. Another section gives detailed highway tours with interesting historical notes interspersed. Excellent maps and illustrations abound. Other state guides, while smaller, follow a similar plan, and are also published as part of the American Guide Series, originally compiled in the 1930s and 1940s by the Writers' Program of the WPA.

So far, all the guides we've spoken of, with the exception of Fielding's, are undated. They are revised at random intervals, as author, publisher, or readership demands. You have to look at the copyright date to tell when the book was published. Many dated guides do come out annually; but because of research and writing time and the traditional autumn publication, much of their material is two years old by the time we're ready to use it. So update guidebook information yourself whenever you can.

Four of the best-known dated annual guidebook series are Fodor, Waldo, Fisher, and Frommer. Fodor publishes a one-volume *U.S.A. Guide*, as well as regional guides to the United States, area guides, foreign country guides, city guides, and such specialized books as *Cruises Everywhere* and *Railways of the World*. The format is a mixture of enrichment material for the entire area, followed by descriptions of the state, province or canton, and specific city, interspersed with "Facts at Your Fingertips" for the area and each of its subdivisions. "Historic Sights," "Seasonal Events," "What to See," "What to Do with the Children," and other helpful sections are accompanied by practical information on hotels, restaurants, and such.

Myra Waldo's guides have a similar format. Both Fodor and Waldo appeal to the middle-class traveler who wants to stay at a good, if not deluxe, hotel, and eat sometimes at a fancy restaurant, sometimes at the nearest coffee shop. This traveler will probably arrive by plane or car (rather than cruise ship or bicycle), and wants to see the major sights and be amused in the most typical fashion, but doesn't feel compulsive about examining every case in the museum.

Fisher's traveler is perhaps slightly more sophisticated, and finds the bright red marginal annotations a novel idea. Although the style is informal, the basics are all there, and the annotations are a plus.

Arthur Frommer, who has been advising his readers for over two decades on how to enjoy travel, first on five dollars a day, then five dollars and ten dollars, then ten dollars and fifteen dollars, and now mostly "Dollar Wise," visualizes a traveler young at heart, if not in years. His language is informal—"Before doing anything hop over to the helpful tourist office and pick up brochures."

Frommer's books are filled—indeed, they overflow—with readers' suggestions. But I have two objections to this system. First, as a traveler, since I know nothing about these readers, their tastes, their travel backgrounds and knowledge, I'm disinclined to follow their suggestions. I would rather hear from Frommer's experienced researchers, even though I realize they may miss some of the goodies that readers can fill in. Second, as a writer, I object to Frommer's form of payment for the published suggestions—a copy of the book that contains the suggestion. **As a travel writer, don't ever give away your good ideas this way.** If you discover some little-known facet of the travel experience, some plus value, blow it up into an article of your own and get paid for it—in **cash!**

Frommer emphasizes accommodations and meals, in addition to telling where to go and what to see. His books court the economy-minded crowd, but include suggestions for those who want to splurge occasionally. Although weakened by lack of indexing, Frommer's books do give a lot of information, such as where to find Dr. Scholl's or the nearest launderette. (His seventeen lines on the British Museum mention the Rosetta Stone, the Magna Carta, and the Elgin Marbles.)

Many guidebooks, while seemingly of interest only to a specific group of travelers, contain material of widespread value. *Saltzman's Eurail Guide (How to Travel Europe and All the World by Train)*, while addressed primarily to the train traveler, and overflowing with authoritative world-wide railroad information, also discusses jet lag, hotel reservations, and what to do if you lose your passport. Its country-by-country section includes maps and sight-seeing material, as well as plans for one-day train excursions and scenic rail trips.

Guidebooks compiled by Harian Publications, the list headed by *Retirement Paradises around the World, Europe at Low Cost, America by Car*, and *Around the World by Passenger-Carrying Freighters*, usually appeal to those with more time than money, but occasionally offer a good universal idea. As the number of traveling retirees grows, more and more guidebooks will be addressed to them; and you, as a writer, will become increasingly aware of senior citizens as a potential audience for travel material.

Let's Go: The Student Guide to Europe, on the other hand, is intended for the young and adventurous. Although some will be traveling by car, this book assumes many will be biking, walking, or hitchhiking. It gives the rundown on student accommodations, food, and sight-seeing. Its advice for England: "The drinking age is eighteen, but this isn't strictly enforced."

At the other end of the scale, the Michelin Guides, red for food and lodging, green for sightseeing, are intended for the knowledgeable and sophisticated motorist. Their red and black symbols of quality have long been a report card the traveler can trust. The Michelin has plenty of maps and city plans, and includes "plain but adequate" hotels and "good food at moderate prices," as well as more deluxe suggestions.

Within the United States, Mobil's regional *Travel Guides* and the AAA's individual state or regional *Tour Books* are geared to the driving traveler, often the driving traveler accompanied by children. The AAA's books are set up with a brief "what to see" in each city in the state, arranged alphabetically, then a chart and information on the recreational possibilities. About three-fourths of the book deals with specific accommodations and restaurants, again in alphabetical order by city. These digest-size books are distributed free to AAA members, as are maps, camping books, and special tour guides.

Mobil's oversize books also list the cities and areas within each state alphabetically, with a very brief "what to see and do" section and most space given over to food and lodging.

America on $8 to $16 a Night lists mostly chain restaurants and motels, with an occasional old inn or family-style diner that gives good value for the money. There are a couple of pages of shopping advice and a "Special Section for Students, Campers, and Super-Budget Travelers of All Ages."

Roadfood is supposed to be a guide to good, inexpensive regional restaurants. But its authors could find only eleven recommendable restaurants in the entire state of California, and most of those were places like Chris's Hot Dogs or Mac's Coffee Break, where the authors say they had a good breakfast but a "disappointing" lunch. A good idea, but the execution is limited. Perhaps some of you will come up with more comprehensive books of this type.

On a more positive note, guidebooks I heartily recommend are Robert Bone's *Maverick Guides* to Hawaii, to Australia and to New Zealand. They give an overall view, then history, airports, transportation, hotels, restaurants, sight-seeing, guided tours and cruises, water sports, other sports, shopping, nightlife, and an address list for each of the six principal islands. The book is well balanced in its presentation of history, sight-seeing, and everyday details.

This barely scratches the surface of available guidebooks. Whether you're a youth hosteler, a garden lover, a tombstone viewer, or a bird-watcher, you'll find a travel guide to help you do your thing. But before you invest in too many general guides, make sure they're the ones whose approach and orientation will really help you and the audience you write for.

Reference Works

At home I use a *World Book Encyclopedia*, purchased when our children were very young and updated annually. It explains most of the things I want to know clearly and reliably, if sparsely and simply. I also occasionally use the encyclopedia my parents bought when I was very young. But these are only preliminary reference sources, since I live three blocks from the main library and two miles from a university library. A more isolated travel writer might want to consider investing in a more comprehensive encyclopedia. However, don't ever hesitate to use a children's encyclopedia or other children's reference books to explain something you don't understand very well.

We'll discuss reference works at the library in Chapter 3. But two books I find indispensable at home are *Webster's New Geographical Dictionary* and *Webster's Biographical Dictionary*, both published by G. & C. Merriam, both thumb-indexed and packed with valuable information. *The Columbia Lippincott Gazetteer of the World* is good, too.

Other handy reference works for the home library are telephone books from areas you call frequently. Your telephone company will get them for you free if you ask. The library and the phone company have additional phone books for numbers you need only occasionally. The *Toll Free Digest* or one of the other directories of 800 numbers, as well as a zip code directory, are essential tools in today's world.

As the flood tide of printed material threatens to engulf us, it becomes increasingly important to know what information is where. Bless the magazines that provide annual or semiannual indexes. *National Geographic*, *Reader's Digest*, *Time*, and others will send them to you free. *Sunset* charges a dollar per index. *Writer's Digest*, *Road and Track*, and *Scientific American* publish their annual indexes in the year-end issue, as do many other periodicals. If there's a publication you find especially helpful, inquire about an index—perhaps they have one. A few years ago I treated myself to the cumulative *National Geographic Index 1947-1976*. This eliminates sixty semiannual indexes when I need a *Geographic* article, and has proved well worth its price.

You probably already own a current almanac. Librarians say nearly 90 percent of reference questions can be answered from an almanac, and I have found this the most important reference book to take along when working as a cruise enrichment lecturer. The *World Almanac and Book of Facts*, *Information Please Almanac*, *Official Associated Press Almanac*, *Reader's Digest Almanac*, and others are all produced annually, all arranged slightly differently, with different emphases. You might want to own more than one. Outside the United States, the *Europa Yearbook*, the *Canadian Almanac and Directory*, and *Whita-*

ker's *Almanac* (for Britain) serve the same function.

You can't be a travel writer without an atlas. True, boundaries and political entities change so fast you need to update your maps almost hourly, but a good basic atlas or two—or three or four—is essential for general geographic information. There's nothing like an atlas to help you decide where to go. If your travel writing specialty is literature, genealogy, history, or biblical scholarship, you'll find an atlas designed especially for your needs. Are you a treasure hunter? The *Atlas of Treasure Maps* shows three hundred locations of buried treasure in the Western Hemisphere, but no guarantee of a *find* comes with purchase of the atlas.

Specialty Publications

Depending on the kind of travel writing you're doing, you'll want to have the most helpful reference materials within arm's reach. A writer who concentrates on the historical aspects of travel needs a historical atlas. This would be supplemented by the *Classical Handbook*, a book on mythology, handbooks on art and architecture, and several standard volumes of world history. Other travel writers might find it more helpful to invest in guides to sports, camping, airplanes, ships, antiques, wild animals, psychology, music, stamps, botany, or the *New York Times International Cookbook*. I have a friend who's under contract for a book on ferryboats of the United States, and he was delighted when I told him about a book on ferryboats in my area. As we focus more sharply on special facets of traveling, we need more and more background material to digest.

Don't overlook those beautiful coffee-table books, from *Persian Miniatures* to *Islands of the Rising Sun*. Expensive, yes, but they give the background and flavor that make destination decisions easy. *Seven Centuries of Sea Travel: From the Crusaders to the Cruises*, for instance, shows the development of sea travel from the fourteenth to twentieth centuries. Its profuse illustrations begin with a scene from the story of Tristan in a fourteenth-century French manuscript, and continue with watercolor sketches of nineteenth-century cruiseship cabins, sectional plans of emigrant ships, paintings of paddlewheel steamers, and menus from the *Lusitania*. Illustrations of hovercraft, hydrofoils, car ferries, and modern cruise ships, with explanatory text, bring the reader's knowledge up to the present.

Ancient Egypt: Discovering Its Splendors tells, in words and illustrations, of the Nile, the Pyramids, the tombs, the ancient gods, as well as of the pleasures of life in Ancient Egypt and the invention of writing. *New Mexico: A Pictorial History* shows the state from the time of the conquistadors, with wars, revolts, banditos, ghost towns, Indians, and Billy the Kid. The Sierra Club's *On the Loose* is a medley of poetry and photography that explores human freedom and the great outdoors.

All these books, with their emphasis on the lasting and the memorable, provide special insights. I even know someone who's found a desperate need for a numbered copy of the limited edition of the *Pictorial Supplement to the Denver South Park and Pacific*. A railroad buff's treasure, it contains maps, timetables, and full-color paintings relating to this narrow-gauge mountain railway.

When it comes to travel artbooks, if you don't own UNESCO's excellent *Art Series* on countries from Norway to Ethiopia, with beautiful plates and numerous drawings and explanations, or some of the other outstanding art books, try to borrow them from your library. Also, in oversize paperback, Lane Publishing issues *Sunset Travel Guides* for such diverse areas as the South Pacific, the Rockies, and Europe, and publishes a series of elegantly illustrated *Sunset Pictorials*, including *San Francisco, Beautiful Hawaii*, and other volumes.

Classics

Have you longed to see Alexandria after reading Lawrence Durrell? Or promised yourself a trip to Spain with a copy of *Don Quixote* on your lap? Are you considering a visit to Colleen McCullough's Thorn Bird country or Nathaniel Hawthorne's New England or James Michener's Hawaii? Some of the world's best travel guides are Charles Dickens and Mark Twain, Ernest Hemingway and Joseph Conrad, Robert Louis Stevenson and William Butler Yeats, Pearl Buck, Lafcadio Hearn, Somerset Maugham, Lord Byron, Charles Darwin, Rudyard Kipling, Jack London, Herman Melville, John Steinbeck, and Washington Irving.

The Complete Traveller, at 199 Madison Ave., New York NY 10016, is one of the first bookstores devoted entirely to travel books. All over the United States travel bookstores are burgeoning now, including on their shelves everything travel-related—from turn-of-the-century out-of-print guidebooks to travel-related novels and stories.

Maps and Brochures

Touring maps of all kinds are the travel writer's tools. As the free ones become ever harder to come by, hoard what you have. Automobile clubs sometimes distribute, in addition to their tour guides, maps and such helpful books as *Triple A Travel Tips* and *A Guide to California's Gold Country*. The British Automobile Association gives facts and figures for hundreds of hostelries in its low-priced *Guide to Guesthouses, Farmhouses, and Inns of Britain* and its *Guide to Guesthouses, Farmhouses, and Inns on the Continent*.

For your travels by car, both the AAA and the National Automobile Club provide custom-made trip kits and strip maps for their members. Mobil also prepares custom trip kits for its customers. Texaco provides city and state, as well as US maps, without charge, and the maps can be marked for you to indicate the most direct or the most scenic route.

Touring materials also include museum guidebooks, which I usually order before the trip. I've learned to order in English. When I wrote to the Louvre in my best high school French, the director replied, in expert English, that he was sending me a Louvre guidebook in "le fran-cais facile." It turned out to be such "easy French" it was a guidebook for young children.

If you plan a foreign trip in the fall, the English language tours may be finished and the government tourist offices have probably run out of travel literature. *Eurail (R) Guide* suggests writing in the spring to the tourist offices of the places you expect to visit, and asking them to send you all their English-language information as soon as they have it.

Periodicals

You'll surely want easy access to newspapers and magazines you expect to write for. You'll doubtless subscribe to or send for samples of many travel-oriented publications, from *Odyssey* to *Geo*, from *Accent* and *Trip and Tour* to *Travel and Leisure* and *Ford Times*. Again, de-pending on your own specialized travel interests, you may turn to *Gourmet* and *Bon Appétit* or to *Surfer* and *Yachting*.

You'll want to read at least one Sunday newspaper travel section and at least one weekly newsmagazine, in addition to the daily paper. A travel writer needs to know what's going on in the world.

Don't forget to subscribe, if only briefly, to a newspaper in the area you're planning to visit. The Philadelphia *Inquirer*, for example, gives you the *feel* of the city, an overview of what it's like, and alerts you to the colorful New Year's Day Mummers Parade, the Little League World Series, or the June celebration when the colonially costumed people of Elfreth's Alley, the oldest continuously occupied residential street in the United States, hold their annual fete.

Other local papers tell you about special activities, so you can plan your vacation or weekend jaunt around the Oyster Shucking Champi-onships in Leonardtown, Maryland; the World Championship Inner Tube Race in Yuma, Arizona; or the Fishworm Judging Contest in Ster-ling, Colorado.

In this climate of exploding city and regional magazines, do try to buy the magazine(s) of the area you'll be visiting, such as the *Colorado Express* and *Savannah Magazine*. This is the kind of background in-formation you need to pursue the live research you'll be doing on the trip itself.

Don't be timid about requesting photocopies of newspaper and mag-azine articles published long ago, when you hear of something that might provide just the research pivot you need. I've found periodicals remarkably generous in filling requests for copies of special stories. Another writer asked, without much hope, for the copy of a magazine article on camels written 116 years ago. Within an amazingly short time this treasure appeared in her mailbox. Usually this service is free; if not, the cost is only a few cents.

US Government Publications

The US government is one of the world's biggest publishers. Take advantage of it. The government even puts out several publications to help you discover what is available:

> *Consumers Guide to Federal Publications* gives three hundred-odd subject lists from architecture and automobile insurance to surveying and mapping, and Spanish publications.
>
> *Selected List of US Government Publications* gives 130-150 publications with wide appeal. Issued biweekly—ask to be placed on the mailing list.
>
> *List of US Government Bookstores*
>
> *List of Depository Libraries*
>
> *The Consumer Information Catalogue* presents over 200 selected federal consumer publications. Published quarterly.
>
> *Government Periodicals and Subscription Services* lists periodicals by various government agencies, from the bimonthly *Cultural Post* published by the National Endowment for the Arts, to the quarterly *Outdoor Recreation Action*, published by the Department of the Interior.
>
> *Select List of Publications of the National Archives and Records Service* is the key to which federal department has what in the way of records.
>
> *Monthly Catalogue of US Government Publications* shows chronologically what has been published.

There are a number of other aids to finding your way around in the maze of federal publications. Write either to the US Government Printing Office, Washington DC 20402, or to the US government bookstore nearest you for prices.

Several other lists and compendiums are especially valuable to the travel writer. *Maps (United States and Foreign)* not only includes weather maps and distribution of various segments of the population, but also lists general reference maps of foreign countries—from Cambodia and Cyprus to Yemen and Yugoslavia. The lists of miscellaneous and special purpose navigational charts, sheets, and tables are helpful, too.

Background Notes are short, factual pamphlets (usually eight pages) written by State Department officers for about 160 countries. The pamphlets, which are invaluable for taking along on your trip, cover the country's land, people, history, government, political conditions, economy, and foreign relations. They also include a profile, brief travel notes, a map, a list of government officials, and an excellent reading list.

More in-depth are the *Pocket Guides*, issued for countries where US troops are stationed. These are small format, 100-200 pages, and cover sightseeing, diversions, etiquette, money, where to find a golf course, what the restaurant menu really says, and a basic language guide.

Much more detailed, the Defense Department's *Area Handbooks* for

105 countries, from Afghanistan to Zambia, are just about the best guidebooks you can buy.

The government also publishes a directory of 1,500 industrial plants and federal installations, including copper mines, breweries, and newspapers, that offer free tours.

The US Travel Service of the Department of Commerce has issued the following free booklets:

Tips for an Energy-Wise Vacation
Getting the Best Value for Your Vacation Dollar
How to Get an Air Fare Deal
Your Rights and Responsibilities—Know Before You Go
Helpful Information Sources
The Benefits of Using a Travel Agent
Helpful Hints for the Older Traveler
Travel Tips for the Handicapped
Traveling with Pets
USA Holiday Planner
Festival USA
American Indian Pow Wows and Festivals
Underwater Recreation
Automobile Museums
Oceanariums
Winter Resorts
Health Resorts
Traveler's Guide to Special Attractions
The Supernatural: Haunted Houses and Legendary Ghosts
Guides to specific areas, from New Orleans to Alaska

You can order all of these from:

Consumer Information
United States Travel Service
US Department of Commerce
Washington DC 20230

Additionally, these booklets and all the others mentioned can also be ordered through the US Government Printing Office or your nearest government bookstore.

If you're traveling near a President's boyhood home, send for the hardcover *Presidents*. *Ducks at a Distance*, a color illustrated waterfowl identification guide, is a bargain. So is the *Guide to Genealogical Records in the National Archives*. *Key Officers of Foreign Service Posts* is a good buy if you think you'll get overseas and need to know the name of your ambassador. The Civil Aeronautics Board will send the free *Fly-Rights: A Guide to Air Travel in the US*, and the US Customs Service will send, also free, *Customs Hints—Know Before You Go* and a booklet on the generalized system of preferences for 101 nations and 36 dependent territories where you're likely to buy certain items. Customs will also help the writer with material on smuggling, tariff laws, and what people try to get away with.

If you like to vacation away from crowds, request information on lesser-used national parks from:

National Park Service   US Forest Service
Department of the Interior   or   Department of Agriculture
Washington DC 20240   Washington DC 20250

The US Department of Transportation's National Highway Traffic Safety Administration issues an excellent booklet on *Travel and Camper Trailer Safety*, and the Bureau of Consular Affairs of the Department of State produces *Your Trip Abroad*, a good roundup for the beginning traveler.

If you're interested in camping in national parks, travel accommodations for the handicapped, international relations, backpacking, Indian ceremonials, or outdoor sports, send for the government booklet that gives you all the details.

The National Park Service publishes reams of helpful information, and also presents the visitor with special leaflets at most of the attractions it administers, such as Valley Forge National Historical Park, San Francisco's Fort Point, and Washington's John F. Kennedy Center for the Performing Arts. The Park Service's *Guide to the Historic Places of the American Revolution* is a gem.

The CIA publishes maps, atlases, and a street guide to Leningrad. *The Atlas of the People's Republic of China* is currently popular; illustrated with many pictures and maps, it summarizes China's geography, economy, history, and culture.

Next time you're in Washington, DC, visit the Library of Congress—it's fascinating. If you're visiting Washington, be sure to write or call your congressman for help in securing tickets to special attractions. Allow plenty of time. Ask your congressman, too, for assistance in finding information about anything connected with the federal government.

Every government department has a public information director and a library, with a clipping file and other special materials.

The Library of Congress Reference and Bibliographic Service will help those outside the Washington area find material for a small fee. You can obtain a copy of anything there unless it's restricted or needs copyright clearance. One writer, doing a roundup of Civil War battlefields, asked for—and received—the Reports of the Secretary of War to the 33rd and 34th Congresses in the 1850s. For this kind of help, get in touch with:

Chief, General Reference and Bibliography Division
Library of Congress
Washington DC 20540

Local Government Publications

Various agencies of state governments also print free or low-cost material valuable for the travel writer, from a beautifully complete, 879-item *California Historical Landmarks* to a leaflet on *Three Lincoln Shrines in Illinois*. South Dakota booklets tell all about the Black Hills and the Badlands, Delaware emphasizes its coastal vacationland, Georgia publishes an outdoor guide, and Oregon has all sorts of literature on forests, trees, and parks, as well as on the Lewis and Clark Trail. *I Love New York* is a comprehensive guide to the state, while the quarterly leaflets, *New York in Summer*, *New York in Winter*, etc., concentrate on the Big Apple itself. Philadelphia also publishes seasonal booklets, as well as *Philadelphia: A City for All Seasons!* California's Department of Transportation issues a *Safety Roadside Rest Area Report*. North Carolina's *One Day at a Time* details eleven different tours to familiarize visitors with the state.

You can also write to individual areas for information. Denver publishes *Mile-Highlights*, Fort Lauderdale recommends the Everglades, and the El Paso Convention and Visitors Bureau publishes *El Paso-Juarez*. Islands, from Martha's Vineyard to Guam, call themselves to your attention.

Worldwide, 140 cities are affiliated with the International Association of Convention and Visitors Bureaus, many of which issue seasonal calendars listing scheduled events. A phone call or postcard requesting the events calendar will put you on their mailing list.

Don't forget historical societies as a source of pretrip research material. The Mount Vernon Ladies Association of the Union will inform you about Mount Vernon, and the Preservation Society of Newport County, Rhode Island, will send you a booklet on six mansions located there. San Francisco's Chinese Culture Foundation has information on the Chinese Heritage Walk and the Chinese Culinary Walk, and the Nevada County Historical Society will bring you up-to-date on Gold Country restorations. The Pacific Area Travel Association can be an invaluable resource.

Sometimes several political entities join together to promote their joint travel-recreation area. They publish huge amounts of material. Pennsylvania Dutch country, Cape Cod, the Redwood Empire, and the Shenandoah Valley all do their best to lure visitors. So do the East African Wild Life Society and the Caribbean Travel Association. The Organization of American States puts out a fine handbook and catalog, and the Pacific Area Travel Association distributes a vast amount of excellent material on its member countries.

Literature From Other Countries

Early in your subject research write to the travel promotion bureaus of the countries you'll be visiting. Every country wants to present—aggressively—its most attractive features. From the *British Tourist Guide to Tunisia*, *A Trip to Italy*, and *Kenya: A Land of Contrasts* to Japan's *Tourist's Handbook*, with "Practical Ways to Relieve Your

Language Problems," and the *Traveller's Encyclopedia of Ontario*, tourist office publications do a fantastic job of telling the rest of the world what they have to offer. A postcard will bring you literally boxes of literature. Read it carefully. A single-line reference may produce an idea that will produce sales. A.R. Roalman, for instance, contemplating a trip to Japan, found in the tourist-office literature a single sentence about the oldest wooden building in the world. Queries to *Popular Mechanics* and *American Forest* netted pretrip assignments, and on-scene research developed three additional noncompetitive stories.

If you read the travel folders—either government or commercial—it's hard to believe in anything but sandy beaches with girls in bikinis and majestic, snow-covered slopes. Everybody seems to live in picturesque thatch-roofed cottages, and picnic in sylvan settings.

To get a more realistic picture and plan intelligently, first cross out all the adjectives in the promotional brochure. Then read the last page for the straight facts. The relationship of one day to another, one country to another, within the tour framework, gives you an idea of what the tour people consider important about the area. Look for the words "We stop at" or "We visit." Without those words, the tour company thinks it only important enough to drive by.

One of the travel writer's most important skills is learning to read *between* the lines. A European tour that gives half a day to Florence and during its day and a half in Paris provides half a day of city sightseeing and a trip to Versailles plus "an afternoon free for relaxing or perhaps a visit to the famous Louvre Museum" is *not* a tour for art lovers. If you're writing an art-oriented article, don't bother reading *that* tour brochure.

Miscellaneous Freebies

Don't spurn public-relations handouts. As a matter of fact, when you're beginning your research, *ask* for handouts. In addition to writing the tourist offices, a good technique is to place a free ad in *Party Line*, a weekly newsletter that goes to hundreds of PR people. Write:

Betty Yarmon, Managing Editor
Party Line
35 Sutton Place
New York NY 10022

There's no cost to media people, only to the PR specialists who buy subscriptions for the privilege of sending materials to writers like you.

In-flight magazines, those publications you find in the pocket in front of you as you struggle into your seat belt, and in-room magazines, which you find on your desk in many hotels, are valuable sources of information for pretrip subject research. When you make your plane and hotel reservations ask for copies to be sent to you in advance.

Although some of the airlines' extensive literature requires a modest payment or is only handed out on the plane, most will appear in response to a postcard from you. Pan Am publishes the outstanding *New Horizons World Guide* and *New Horizons U.S.A.*, while TWA translates menus, advises on *Climates and Clothes*, and publishes *Business Travel Tips*, *Getaway Books* and *Pocket Guides* to various countries.

KLM provides a *Motoring Guide to Europe* and *Surprising Amsterdam*; Japan Airlines passes out helpful city guides and a *Guide to the People's Republic of China*. Continental's *Wings Over Paradise* is a beautifully illustrated history of Micronesia, and Quantas sends prospective tourists a variety of literature, ranging from *100 Things to See and Do in Australia* to a slick-paper, color-photo book of *Unique Tours to the Island Continent* and a pocket-size *Understanding Down Under*.

United Airlines has an interesting brochure on baggage, American Airlines concentrates on *The Art of Traveling*, and Sabena's *Helpful Hints for Your Trip to the Common Market Countries* is full of good advice on metrics and other nitty-gritty. SAS provides *City Portraits* for all its destinations, which include hotel lists, city maps, a brief roundup of advice on food and money, a review of the sights, and what to do during your first hour. Air France provides three extremely helpful booklets—*Inexpensive Restaurants Near Famous Monuments*, *Business Traveler's Guide to Pairs*, and *BonJour Paris*, an English-French dictionary with the phrases arranged according to where you would use them.

Although resources proliferate, they aren't all necessarily helpful and accurate. The travel writer has to approach pretrip research with discretion. Some of what you read is good—some of it is garbage. For instance, I read a book for women travelers on cruises that advised those with children to try to engage the children's counselors as baby-sitters in the evening. If this is not possible, suggested the author, perhaps you could persuade your room steward or the purser to sit with your children. *The purser!* I knew instantly that that author had never been on a cruise, and immediately lost faith in anything else the book said.

However, the more involved you become with travel writing, the more convinced you will be that you can never do *too much* research. As you learn to use what you glean from both formal and informal sources, you'll realize that the information overload makes destination decisions easy and constitutes an unmistakable plus value.

As we consider what to do before your trip, while traveling, and after your return, we'll look into other forms of research, such as telephone interviews, face-to-face interviews, questionnaires, and on-the-scene observation. But in the next chapter let's consider some of the valuable aids the travel writer can find at the public library.

3

Your First Trip Is to the Library

ibrary research!" My friend threw up her hands in amazement. "What do you mean—*library research!*" You're going there, aren't you? Isn't that enough?"

Going there is seldom enough for the travel writer. Nobody but another writer seems to realize that travel articles require subject and market research before you go, while you're traveling, and after you return home.

Subject research is the glue that holds your story together. It's the credibility you achieve by presenting someone else's opinion, along with your own. It's the way to understand what you're seeing before you see it, while you're seeing it, and after you've seen it. Subject research is the keystone of the writer's craft; it's a big part of the plus value.

Are you beginning to think the travel writer spends a lot of time at the library? You're right. Several years ago my article in the *Seattle Times Magazine* indicated only that I lived in Palo Alto, California. An envelope sent to the Palo Alto Public Library enclosed the article with a note requesting that the accompanying letter be forwarded to me. Next day the letter arrived at my house with a word of explanation from the head librarian. The letter's criticism of my article was tempered by the astuteness of its author in assuming a writer would be well known at the local library.

Does it all sound formidable? Really it's not, because a lot of the topics we'll cover you've probably known about for years—you just never thought of them as *research*. This chapter introduces you to the library, and shows how it can provide a firm framework for other reading and ongoing face-to-face research. Be sure to read enough so you're

Gothic Cathedral in Lausanne, Switzerland

getting several opinions, not just one, from which you can form your own and start out with a new approach.

When it comes to subject research, a travel writer cannot exist without the library. As Hayes Jacobs remarks about libraries, "If a writer lives near a good one, he is specially blessed; if he lives near a poor one, he ought to think about moving."

Entire books have been devoted to the description and use of library resources, but this is only a quick guide to finding what the travel writer needs.

Our most valuable resource is the *reference librarian*. Librarians exist to provide information. They are delighted to provide that information. I have researched in many libraries—public, university, and special, in the United States and abroad—and I've always found librarians helpful and eager to supply whatever I requested. You'll find help at the library, too. First introduce yourself to the librarian. Explain that you are a writer. You'll find that nothing is too good for you. You're important to the library—you create library material.

Often a phone call to the reference desk will answer a simple question. Are you interested, for instance, in how your own money lines up with the cruzeiro, krone, rupee, or baht? If your local paper doesn't have a complete foreign-exchange column and you don't subscribe to the *Wall Street Journal*, the reference librarian may look it up for you. Be sure your question is specific. *Not* "Tell me about Thailand" or "Tell me about polygamy," but "Does the present king of Thailand have more than one wife?" Here's a sample of some of the questions I've asked over the years:

What are the opening words of Sweden's national anthem?
Which is bigger—Disneyland or Disney World?
How does the travel industry rank in importance among US industries?
What is the weather like in Trieste in January?
Which airlines serve Sun Valley?
What do they call the schools where Muslim boys study the Koran?
Where was the world's first travel agency established?
Who originally built Tree Tops in Kenya?
Was it sunny or cloudy on May 14, 1607, when Captain John Smith landed at Jamestown, Virginia?

Once the entire library staff spent a week trying to find out for me what the ancient Greeks used for theater tickets.

If you're not familiar with the vertical file, ask your librarian where it is. The file may or may not be physically vertical, but it will surely contain maps, guidebooks, menus, museum catalogs, photographs, theater programs, and hundreds of nonbook items that will help in your pretrip research.

Through your librarian discover what interlibrary loan can do for you. I once found a book in Sydney, Australia's main library that I later wanted to refer to at home. My local library queried regional libraries, the California State Library in Sacramento, and the Library of Congress. Nobody had the book. But the local library finally found it and borrowed it from a special library in Toronto.

Sometimes you have to be a supersleuth to find what you're looking for. You probably understand about the card catalog—an author or main-entry card, plus a title card, plus (for nonfiction) at least one subject card, for each library item. And you probably realize that often these are all filed together in one alphabetical listing, but sometimes there are separate author, title, and subject catalogs. (With new processing methods we see more libraries switching from *card* catalogs to computerized *book* catalogs.)

But you may have difficulty finding the heading the library cataloger used for the subject you're trying to find. Will it be under "archaeology" or "history" or "ancient history" or "European history"? Ideally, it will be under all of them, each with a "see also" reference. But sometimes you have to work hard to come up with a synonym that you and the cataloger agree is what you're looking for. Consulting *Subject Headings Used in the Dictionary Catalogs of the Library of Congress* may send you off in the right direction, but even so it's confusing.

Do you need something on the Peace Corps, for instance? Don't give up too easily. Try "United States—Peace Corps." Sometimes there'll be a cross-reference card telling you to see a different subject heading or to see an additional subject heading. Persistence pays off.

You probably know that most libraries file their materials according to either the Dewey decimal system or the Library of Congress system. At the Lenin Library in Moscow, however, when one of my daughters asked the librarian whether they use Dewey, the reply was, "No, the Russians have something better than the Dewey decimal system." We later found out that most of their filing is by size. Unwilling to waste a twelve-inch shelf on a nine-inch book, they arrange their closed stacks according to the books' size and shape. It takes hours to page a book from the loan desk.

In most countries the card catalog shows the books that particular library has. If it isn't there and you want to know if the book exists, turn to *Books in Print*, published in three two-volume sets, by author, by title, and by subject. And don't forget about the volume of *Paperback Books in Print*.

One of the library's most valuable tools is the *New York Times Index*. This multivolume, frequently indexed series gives you the exact date, page, and column for articles on your subject in the New York *Times*. It also gives a synopsis of the article that may answer your question, so you don't have to look up the newspaper itself. I didn't have to look through months of newspapers to find out, for instance, exactly when the Pope visited Ephesus—information I needed for half a sentence of a major travel article.

If you do need to look further, the New York *Times* offers complete transcripts of Presidential press conferences, full texts of important speeches and legislation, voluminous amounts of data of all sorts. Many libraries have physical copies of back issues of the *Times* or copies on microfilm or microfiche. In any case, you can copy the page you need. Even more important, perhaps, if you need a national or international story from your unindexed local newspaper, you can assume the story appeared approximately the same day it appeared in the New York *Times*. Once you know the date, it's easy to find the paper in the file at your library or local newspaper office.

The *London Times*, the *Christian Science Monitor*, and the *Wall Street Journal* also publish helpful indexes, and *American Newspapers* tells you which libraries, historical societies, and other organizations have which newspapers, if you're looking for something special.

Large libraries often have newspaper rooms, where back issues of the world's leading papers, either physical copies or microfilm or microfiche, are kept for many years. That's how my husband and I found out about the *Frank H. Buck*. Our research on the Standard Oil tanker *Lyman K. Stewart* that collided with the freighter *Walter A. Luckenbach* and sank in San Francisco Bay in 1922 turned up information about the *Stewart's* sister ship, the *Frank H. Buck*. After some digging we discovered that she, also, met her end on a foggy Saturday afternoon in San Francisco Bay. The *Buck* collided with the luxury liner *President Coolidge* at nearly the exact spot where the *Stewart* had met the *Luckenbach* fifteen years earlier. Both ships spilled oil all over the bay as they were buffeted against the Land's End rocks, where their remains rust today. We did most of the research in newspapers published at the time, and the story turned out to be bigger than we expected.

City directories, both old and new, in addition to the telephone books, help you track down the exact fact you're missing. They not only give information about each household, but often include listings by addresses and by telephone numbers, supplemented by maps and general facts about the area.

William Rivers tells of a researcher trying to retrace the steps of Mark Twain in Hawaii:

In one of his "Letters from the Sandwich Islands" . . . Twain mentions a wonderful party at "Sam Brannon's bungalow." The problem: Where was Brannon's bungalow? A hundred years had passed, Honolulu had changed, and everyone living in Brannon's time was dead. . . . If he [the researcher] had been looking for a living resident of Honolulu, he would have needed only a City Directory and a map. He needed no more to fix the location of Sam Brannon's bungalow. The City Directory of Honolulu for 1865 lists Brannon and his address, and a map shows the precise location.

Another travel writer's tool, *Facts on File: A Weekly World News Digest with Cumulative Index*, a classified loose-leaf digest of news arranged under broad subject headings, is an index I always consult when I begin an article on a country I haven't done for some time, just to be sure I've kept up with what's been going on in that country.

Facts on File has another advantage—it's more accurate than the daily newspaper, put together at top deadline pressure, can hope to be. We all know that newspapers give us many clues, but are usually not scholarly authorities. Books, on the other hand, present a problem to the library in many fast-changing fields. They're obsolete almost as soon as they're printed. For this reason, libraries tend to spend greater and greater proportions of their budgets for periodicals, where the time lag is not so great. Books on some subjects, however, provide valuable information even when their copyright dates aren't current. The rule of thumb for accuracy is, if three people say it's true, it's likely to be.

Some books, of course, are definitive, regardless of their age. Need to know anything about food? *Larousse Gastronomique* should give you the word, and they say if you need to ask what it is, you aren't ready to use it. The thirteen-volume *Mythology of All Races* is well illustrated and what you want is easily located therein. Helen Gardner's *Art Through the Ages* is an old standby. One of the world's best reference books for the travel writer is the *World Travel Directory*, which is updated annually. It not only lists travel agencies, wholesale tour operators, and local sightseeing companies all over the world, but tells you, state by state and city by city, about newspaper travel sections, hotel and travel media, and all sorts of people and companies connected with the travel industry. Other useful books include:

Reference Guide for Travelers is old but still helpful, with guidebooks and reference books arranged by country.

Statesman's Yearbook: Statistical and Historical Annual of the States of the World gives statistical and descriptive data about world governments.

Statistical Abstract of the United States and *Historical Statistics of the United States, Colonial Times to 1957: A Statistical Abstract Supplement* are published by the US Bureau of the Census and provide statistics on political, social, and economic aspects of the United States.

Joseph Nathan Kane's *Famous First Facts: A Record of First Happenings, Discoveries, and Inventions in the United States* is handier than you might think.

The Guinness Book of World Records

Yearbook of International Organizations

The Climate of the Continents

A Dictionary of Geology

Chase's Calendar of Annual Events tells what's happening when, and gives special days, weeks, and months.
The American Book of Days
Field Guides to birds, wildflowers, trees.

Want to know something about specific people? Perhaps the address of someone still alive? Try the British *Who's Who* or the Canadian *Who's Who* or *Who's Who in Canada*. *Who's Who in America* is supplemented by *Who's Who in the West, East, Midwest*, etc., and *Who's Who in American Law, Government, Religion*, etc., as well as the *Directory of Medical Specialists* and *Who's Who of American Women*. *Current Biography* sketches persons of many nationalities prominent in the day's news. The *New Century Cyclopedia of Names* gives brief information on over 100,000 people both living and dead.

While not as useful when it comes to contacting research sources, there are several directories of notable Americans, Britons, and Canadians of the past. *Who Was When? A Dictionary of Contemporaries* places subjects in historical perspective. It may come in handy to know that Abraham Lincoln lived at the same time as Emperor Maximilian.

Some libraries are full or partial depositories for federal or state publications, and these materials may be cataloged and shelved like other library books or may be classified as government publications and arranged alphabetically or numerically in a separate place.

Of course you're not going to read *all* of this literature for any one article or even any one subject. Much of the research material you find will be repetitious. And yet, here at the library, the "memory of the human race," you're bound to find, among the morass of superfluous and useless information, the kernel of a fresh idea, the perfect quote, the reference to the authority you didn't know existed, the very special something that provides the plus value for your story.

Quickly finding exactly what you need at the library is an art that comes with practice. Soon you'll learn how to flip through an index and see if there's anything you want, look over an entire section of books and pull out only the single most authoritative one. You learn, too, to skip over material that's unwanted *now*, while making a mental note (perhaps also a physical one) about where to find it, in case that's the very thing you need next month or next year.

If you want a guide to the reference works at the library, Eugene P. Sheehy's *Guide to Reference Books* (with *Supplement*) is the one librarians use. Less comprehensive, but still useful and good reading are *Guide to the Use of Books and Libraries* by Jean Key Gates and *Reference Books: A Brief Guide for Students and Other Users of the Library*, published by the Enoch Pratt Free Library. For research in general you can't beat William L. Rivers's *Finding Facts*.

Obviously the travel writer's reference books I'm mentioning here are merely a sample—materials I've found especially helpful, and a guide to further exploration of the library. Some of them you'll find you use so much you'll want a copy at home.

Encyclopedias we all know about—or at least we think we do. Most libraries have both the *Encyclopaedia Britannica* and the *Encyclopedia Americana*. The *Britannica*, especially, has changed greatly in its new edition, with the facility for quick answers to quick questions in the Micropaedia, more complete answers in the Macropaedia. These are general encyclopedias, as are the single-volume *New Columbia Encyclopedia* and the multivolume *Colliers, Chambers's, Compton's, Academic American*, and *World Book Encyclopedias*. Every discipline seems to produce special-subject encyclopedias of its own. Some of the more helpful include the multivolume *McGraw-Hill Encyclopedia of Science and Technology, McGraw-Hill Encyclopedia of World Art*, and *Encyclopedia of the United States*. If your special travel interest encompasses sports, religion, archaeology, psychology, oceanography, or politics, you'll find an encyclopedia designed for you. The two-volume *Encyclopedia of World Travel* is, however, disappointing in its brevity of treatment.

One of the most valuable tools at your library is *Kruzas Directory of Special Libraries and Information Centers*, which lists thousands of specialized libraries all over the United States, from the library of the American Kennel Club to that of the Voice of America. Did you know there are entire libraries devoted to sailing ships or Shakespeare, American Indians or American wine, insects or international trade? You'll get all kinds of ideas just browsing through the *Directory*.

These special libraries are maintained by professional organizations, charitable foundations, trade associations, consulates, labor unions, and sometimes by the estates of private individuals. From the Folger Shakespeare Library in Washington to the Joseph Conrad Library at the Seamen's Church Institute in New York, special libraries are a windfall for the travel writer. If you live near one, it's usually not too hard to secure permission to inspect its treasures.

Sometimes, too, you can obtain special privileges at a nearby university library, or perhaps at the morgue of your local newspaper. In any of those circumstances, be sure to express your appreciation for the opportunity and try to be as little trouble as possible.

Once you begin your library research you have to decide how to arrange the information you're accumulating. If it's a borrowed book, you're not going to mark it up, of course; but develop the habit of reading with pen in hand. Insert paper bookmarks with directions to yourself to send for or look up additional information, or to photocopy the page or make a special note for a special article. Try to include all pertinent information—dates, call numbers, authors' names—to make refinding the material as painless as possible.

Be sure to indicate whether the gem of information you're jotting down is a direct quote from someone else or has been paraphrased into your own words. Even paraphrased, you may need to give credit if what you're using is a proprietary fact—something which that particular author dug out for himself, something nobody else knew about, as opposed to a common fact, which can be found many places and is known to many people.

Whether you outline your story first, then key in the various fragments of research material, or collect the fragments in separate file folders, or color-code with a rainbow of pens, or make a separate file card for each fact, or devise some more acceptable system of your own, getting your research together is a hard job. A number of travel writers admit, "I do a lot of filing on the floor while I'm working on a project!"

You'll find extensive cross-indexing worthwhile, if you want to find all the information you've squirreled away. Never be tempted to file anything under "miscellaneous." If it's worth noting, it's worth labeling.

None of the travel writers I interviewed for this chapter seemed thoroughly satisfied with present methods of accumulating and arranging information. Each one said, "If you find a good way, please let me know!"

Do you now feel as though you know everything you need to know about researching your subject? Wait! Don't leave the library yet! Not until we discuss the value of the *Reader's Guide to Periodical Literature*, which tells you where to find magazine articles on your subject. The *Reader's Guide* does three things for you: It tells you what else has been published on your subject and where and when; it tells you whether or not your target market has published anything on your subject recently (which we'll discuss further in Chapter 4); and it provides additional research resources by showing you where to find articles that may teach you something about your subject. As a footnote to the advantages of magazine articles as research resources, let's not forget that the authors of those articles are often available to provide additional information or fresh quotations.

Most large libraries subscribe to all the periodicals listed in *Reader's Guide*—from *American Artist* to *World Tennis*—but very small libraries only purchase the abridged *Reader's Guide*, which indexes fewer periodicals, and subscribe only to those periodicals. In both *Guides* articles are listed by author and subject, and page numbers, as well as dates, are given. Entries also indicate which of a magazine's regional editions is indexed.

In looking for magazine articles you'll have to define your subject in the same terms the cataloger uses, but there are hints in the *Guide's* cross-references. If you find nothing in *Reader's Guide*, even after you've considered several synonyms for your subject, you may need a different guide. Is your subject very scholarly? The *Social Sciences and Humanities Index* covers the scholarly journals. If your subject is more likely to be found in specialized periodicals, try the index that lists articles about science, art, music, business, psychology, or engineering. Another indexing service covers such popular publications as *Woman's Day* and *Weight Watcher's Magazine*. If your subject is likely to have appeared in a Catholic, British, literary, or nineteenth-century magazine, a special directory will help you find it.

A newer indexing service at the library, the *Magazine Index*, is a computerized arrangement of several hundred periodicals. While it covers many more publications than *Reader's Guide*, it only goes back a few years.

Send to the H. W. Wilson Company, 950 University Ave., Bronx NY 10452, for a free pamphlet on using the *Reader's Guide*. Other indexes are handled so similarly, the information is universal.

These *Guides* for readers are also tremendously important in market research, as we'll see in Chapter 4. There's no doubt that the quantity and quality of the market research and the subject research differentiate the amateur, who says, "Some day I must get around to writing up the story of my wonderful trip to Paris and send it to one of the big magazines—I'm sure they'll buy it," from the professional, who says, "I want to be sure I have all my facts straight on the Paris Sewer trip—what time it leaves, how much it costs, and the other details. Then I'll see what the card catalog and the *Reader's Guide* have on Paris sewers—I could use a few anecdotes and quotes and a little historical background to spruce up my story."

With guides to tell you what has already been published on your subject and reference books of all kinds to increase your knowledge and information, you'll be glad if, before you begin to travel, you take a trip to the library.

4

Study the Marketplace Before You Start

mateurs talk about writing; professionals talk about marketing" is a cliché well known to writers—well known because it's true.

Again and again I've heard one professional writer respond to another's description of a project with, "Good idea. Where are you going to send it *first*?" And again and again I've heard one pro respond to another pro's tale of rejection with, "Too bad. Where are you going to send it *next*?"

Ask an amateur who he's writing the article for, and he's likely to reply, "Oh, nobody special. I'm just writing it kind of generally." **There is no such thing as writing generally.** Successful writing is always for somebody. It's for a particular publication, a particular reader. Successful writing is aimed and slanted, facts astutely selected to appeal to a well-defined segment of the reading public.

Practically any publication will be receptive to travel material, if the material is geared to its *specific* audience. In a minute we'll take a typical travel story and consider where it might sell. But first—how do you go about finding that audience? You begin with marketing manuals. Study them at the library before deciding which is most convenient and complete for your needs.

Writer's Market and *The Writer's Handbook* are the most familiar to freelancers.

Writer's Market contains listings for more than 4,000 periodicals, publishers, and organizations that are potential buyers of freelance material.

Travel material can be packaged and presented in a multitude of forms, but the most familiar is the newspaper or magazine feature. Po-

Castle on the Rhine, Germany

tential travel article buyers appear in *Writer's Market* under three basic headings: consumer publications; company publications; and trade, technical, and professional journals. The market lists are updated via the monthly magazine *Writer's Digest* and the annual *Writer's Yearbook*, published about halfway between *Writer's Markets*. Each listing gives the publication's address, the name of at least one editor (sometimes of several in charge of different types of material), the publication's emphasis, and its readership. The listing also mentions the number of freelance manuscripts used, the kind of material the publication will consider buying, rights purchased, normal reporting time, and how the freelance writer should get in touch.

Merely browsing through market manuals will give you many ideas for articles, as well as introducing you to hundreds of publications you're unaware of. You'll find many pleasant surprises as you thumb through them. They will give you a springboard, a jumping-off place, to marketing ideas of your own, as well as ideas for shaping and writing the piece, itself. If one of these publications should not happen to work well for you, still it catalyzes the recognition of another that may turn out to work better.

The Writer's Handbook, published by *The Writer* magazine and updated through monthly market lists in the magazine, has a slightly different format. Its hundred articles on various types of writing fill three-quarters of the book. The rest deals with specific markets, categorized by type of material, such as "Fiction Markets," "Article Markets," "Reprint Magazines," etc.

Literary Market Place (LMP) is also popular. Its comprehensive coverage of the whole publishing world—everything from book review syndicates and multimedia materials to bookbinding and messenger services—is invaluable.

Its magazine section not only provides an alphabetical roster with addresses, phone numbers, and editors' names, but also a listing classified by subject interest. Newspapers are arranged by states and alphabetically by cities within the states. But no information is given about the freelance needs, prices, or modus operandi of these publications. The *International Literary Market Place* is arranged alphabetically by country, with information on each about public holidays, mailing requirements, literary agents, major libraries, translation agencies, and a vast amount of other material.

Both *Ulrich's International Periodicals Directory* and the *Standard Periodical Directory* list their 60,000-odd entries under about 250 "field of interest" classifications. Browse through them next time you're at the library. Look over the *Ayer Directory of Publications*, the *Directory of Publishing Opportunities*, and the *Editor & Publisher International Year Book*, too. Each approaches its periodical listings from a different direction and includes different information.

The five-volume *Working Press of the Nation* is designed for publicists but can be extremely helpful to freelance writers. Volume 1 covers all the daily newspapers published in the United States and Canada and includes the names of their travel editors. Volume 2, the Magazine Directory, gives information about many of the magazines published in North America. Volume 3 is the Radio and Television Directory, and Volume 4, the Feature Writer and Syndicate Directory. Volume 5, the Internal Publications Directory, covers 3,400 in-house communications, and replaces the *Gebbie House Magazine Directory*. Regional marketing information appears in such publications as Frances Halpern's *Writer's Guide to Publishing in the West*.

With thousands of periodicals publishing all sorts of material, whatever kind of travel story you write, there's a market for it *somewhere*. As you pore over the various marketing aids, jot down the names (and page references) of the likeliest prospects for the subject(s) you have in mind. Then read copies of the publications themselves.

There is simply no substitute for studying at least three or four recent issues of each of your target markets. This not only tells you whether or not this publication *is* a likely buyer for your idea, but actually helps you shape the idea. Read each issue from cover to cover, including the ads. The ads, often designed by professional readership analysts, provide strong clues. Are these readers more interested in saving money or in having the best? Are they in need of more tax shelters or more ways to fix hamburger? Are they tennis players or wheelchair users? Scrutinizing the advertisements and editorial material is the best way of judging what each market is likely to want.

Many of these magazines are available at the library. Others can be purchased at the newsstand. But how can you obtain copies of the more obscure publications?

There are a number of ways. One is by studying the *Writer's Market* listings that say "Free sample copy on request." I underline those as I go through the book, then have a helper address postcards to the seven hundred or eight hundred I want, pressing onto the other side of the postcard a label with the message "Please send a sample copy and information on your requirements as suggested in *Writer's Market*. Thank you." I sign them. For publications that charge for sample copies, I write a letter with a similar message, adding "fifty cents enclosed," or whatever. If a magazine doesn't say anything in its listing about sample copies, I send a form letter requesting them, which usually results in their arrival. (If you're thinking only of yourself—not classrooms full of students—your sample copy needs might be more like seventy or eighty, or even seven or eight.)

What are some of the other ways to find obscure magazines, not generally available at the library or on the newsstand?

Ask Your Friends

Tell everybody, "Never throw away a magazine. Whatever it is, please let me look at it first." My mother used to live in a large apartment house where residents placed their old magazines on a shelf beside the incinerator. Every time she heard the incinerator room door closing, Mother dashed out to look for treasures. That's how she happened to bring me *Aramco World*, published by the Arabian American Oil Company for libraries and researchers, as well as for Aramco's friends. When I saw they used in-depth articles on the Middle East, along the lines of what I was writing, I checked into it further, and *Aramco* proved a good market for me. Ask your barber, your hairdresser, your dentist, your doctor—anybody—to save magazines for you. Ask friends to give you their old trade journals, company publications, religious magazines, hobby periodicals, and club and association magazines. You'll be surprised at some of the unusual markets you'll find.

Never pass up a rummage sale, thrift shop, or flea market. Your traveling companion may tease you about hoarding for paper drives but when you think of those old magazines as potential *markets*, you're glad to give them a little space. Don't overlook the Friends of the Library sale or the Post Office distribution of undeliverable magazines. There are other places to look for discards, too. As we stood on a Los Angeles street corner awaiting the bus to take us to the Rose Bowl, I glanced at the mesh trash can beside me. When I saw three hard-to-find magazines in a paper bag, I fished them out. (I won't tell you what my husband had to say about *that*!)

Look for Other Opportunities

Always search for hidden markets. You'll build up an "old boy"/ "old girl" network as you move along in freelancing, but meanwhile take advantage of whatever you can find. The *British American Magazine*, for instance, advertised in the newspaper classifieds for writers, so I called it to the attention of a student who had just returned from England. When the editor of *Guest Informant* (which you often find in your hotel room) told me how desperately she needed writers in a couple of cities, I was able to give her the name of a friend in one of them, which was the beginning of a mutually satisfactory literary relationship for them. There are markets and there are ways to find them.

Market research not only helps you find the obvious and hidden markets and shows you what else has been written on your subject, it helps you to know *how* you should write for your target markets. Your final target will determine your *exact* focus and slant, but you'll be doing your general planning well in advance. Will your piece be in first person, in third person, in a combination "I-you," or in a hidden viewpoint that takes the reader right on-scene without revealing who is giving the information? Will your language be formal or informal? Your tone serious, helpful, nostalgic, humorous? Will you use quotes, anecdotes, fictional techniques? Do the markets you have in mind require more research than you will be able to complete? Is the approach you intend to take appropriate for the age, sex, political inclination, financial condition, and educational level of the readership you seek?

Plan Your Article Itinerary

Analyze the stories in your sample publications and begin preparing an itinerary for your manuscript. Where will you send it *first*?

Then where will you send it *next*?

Psychologically, an itinerary for each story you're contemplating is one of the travel writer's most valuable supports. When you have all possible markets listed on your itinerary sheet, if your query or your story gets a "Sorry, no thanks," you already know where you're going to send it *next*. This is not only an important time-saver for a datable subject—you just type out a fresh title sheet, put the package in a fresh envelope, and drop it back in the mailbox—but it alleviates the "I'm not much of a writer, they didn't like it, after all, nobody's ever going to buy anything from me" blues.

After arranging your preliminary itinerary, return to the *Reader's Guide* and other magazine indexes. How recently have your target markets covered your subject? Is it too soon to suggest that subject again? If there have been a great many stories, you may feel the marketplace has been saturated, unless you have some new, absolutely irresistible angle. If you find *nothing* on your subject, you may wonder whether for some reason that subject is taboo among major magazines, or whether you've looked it up incorrectly and should search for a synonym for the heading you're looking under. Or this may be a lucky accident for you to be first with the story.

Once you've researched your subject's recent publication history, you can plan a firmer itinerary.

There are several ways of devising an itinerary. If money is your primary goal, the first publication you send to would be *Reader's Digest*, perhaps, or *Playboy*, or *McCall's*. Your descending order would list lower-paying markets, on down through the cent-a-word possibilities. However, there's another factor to consider: Does the magazine pay on acceptance or on publication? *On acceptance* means you'll get your check a couple of weeks after you get the "Yes, we want it." *On publication* means you'll get paid when and if your piece appears in print. Some editors are very fair about this and only accept material they know they'll be using in the near future. Others are tempted by the opportunity to build up a free inventory, and your story may sit "in inventory" for months or years. In general, an editor is more likely to publish promptly something he's already paid for. Sometimes a periodical will pay immediately for the article, but will hold all the photographs you've sent until the staff is actually laying out the issue. Then they'll return the unused photos and send a check for those they use. That seems reasonable, doesn't it? But if you're the kind of writer who doesn't really believe it's *sold* until it's *paid for*, beware of pay-on-publication involvements.

If prestige and the respect of colleagues and peers would please you most, you'll begin your article's travels with the *Journal of Archaeology*, the *Journal of American History*, *Scientific American*, or some other prestigious publication, whether or not they pay at all, then move on to more popular markets.

If, on the other hand, you want to sell the piece quickly, you might begin your itinerary with the publication that seems to you a most likely market for this particular story. After you've done your market research, read several copies of your selected targets, and eliminated those that have recently used your subject, you should be in a position to judge which publication would most want what you have to offer, and which publication would be the next most probable, on down to the long shots and the lucky accidents. Your individual itinerary will show some combination of these.

Plan Your Markets When You Plan Your Trip

Let's take a *Writer's Market* and a mythical trip and see what we can do about finding candidates for a marketing itinerary. In thumbing through *Writer's Market*, don't merely turn to the section titled "Travel, Camping, and Trailer" and stop there. *Every* section lists publications likely to buy travel material. From *Baby Talk* to *Modern Maturity*, hundreds of periodicals are potential markets for your work. So study *Writer's Market* carefully, and creatively. Do this as soon as you know you'll be traveling, to identify all the possible audiences for your trip story.

Say you're scheduled to take a cruise on the *Mississippi Queen*, a paddle wheel steamboat—fourteen days on the Ohio and Mississippi Rivers, from Cincinnati, Ohio, to Minneapolis/St. Paul, Minnesota. Traveling with you and your spouse will be your three children: Mike, a high school football player; Melanie, an inquisitive nine-year-old; and Brucie, a toddler in diapers. You will also be accompanied by your eighty-four-year-old mother-in-law and your recently divorced thirty-two-year-old sister, a bank executive in training. You will *not* be accompanied by Butterball, your golden cocker, whom you've left in a kennel, or the tank of tropical fish a neighbor boy is supposed to feed.

Both you and your spouse get three weeks' vacation, so you'll travel a thousand miles to Cincinnati in your RV, taking six days to see the sights along the way. After the river trip, some members of your party will fly home on a commercial plane from the Twin Cities, while some of you will fly in a friend's private plane back to Cincinnati, where your camper awaits you. This time you'll cover the thousand miles in two and a half days, so you'll be ready for work Monday morning.

How many periodicals would be interested in some kind of story related to your *Mississippi Queen* trip? Hundreds!

Let's do this systematically. Turn first to the Consumer Publications section in *Writer's Market*.

Would an **animal** publication such as *Animal Review, Animal Lovers Magazine* or *Family Pet* be interested in your efforts to find the perfect kennel for Butterball while you're traveling? Is there a story in the neighbor boy and the tropical fish?

Would **art** publications like the *American Art Journal, Arts Magazine* or *The Original Art Reports* publish something on Cincinnati's Taft Museum, the Walker Museum of Art in Minneapolis, or Carl Milles's thirty-six-foot onyx Indian statue in St. Paul?

The **association, club, and fraternal** magazines are concerned with the ideals, projects, and activities of the sponsoring club or organization. Any of these become excellent markets for the freelancer familiar with the area where the organization will be holding its next convention or the area where the group sponsors a particular project.

Even stories on the environs of the convention city are popular with association editors. If the Elks or the Lions, members of Kiwanis or Rotary or one of the other associations happen to be planning a convention for Cincinnati, Louisville, St. Louis, St. Paul, Minneapolis, or even some nearby city, wouldn't some of its members be interested in extending their convention trip with a vacation on the *Mississippi Queen*? Aren't you the logical one to tell them all about it in the association publication?

The **automotive and motorcycle** section mainly lists those publications concerned with the vehicle as a hobby or sport. (Publications in the travel, camping, and trailer section deal with the vehicle as transportation or shelter.)

Is the friend who's piloting you back to Cincinnati an **aviation** personality? Or will the trip be an especially interesting or unusual experience? If so, perhaps *Air Line Pilot, AOPA Pilot, Private Pilot* or *Plane and Pilot* would take a story.

If you're black, a **black** publication might like to hear about your trip. For one of the **business and finance** publications—thirteen pages of them—you'll have to think of a special angle. Maybe your sister will come up with just the thing. If CB equipment is part of your travels, one of the CB radio magazines might be interested.

Surely travels with a toddler on a river steamer would make a story for one of the **child care and parental guidance** publications. *American Baby, Baby Talk, Baby Care, Home Life, Mothers Today, Parents' Magazine*—any of them would welcome your advice.

Perhaps someone you'll meet on the trip or some project you'll happen upon would make a good story for one of the **college, university, and alumni** publications. And don't overlook **consumer service and business opportunity** publications. *Buyways*, published for members of the National Association of Consumers and Travelers, is an excellent vehicle for travel material that emphasizes getting your money's worth. **Education** publications? Select one that looks for travel articles that show the educational value of the experience for the child. You hope the meals aboard the *Mississippi Queen* will be appropriate for inclusion in *Gourmet* or *Wine World Magazine*, which are natural choices in the **food and drink** category. Reading *Bon Appétit's* "Eating, Drinking and Cruising on the Thames" may inspire you to consider writing "Eating, Drinking and Cruising on the Mississippi."

General interest publications and **miscellaneous** publications run the full gamut of reading material. And practically all of them publish travel stories in one form or another. (*Accent*, for instance, a magazine purchased by various businesses to distribute to employees, customers, and friends, is in the market for lively travel vignettes that are short but informative and of lasting interest, and prefers US destinations. Its editors buy ten to twelve articles and thirty to forty photographs from freelancers every month. The preference in photos is for those without people, "unless actively engaged in interesting ways.") *Easy Living*, for instance, is distributed quarterly by Creative Marketing Enterprises, Inc., is read by savers club members. (Savers club publications seem to use a lot of travel pieces. That's natural, I suppose, since the thing that many people are saving for is a trip.)

National Geographic tells the writer not to worry about submitting photos, as these are handled by professional photographers. On the other hand, its listing suggests that photographers submit a generous selection of transparencies. "The use of many clear, sharp color photographs . . . makes lengthy word descriptions unnecessary," warns the *Geographic*, indicating also that historical background be kept to a minimum. The magazine is, it says, "seeking short American place pieces with a strong regional 'people' flavor." Doesn't that sound like a natural for a travel writer aboard the *Mississippi* Queen?

A *Signature* editor once wrote me:

> Our editorial format is such that our travel stories are not usually run just because a place exists. We demand a heavy element of reader service in our features; whether the vacation site is a new one filled with exotica, or an old favorite spot which is presented in an offbeat way. We try at all times to have an unusual premise on which to take our tack. . . . We told our readers not just to go to the Greek Islands, but how they would be able to buy a part of them for a reasonable sum.

Signature in the **general interest** section and *Travel and Leisure* in the **travel, camping, and trailer** section are sent to holders of travel credit cards, presumably among the world's most sophisticated travelers. The focus and tone for these publications would be entirely different from the focus and tone for readers of *Sunshine Magazine*, *Good Reading*, or *Readers Nutshell*, modest publications that deal in upbeat, inspirational themes. The estate-oriented reader of *Town and Country* is a very different person from the small-town reader of *Grit* and the rural reader of *Capper's Weekly*. It's up to you, the writer, to discern these differences, and pinpoint ideas that will appeal to the specific audience. *Saturday Review*, an intellectual biweekly, might be interested in a *Mississippi* Queen story. So might the *Star*, a weekly tabloid. But they would want quite different stories.

The rejuvenated *Saturday Evening Post* can be a good market. *Reader's Digest*, at the top of the pay scale, often runs original "Armchair Travelogues." Not an Armchair Travelogue, but more like an ode to a river, "Life on the Mississippi—Revisited," condensed from Ben Lucien Burman's *Look Down That Winding River: An Informal Profile of the Mississippi*, is the story of a journey aboard a barge-pushing towboat. Perhaps the *Digest* would be interested in your journey.

A high-quality historical, artistic, or scientific piece would be perfect for the *Smithsonian Magazine*, which ran "Feisty Fink, King of Battling Boatmen on the Big River," about a legendary keelboatman on the Ohio and Mississippi Rivers over a century ago. *Ford Times* wants "almost anything relating to American life, both past and present, that is in good taste and leans toward the cheerful and optimistic." "My Old Kentucky Home," a story about the state shrine and park commemorating Stephen Foster, ran in the same recent issue as "Go Exploring with a Pocket Lens," an illustrated article about the wonders of dandelions, thistles, red clover, and other common items, as seen through a pocket magnifying glass. Could you have written one of these stories after your mythical trip?

First-rate and prestigious, *Geo*, which has expanded from Germany to a US edition, vibrates with elegance and excitement. Its long features explore every facet of the geographic subject under discussion and enhance the copy with outstanding photography. An environmental approach might work here. Treatment is more twenty-first-century than *National Geographic*'s, but subject matter is similar, and it's the sort of publication people put out on their coffee tables.

Health publications? Well, if your mother-in-law has an incapacitating illness, *Accent on Living* might be interested in how she gets along. *Bestways, Health, Your Life and Health, Weight Watchers Magazine*, and a whole covey of fitness publications would all respond to some kind of a health angle—maybe something on food, exercise, or recreation aboard the *Mississippi Queen*. The weight-watching magazines usually carry staff-written diet material, but like to fill in with interesting non-diet stories from freelancers. *Goodstay* is distributed to people in the hospital—its purpose being to cheer them up.

Among the **history** publications, *American History Illustrated* welcomes suggestions for illustrations, but usually doesn't buy photographs. *American West* limits its coverage to "anything west of the Mississippi River," so you'll have to be careful which riverbank you're talking about if you try to do a historical piece for them. *Chicago History*, or *Historic Preservation* might be interested in the Nauvoo, Illinois, Mormon community or the Indian battles at Dubuque, Iowa, or the Indian games in La Crosse, Wisconsin, or other vignettes of history encountered on your trip.

The thirteen pages of **hobby and craft** publications include many unexpected titles. *Treasure* and *Lost Treasure* would be interested in the history of Cave-In-Rock, Illinois, if there's even the slightest hint that some of the unsavory characters who once peopled the rock left some hidden treasure behind. *Early American Life* is an excellent market for stories about visits to historic sites.

An amazing number of **home and garden** publications run some kind of travel article every month. Each travel article is, naturally, geared to that publication's readers, so the same idea wouldn't work for *Metropolitan Home, Flower and Garden Magazine*, and *House Beautiful*. *Better Homes and Gardens* ran a series on "Learn-To-Do-Something-New," and one article in the series was "Vacations." The

"Something New" was guided nature expeditions. *Better Homes and Gardens*, however, is probably not a good market for your *Mississippi Queen* story yet. *Reader's Guide* leads you to the June 1978 issue, which included a huge feature on exploring the Mississippi, as well as an extensive report on the *Mississippi Queen*. You might, however, want to use this issue as a reference for your own article, making sure there's nothing you've left out, and you might want to write to the author of this story, requesting additional information or a fresh quote on the pleasures of cruising the river. But *Better Homes and Gardens* would probably wait a while before considering another Mississippi story. "How to Choose a Boarding Kennel," ran in the June 1977 issue, but they might be getting ready for that theme soon again.

Poolside Living, somewhat surprisingly, in its Spring 1976 issue, featured "The River." The blurb quotes Mark Twain, " . . . the great Mississippi, the majestic, the magnificent Mississippi, rolling its mile-wide tide along, shining in the sun. . . ."

Beautifully illustrated, the story continues for four pages, and when it says on the second page, "In one way or another, directly or indirectly, the Mississippi River system touches the lives of all of us. . . . It is a piped, controlled and limitless commodity that slakes our thirst, waters our gardens, fills our pools and serves our industries," we turn back to the title page. Oh yes, the magazine is published by the Monsanto Company in St. Louis and is, of course, addressed to swimming pool owners.

Many home and garden readers would like to know what you think about the beautiful homes and gardens of St. Genevieve, Missouri, or the seasonal floral display at the Jewel Box Conservatory in St. Louis.

In-flight publications like travel material—*sometimes*. All of them, and their advertisers, court the affluent business travelers, who make up over 50 percent of the plane's load, so it's a special kind of travel material. No first-person accounts, no camping out with the children, no long-winded sagas for what may be a fifty-minute ride. Naturally, in-flights try to appeal to the reader who *flies* to his destination—unlike *Ford Times* and Chevrolet's *Friends*, which extend friendship to the reader who *drives*; *Hertz No. 1*, which includes sight-seeing information for the reader who *rents* and drives; and *Go Greyhound*, which features historic, scenic, or entertainment attractions accessible to the reader who leaves the driving to *them*.

Although the different in-flights vary somewhat in their approach, most want stories only on the destination areas they service, and all prefer a cheerful, optimistic, upbeat approach.

In-rooms, similar to in-flights, are found in many large hotel chains. The Webb Company produces several of the airline and hotel publications, and East/West Network, Inc. puts out a number of them, so if your story doesn't quite fit the target market you select, it's passed on to a sibling periodical. (East/West, incidentally, is binding into its magazines a new twenty-four-page supplement, *Scoops*, geared to the female business traveler.) In addition to Webb and East/West, Ameri-

can Way might provide a home for a *Mississippi Queen* story compatible with their destinations.

Juvenile publications and **teen and young adult** publications use travel material in two ways—stories introduce young people to the experience of traveling; and they teach about children from other countries and other cultures. Many of them emphasize the values in other cultures, helping young people to realize that other people are *different*, but not *inferior*. *Cricket, Highlights for Children, Touch*, and any of the *Scholastic* magazines would be good candidates for the *Mississippi Queen* experience from the child's viewpoint. Flora and Fauna in and around the Mississippi, What It's Like Traveling on a Big Ship, The History of the River, What Would Mark Twain Say if He Could See Us Now? would all make good themes. So would caring for vacationers' pets. Try your story out on Melanie, and see if *she* likes it. *Circle K Magazine* wants travel material "from a student's angle: how to budget, what to take, where to go, etc." Could you adapt your material with son Mike's help? *Seventeen* likes to advise female teenagers on travel. *Ranger Rick's Nature Magazine*, published by the National Wildlife Federation, would certainly consider a story on the Upper Mississippi River Wildlife and Fish Refuge, a 196,000-acre preserve where Canadian geese, blue herons, bald eagles, beaver, and deer can be seen. *National Geographic World*, published for young readers, would like this type of story, as well as a host of other stories you might get out of this trip. The *Friend, It's Our World* and the *Vine* are possible juvenile markets, too, although they might be more interested in foreign travel.

The Wildlife and Fish Refuge story, slanted differently, of course, would be ideal for some of the **nature, conservation, and ecology** publications, such as *Audubon, International Wildlife*, the *Living Wilderness, National Parks, National Wildlife, Natural History*, and others. One of the best travel stories I've ever read appeared in *Pacific Discovery*; zoologist Steven Anderson describes the people and the animals marching in marble-carved relief down the Apadana Stairway at Persepolis.

Slanted still differently, your *Mississippi Queen* experiences might go to a **sports and outdoor** publication such as *Field & Stream, Illinois Wildlife, Michigan Out-of-Doors, Outdoor Life, Outdoors Today*, or *Wisconsin Sportsman*. Is there good fishing along the way? Good hunting? En route to the Mississippi did you stay at special campsites? Encounter any unusual hunting and fishing laws? Did you, yourself, have an extremely successful fishing session with new or unusual equipment? A *Sports Afield* editor says, "We're emphasizing travel and where-to-go articles. . . . We want to know about little-known, new or reborn 'hot spots'—anywhere in the world." *Sports Afield* likes lots of information and how-to, and soft-pedals "true-life" adventure.

Sports Illustrated is a wonderful market because of its *weekliness*— it uses four times as much material as a monthly! Sometimes what it uses is amazing—everything from "Sail a Slow Boat to See," a charmingly illustrated journey along the canals of France, to an early-in-this-century story of two small boys who crossed the continent on horseback, to the origin of Australia's theme song, "Waltzing Matilda," to "America Is Formed for Happiness," a story from the diaries and letters of British travelers who toured the colonies before the Revolution. A history teacher friend says *Sports Illustrated* publishes "some of the best history articles around."

In that same sport section, many of the boating magazines, from *Boating* to *International Yachtsman*, would be good markets for the *Mississippi Queen* story. Readers—and editors—who are interested in boating are interested in any type of waterborne holiday. Archery, bicycling, gambling, hunting and fishing, swimming and diving, and other sports categories might tie in, also, and son Mike might have ideas about still other angles. If your travels take you where some sport will be holding a championship meet, you may have a story. The idea is, of course, to urge those interested in the sport to attend the championship event. The November 1977 issue of *Skating*, for instance, begins its story "On the Oregon Trail" with:

> Portland, Oregon, host to the 1978 United States National Figure Skating Championships next February 8-11, is more than just a city, it is an idea, an experience. Portland is a potpourri, spiced by variety. But Portland has something else undefinable but perhaps best called personality.

(It doesn't take much insight to figure out that this was written by the Portland Chamber of Commerce—but it does prompt the freelancer to look out for future championship areas.)

The twelve pages of **lifestyle** publications include some that are anti-establishment, some that pay only in copies, some that are transitory and ephemeral in nature. But *East West Journal, Harrowsmith Magazine, Mother Earth News*, and *Natural Life Magazine* are all substantial publications, all interested in organic gardening, rural living, homesteading, natural foods. Will you see stories along the way that would be suitable for one of them? Perhaps you'll buy eggs at a dilapidated farm just purchased by a young couple beginning to restore it, or you'll notice a hundred miles of roadside vegetable stands with signs advertising their wares as organically grown, and you'll stop to interview several of the farmer-greengrocers.

Back in the **literary and little** publications, nearly forty pages of small-magazine listings provide a number of possibilities. Many, however, pay only in contributors' copies. The travel writer who feels a desperate need to be published—regardless of pay—might consider these as beginning markets.

With the right angle to your river trip story, you should be able to make it at **men's** publications like *Playboy* or *Gentlemen's Quarterly*. Would *Esquire* like a story about the business of running the *Missis-*

sippi Queen similar to its story on Aspen, "The Business of Running a Ski Mountain?"

Military publications? In addition to the purely professional periodicals, a number of these are interested in historical pieces, although *Army* states emphatically, "No rehashed history." *Battle Flag*, on the other hand, wants features on little-known battles, ancient warfare, and weapons of war. How about something on those Indian battles in Dubuque? The *Retired Officer Magazine* reaches a slightly different group, and often is similar in content to other retirement magazines.

Ladycom, Military Living, and *Military Living and Consumer Guide's R&R Report* appeal mainly to the distaff side of the military, while *Off Duty* tries to please the women *and* their men. Published in three editions (Pacific and US West produced in Hong Kong, and European produced in Germany), *Off Duty* also divides into "A" and "B' splits. The "A" edition is geared to the mature military man and his family, the "B" edition goes to single, often younger, servicemen. Travel stories are usually published identically in both editions, but the movement is away from destination stories; the present preference is for stories with an extra element of something to *do* besides just sight-seeing. Two weeks on the *Mississippi Queen* might be an especially appealing story for *Off Duty*'s US West edition. *Overseas Life,* also published in Germany, and also beamed to US military men, thinks of its audience as somewhat younger, with fewer married, and more on limited funds. But the editor reports a strong need for US-based material, since many readers are interested in what's happening back home in America.

The entertainment aboard the *Mississippi Queen,* which is often spectacular, may inspire you to search for one of the **music** publications or one of the **theater, movie, TV, and entertainment** publications as markets for your stories. In music, especially, you have a wide choice for reviewing the entertainment or interviewing the entertainers, from *Bluegrass Unlimited,* to *Modern Drummer, Guitar Player Magazine,* and *Keyboard Magazine.*

Newspapers and weekly magazine sections are among the best travel markets in terms of volume, although their pay is often modest. You can, however, usually sell the same piece over and over again, marking it "exclusive your circulation area," and sometimes it builds up quite a nest egg. Better still would be to make an arrangement with a syndicate, but that's sometimes harder than it appears. Newspapers will often have special theme issues, such as the *Los Angeles Times* with its annual plans for International and Europe; Alaska; Canada and the Pacific Northwest; Summer Vacations; Hawaii and the Pacific; Mexico; Cruises; and Caribbean issues. Many weekly travel sections run annual cruise issues and vacation issues.

Magazine supplements and Sunday supplements often produce a travel edition in early spring and a vacation-resort edition shortly before school closes. Often the editorial material has some connection with the areas, accommodations, or means of transportation being advertised. If you have file cabinets bulging with travel research and photographs, let your local editors know where they can call you when they need to cover a particular area. Or find out when they're likely to be ready for a story you would be able to produce. If the *Mississippi Queen* Company wants to buy an ad in your local paper, your editor may assign you a story.

Monthly and bimonthly magazines, incidentally, have in-depth issues on specific themes, too—a certain area of the world and all its various charms, or a certain activity, like skiing or golf, and all the places it can be pursued. If the area, the site, or the activity is familiar, find out about these in-depth or theme issues ahead of time and see if you can fit what you know into what they want. Get in touch with suggestions before you begin your river trip. It's highly likely that somebody will be planning an in-depth boating issue, a special Mississippi River issue, or a complete roundup of recreational activities in the area you'll be covering.

Editors of the *Christian Science Monitor* usually insist on a degree of exclusivity, and you may be disappointed in the size of their check. However, their quality demands are high, and publication in the *Monitor* adds to your reputation. Publication in the travel section of the *New York Times* is also prestigious, and they also want all rights. At the *Times* they say, "Write what you have to, and then get out," but most newspapers insist that a writer keep under their maximum word length, usually about eight hundred words, hardly ever more than fifteen hundred, sometimes as short as three hundred. More and more newspapers are accepting color photographs now (for discussion of photography see Chapter 15), but all prefer some kind of photos, either color or black and white, to accompany the story.

A new wrinkle is the travel supplement that goes out with a number of papers, such as the *Travel Informer*, published three times a year for six Southern California towns, and *Travel Illustrated*, a monthly four-color publication featuring domestic and international travel, distributed with a dozen newspapers throughout the country. A riverboat story might go over well there, and it certainly should be welcome at newspapers in states where the *Queens* travel.

If you're clever with a camera, any of the **photography** publications will welcome your *Mississippi Queen* story. Photographs are an important plus value for any story, so keep your camera handy. Perhaps the picture-taking possibilities will give you ideas for writing, too. **Poetry** and **puzzle** sections are so specialized, you'll have to work extra hard to tempt them. Wouldn't it be fun, though, to drift through a somnolent afternoon on the river, sitting in a deck chair composing a verse or constructing a crossword puzzle?

The **regional** and city publications, have, as you know, been booming—multiplying and expanding. They don't all always stick precisely to their own areas, but they do try to publish articles that will interest their readers. So your trip might make an intriguing story for the affluent, leisured readers of *Palm Beach Life*, published in Florida, or the venturesome, travel-oriented readers of *Westways*, published in Southern California.

By carefully reading the *Writer's Market* listings, we discover that *Bend of the River, Cincinnati Magazine*, and *Ohio Magazine* sound like good markets for your trip story. *Chicago Magazine* and *Avenue M* seem possible. *Missouri Life* and might publish a piece about your trip, and *Wisconsin Trails, Madison Magazine*, and *Inland Shores*, as well as *Mpls. St. Paul Magazine* all sound like good prospects. So do *Louisville Today* and *Back Home in Kentucky*. Don't overlook the geographically related areas served by *Indianapolis Magazine, Outdoor Indiana, New Orleans Magazine, Nashville* and *Pittsburgh Magazine*. Would an article on choosing a kennel appeal to all of them?

Bend of the River specializes in Ohio history and antiques, and, indeed, seems to be living in a historical era, offering as it does five dollars minimum, on publication, for an exclusive 1,500-word article, and a dollar per black-and-white photo, with caption. Other magazines in these two groups pay more, some of them much more. Practically all of them say they want history, nostalgia, humor, and travel pieces, and many would like photo essays. Understandably, *Chicago Magazine* has a more urban outlook than *Wisconsin Trails*, but most of them speak of their readers as upper middle income, college educated, interested in the arts and in travel to nearby areas.

Writer's Market's twenty-four pages of **religious** publications include magazines of all denominations. The material doesn't have to be *too* religious in theme, but it can't be *anti*-religious. Here again, each periodical is especially concerned with its convention site or the area of a special project. Some of the religious magazines pay very modestly, others are competitive with general publications.

Saint Paul's Cathedral, styled after Saint Peter's Basilica; the Mormon buildings in Nauvoo, Illinois, built by Joseph Smith and his followers; the buildings of the communal society at New Harmony, Indiana—all would fit into a religious publication. I have sold articles to religious magazines of all denominations on such subjects as: Olvera Street, the Mexican quarter of Los Angeles; the Junior Museum of Palo Alto, California; the largest all-women's college in the world, Ewha University of Korea; and "How Far Does Your Dollar Travel?"

Another travel writer says he has revised some of his nonselling travel articles to emphasize the religious peg, thereby making them appealing to this group of magazines. He wrote about religious statues adorning an Arizona site that were built by a man fulfilling a World War I vow, and an Indian pueblo once destroyed because its inhabitants professed Christianity. Study the religious markets. You'll get lots of ideas for stories for them about the *Mississippi Queen* trip and your travels before and after.

Retirement publications gain in importance as the average lifespan increases: More and more citizens retire earlier and live productive and interesting lives for longer and longer periods of time. Travel is an important part of those productive and interesting lives. There are four major magazines in the retirement category. *Dynamic Years* is for preretirement planners. "Exciting use of leisure" is one area of its subject matter. Wouldn't your story qualify? *Dynamic Years* stories all have an upbeat, optimistic note, like "Riding the High Country: Trail rides lead the way to the unspoiled beauty of high wilderness" or "Is a Cruise for You? Those adventuresome cruise ships can take you on a nonstop vacation." Could you work out something like "Drifting through Yesterday: A Mississippi Riverboat Is an Experience for Today"?

Modern Maturity, the vehicle of the American Association of Retired Persons, is for those who have already retired. While AARP runs its own tours, and much of the travel material in the magazine relates to the trips it's promoting, there's still room for the freelance travel writer. Two series seem to be ongoing: "Let's Explore America" and "Invitation" to such attractions as Yuletide at Yosemite or to the Pompeii show in various American cities. Your river trip might fit into one of these series or might emerge as a straight nostalgia piece.

Fifty Plus, which used to be *Retirement Living*, has a strong travel emphasis these days. It sees its readers as "alert, active, forward-looking." "No nostalgia" is the word here, and the preference is for "unusual travel stories."

Prime Time, one of the newer publications, is designed for people in the forty-five to sixty-five age group who are "ready for the rewards, excitement, and adventures that come with the second half." Many of its articles deal with travel-related subjects (restaurants, resort time shares, winter vacations without skiing, house swapping, and "Tourism Without *Turista*"), and there's a major travel feature each month.

In addition to the big ones, *Mature Catholic, Mature Living*, which is Baptist, *Mature Years*, which is Methodist, *New England Senior Citizens/Senior American News*, *Retirement Life*, *Senior Exchange*, and *Senior Advocate* address themselves to the older American, and that older American usually likes to travel. The story of a trip where you're housed and fed in comfort and only have to unpack once is bound to appeal to a senior audience. Your mother-in-law probably has some good ideas, too, about which facets of the *Mississippi Queen* cruise would be most interesting to those of her generation.

Among the **science** publications, you'd probably have to introduce a really special angle to sell to some of them, like *Astronomy* or the computer or electronics magazines. However, *Popular Mechanics* ran "Bargain Float Trips near Home" not long ago.

Probably the greatest diversity within a category is found in the **women's** publications section. You doubtless know the big traditional publications, all of which use travel stories sometimes. The pitch would be different if you're trying to sell the story to *Ms.* than if you're aiming for *Cosmopolitan*, still different if you're seeking publication in *Playgirl*, and even more different for *Farm Wife News*. *Bride's* and *Modern Bride* might want to consider the *Mississippi Queen* for honeymooners. *Women Today, McCall's, Working Mother, Working Woman, and New Woman* are all unique and would require special

Mississippi Queen stories. All of them, however, would be interested in how to save money while traveling, how to pack, what travel documents you need, or other general themes shaped for them. *Women in Business* runs an annual March/April travel issue that features the American Business Women's Association convention site and adds some travel how-to-do-its.

One of the biggest buyers of travel material is *Redbook*, whose readers are eighteen to thirty-four, most of them young mothers. From time to time there's a special "Redbook Traveler" section, which includes a variety of themes: "The Adventurous Life"; "Unusual Vacations"; and "Vacations to Remember." Your river trip might be adventurous enough or unusual enough to fit and presumably it will be memorable. What will the "Redbook Traveler" be doing next? If you think your family's vacation would interest other families, why don't you inquire?

The **travel, camping, and trailer** publications cover a broad range of periodicals. In addition to the AAA publications, other automobile clubs, both US and Canadian, publish similar magazines. Insurance companies and oil companies vie for the traveler's attention. There are several newsletters of travel advice, and a whole host of possibilities among the RV publications. As one editor states, "Freelancers are very important to national special interest publications, since it is economically unfeasible for magazines to have staff writers cover such a broad geographical area." He says that in addition to articles written by experts, he also needs travel pieces with an enthusiastic approach. During your RV trips to and from Cincinnati, will you find something boat-related to approach enthusiastically?

Travel/Holiday, "The Magazine that Roams the Globe," is a large-circulation periodical that looks for "smashing photography."

They want "destinations and activities the reader can duplicate." Your trip qualifies on that score. With the good photographs you're going to take and the lively story you'll promise to write, you're likely to get an expression of interest here.

When you turn to the *Writer's Market* section on **company** publications, you'll be astonished to find so many of them excellent travel markets. Company publications (also known as house organs) are sponsored by a particular company to keep employees, customers, stockholders, salesmen, and dealers aware of what's going on in the organization. Some companies publish several magazines—one for customers, one for stockholders, and another for employees, for instance—while others distribute the same periodical to everybody. Does the organization you or your spouse work for publish a house organ? Would the story of your adventures aboard the *Mississippi Queen* find a good home at one of them?

The emphasis varies tremendously. Some insist on every word being company-related, while others barely mention the sponsor. Volkswagen's *Small World* steers a middle course—the editor says he wants "interesting stories on people using Volkswagens. Our approach is subtle, however, and we try to avoid obvious product puffery." Was a VW the star in any of the stories you saw en route to the *Mississippi Queen* or during your cruise?

Other good market possibilities among the company publications would be *Compass* (Mobil Oil) or *Go Greyhound*.

In the March 1979 issue of *American General Journal* (American General Life Insurance Company) you see a story on "Music, Music, Music: From Bluegrass to Beethoven, Music Is a Way of Life in Virginia." Does that give you any ideas? Where else is music a way of life? Many company publications are searching for good all-around articles, so don't overlook this area of the marketplace when it comes to placing a travel story.

Don't overlook the house magazines, purchased in bulk by travel agents to send to their best customers. They need stories that lure the sophisticated traveler into planning yet another trip; and the trip has to be of the type to generate travel agents' commissions. These periodicals come and go, but while they're publishing they make good markets, so seek them out.

Writer's Market's 154 pages of **trade, technical, and professional journals** offer a huge number of possible markets, too. These publications are produced for people in a certain trade, industry, or profession, and while their emphasis is on technical expertise, many of them fill their pages with interesting, only slightly related stories as well. Does your trade or profession publish a journal? *Instructor Magazine* likes travel stories the teacher can use in the classroom and those that help the teacher in planning his own vacation. Your *Mississippi Queen* story could work either way, couldn't it? *National Future Farmer* likes outdoor activities and the photography trade journals are good for the travel writer-photographer.

Is there some way you could work out a brief story for a business education magazine that could be translated into shorthand for a skills exercise? Anything for *Dental Economics, RVBusiness, Camping Industry, Modern Veterinary Practice?* How about *Ground Water Age*, which asks for "general interest; historical; nostalgia; personal opinion; photo features; profile; and technical" for its well-drilling contractor and water systems specialist audience?

Trade journals within the travel industry, such as *Asta Travel News*, the *Travel Agent*, and the *A.S.U. Travel Guide*, also rely heavily on freelance material. Functions of these publications range from helping the travel agent to do a better job to telling the airline employee where to find the best vacation. Somewhere in this range you and the *Mississippi Queen* must fit.

Whether you travel aboard the *Mississippi Queen*, or choose a vacation closer to home, or farther away, the travel story you write can be published. Nearly all the publications I've mentioned here are listed in *Writer's Market*. And practically all of them pay *something*. I'm not really mercenary, and I don't feel a writer's soul should have a price tag, but on the other hand, a travel writer is a professional, and is entitled to be paid a fair price for a job well done. The trick, of course, is finding the right periodical for your particular story, and studying the markets before you mold your material. This will pay big dividends in terms of selling what you write. Recognizing the wide world of travel writing markets can turn the story you write into the story you publish. After you've completed your preliminary market research and your itinerary, you'll be ready to tackle the ultimate sales tool, the query letter, which we'll discuss in Chapters 11 and 12.

5

Getting Ready to Go

You'd think those who travel for a living would always be on their toes about what they'll need; letter-perfect in their preparations, and ready for the summons to adventure. They would think so, too—but they know better.

Georgia Hesse, travel editor of the *San Francisco Examiner*, wrote a bittersweet column a few years ago about meeting her friend the travel editor of the *Chicago Tribune* in Sri Lanka. His arm was red and swollen. Why? Because although he had completed his shots before leaving home, he had misplaced his "yellow card" (International Certificate of Vaccination). Border officials insisted on duplicating the shots. Georgia Hesse was amused at the time, but admitted she found the situation less amusing a few days later, when she arose at three a.m. for a trip across the island of Mauritius to make a six a.m. flight to the Malagasy Republic. Authorities refused to let her board the plane. Why? Because she had no visa for Malagasy. When she'd looked up the requirements in San Francisco a week earlier it seems she'd mistaken Malagasy for Mali.

Whether you're going to Malagasy or Mali, whether your journey is to the next town or across nine time zones, do as much homework as you can when you're getting ready to go. Otherwise you're likely to be disappointed in dozens of wretched little ways—and plenty of big ways, too.

If your "getting ready" involves planning with a travel agent—and there are those who think this is wise and those who think it's foolhardy—be honest with him. How much money and how much time do you really have to spend? What do you really want to see, and how do you want to see it?

Gigantic statues of Ramses II, Abu Simbel, Egypt

And insist that the travel agent be honest with you. Ask "What is the 'half day of sight-seeing'—is it four hours or only two and a half? What is a 'transfer' supposed to do—meet me at the plane and assist me through customs and immigration, or meet me at the taxi stand and put me in a cab? Does this price include all gratuities? Will my sight-seeing tours be in English *only*? Does a 'driver guide' know enough to help me with my research? Would reversing the itinerary be desirable?" (Always request separate vouchers for each person and each item, so if you decide not to do something it will be easy to obtain a refund.)

Traveling with a group is usually the easiest, in terms of planning and executing. Traveling on an FIT (Foreign Independent Tour) arranged by a travel agent also features prepaid arrangements tailored to suit you with more freedom and responsibility. Giving you still more freedom and more responsibility for taking care of yourself is the kind of trip with no prepaid reservations, no arrangements made for you—you go as you please each day.

Whether you use a travel agent, accept a hosted trip or do it yourself; whether you have assignments, go-aheads, or just something you want to see, always consider your sight-seeing plan very carefully. It is the single most important feature of any trip. Sight-seeing can be dull and dreary, hurried and half-baked; or, with intelligent arranging, it can provide maximum writing and research value as well as personal pleasure and enrichment.

Your sight-seeing program is not something to arrange casually, trusting to luck that you will see the best things in the easiest way at the cheapest price. Too many people select the wrong trip for the wrong reasons. They ruin any chance of writing about their travels because they don't ask the right questions when they're getting ready to go. Sight-seeing plans are geared to particular people, particular places, and particular pocketbooks. If you know the full range of what's available, you'll be able to select your own ideal plan, whether solo or in a group.

Ask yourself, "Why am I traveling? For adventure and discovery? Or for relaxation and diversion? What kind of readers will my stories appeal to? Why will *they* be traveling?"

There are other questions: Is the getting there or the being there more important to you? Are you traveling to find new ideas for your writing, or to give your ideas a rest? As Lawrence Durrell says, travel is "one of the most rewarding forms of introspection."

Are you pursuing the Holy Grail of some long-cherished dream? Will you be satisfied only if you see London's Old Curiosity Shop, or the Mark Twain Museum in Hannibal, Missouri?

Do you want to know how people live in other parts of the world? Are you hoping to make new friends? Or mere acquaintances for the duration?

Do you want to travel with other writers? With other photographers? There are a few tours geared especially toward writers and/or photographers (usually listed in the May issue of *Writer's Digest*), as well as many work-play conferences. If well run, these can be stimulating and rewarding. As at a writers' conference, the shop talk is valuable in itself and the entire trip is slanted to your purposes.

Perhaps you've already arrived at that lofty peak where the editor calls *you* for a story on the new Robert Trent Jones golf course at Xanadu, scheduled for the next issue. Can you make it to the airport by five? Your first-class air tickets and hotel vouchers await you there. At Xanadu's capital you'll be met by the press chargé d'affaires, who will conduct you, via camelback, to the third, sixth, and seventeenth tees. Send the story by Friday.

In such cases, your sight-seeing plan has selected *you*. Sit back and enjoy it. But if you're the one choosing what you will see and how and with whom you'll see it, be sure to consider what kind of person you are.

Take into consideration your habits and characteristics. Your sight-seeing choice, if you like to get up early and be on your way by eight, will be different from that of someone who prefers to review the night-club circuit. If you are compulsive about eating at definite times or need to rest after lunch in hot weather, you must take this into consideration. If you feel lonesome unless lots of other people are sharing your experience, or you're out of sorts when you have time on your hands, your sight-seeing program won't resemble that of the person who's bored hearing someone else's opinion and gets disgruntled when every minute's arranged for. Do you like to laze in the sun, ride a horse, dress for dinner? Do you like to drive or be driven? Are you impulsive, eager to do what you want to do, when you want to do it? Do you detest regimentation? Remember what you are like when you plan your sight-seeing program.

Two writers comparing trip notes discovered that each had had a wonderful time traveling to the same area—although one covered every cathedral and museum and spent evenings at the theater, while the other shunned cities and tramped backcountry roads, staying at country inns in medieval villages. Each had planned a sight-seeing program that covered exactly what she considers a good time and likes to write about.

Each of these women traveled alone, because each was very sure of what she wanted to do and unwilling to make compromises. If you're an independent kind of person, never bored by your own company, consider solo traveling. Going alone, or with a known traveling companion, or perhaps with several well-chosen ones, may work out best for you. If you and your traveling companion(s) don't agree about the ratio of time and money to be spent on various stages of the trip, you'll have to work out compromises. If you want it to be a good trip, negotiate these matters *before* you go. If you intend this to be a business trip for you, what will your traveling companion do while you're tracking down all the facts a travel writer needs? Your traveling companion may or may not feel the benefits are worth the sacrifice of your company, the early morning phone calls, the late-night research and writing sessions. Perhaps you can persuade him or her to become part of the project—by taking photographs, for instance. If you join some group of congenial traveling companions, such as an alumni tour, you'll have to conduct your own business within the framework of the group arrangements, without inconveniencing anybody else.

No matter how much information you unearth, and no matter how enthusiastic you try to be, you'll never convince your readers it's a great place if you aren't having a good time. So take into consideration your personality, the things you like to do, your special interests, and your physical condition. Consider, too: Is this likely to be your only trip to this area? If so, perhaps you'll want to see the "musts." However, don't overlook the advice of Dr. Ralph Crawshaw, who says you should limit your goals and expectations. "You can't see or do everything there is to see or do in a few days, so focus on some special interest." In the Netherlands, for example, he began with Rembrandt's home in Amsterdam, and "went on trying to visualize the city as it must have appeared to him around 1650. I didn't frustrate myself by trying to gulp down the Dutch nation's whole history and cultural development."

I once met a charming, sophisticated woman, a buyer for Sears Roebuck, who had traveled throughout the world. "I've probably been in more foreign cities without seeing the most famous landmarks than anybody you've ever known," she said. She spends her free time sunning on beaches and exploring back alleyways. She added, "I'm past the stage where I feel I have to see something just because three generations of travel writers have stamped it with approval."

Discuss with your travel agent, or with your prospective companion(s), or with yourself whether you want to join a tour group, design an FIT, or just amble unscheduled from day to day. Different traveling writers have different needs.

There's a tour to fit every possible interest or affinity, whether you're a nonsmoker, a wheelchair traveler, or a ballet buff; whether your particular desire is to concentrate on "The Train in American Culture" (a nineteen-day cross-country railroad odyssey), "The European Approach to Policing" (with visits to Interpol and Scotland Yard), or "Surfing in Hawaii."

In choosing a tour, consider not only your assignments and planned stories, but also your other interests and hobbies. Do you think you might find interesting and valuable a tour designed for those studying gourmet cooking, international theater, music festivals, local crafts, viticulture, or stamp collecting? Your pretrip homework for the tour will probably be designed by the tour leaders, who will send you informative study material in advance. Then they will take care of most of the everyday arrangements, which the solo traveler has to work out for himself.

Even if your temperament is anti-tour, for certain destinations at certain times a tour may be the best answer. The Student Travel Catalog, published by the Council on International Educational Exchange, makes note of the fact that its users may ordinarily "avoid 'tours' like the plague!" It goes on to describe the "unique opportunities" of overland tours from Europe to Asia and throughout Africa, but points out bluntly, "If you love your creature comforts, DO NOT BOOK on one of these trips."

Equally candid is Pan Am's brochure encouraging travelers to join its excursions to Mainland China. It recommends "a little homework before you depart" and "a flexible and positive attitude."

> The accommodations tend to be adequate to modest. If you find unanticipated changes unpalatable or cannot accept accommodations considerably less than you would normally prefer, you may not wish to participate in this program. It requires a sensitivity to the customs of the people and a willingness to accept the tour arrangements "as is" regardless of your particular interest or taste.

At least you *know* before you go!

How do you select the best tour? Al Stich, a travel photographer, charted the seven most appealing tours for the area he wanted to visit at the time he wanted to go. By listing in graphic form the airlines and equipment used, the number of meals provided, the number of days, the type of hotels, the points of origin and return, the side trip options, the actual cities and areas visited, and the price, he figured out which of the tours would be best for seeing the places he and his wife had in mind, and which would give the most value for the money.

As one travel writer says, "There are no bad tours—only unfortunate marriages of tour and tourer."

Do You Need a Guide

Your "getting ready" preparation helps you decide on sight-seeing arrangements of all kinds. Aboard ship, for instance, you'll plan whether or not to take the shore excursions. Some ports of call aren't worth a tour—just walking around will show you more than a bus ride would. Others have so much to offer that if the ship is in long enough you would do well to hire a private car and driver.

By yourself with private car and driver is, of course, the most luxurious way to sight-see. If money is no object, you can tour the Rockies in a Cadillac limousine, complete with driver-guide and no worry about gas lines.

Sometimes the money for a private car and guide is money well spent. I was in Milan only once, twenty years ago, between trains. Yet, I'll never forget *The Last Supper*—thanks to the knowledgeable young man who met our train, whisked us out to the refectory of Santa Maria delle Grazie, and then back to the train for Lake Como. His sensitivity, his awareness, his education in art, his ability to communicate the artistic experience, gave me a lifetime memory of da Vinci's masterpiece. That brief visit to Milan was expensive, but it was a bargain.

If you plan to concentrate on scenery, you won't need a guide, except for reasons of safety in wild and remote areas. Unless you feel compelled to know the height of every mountain and the depth of every sea, you can enjoy the Appalachian Trail or Washington State's San Juan Islands without explanation. You move at your own speed, take all the pictures you want, and stop to eat when you feel like it.

Other times, the guide will be the key to your sight-seeing program. Find out which sites have built-in guidance, such as the Panama Canal, where the "talker" comes aboard your ship and explains everything as you sail through the locks, or the French châteaux, where they hand out mimeographed information in your own language. Allow enough time for Gettysburg, where buses take you on regular guided tours of the battlefields, and Williamsburg, where the buildings are attended by knowledgeable costumed hostesses. Today many museums, from Paris to Hiroshima, lend or rent cassette recorders with taped commentary on the exhibits. If you're touring some US or Canadian national parks, or driving from San Francisco to Monterey, or from County Cork to County Clare, or to and from a variety of other places, you can buy taped tours that run on an ordinary cassette recorder and lead you to all major sights. They set forth the history, culture, and folklore of the area, along with shopping tips and sports advice. One of the several suppliers of these tapes is:

CC Inc. Auto Tape Tours
Box 385
Scarsdale NY 10583

Many large cities, as far-flung as Wellington, New Zealand, and Göteborg, Sweden, provide city tours in municipal buses, and Melbourne, Australia, does it with a harbor tour on a city-owned boat. The independent travel writer can build a sight-seeing program around these possibilities.

For developing countries, however, where the language and even the alphabet is often extra-difficult, where all facilities are expensive, where arrangements are complex and time-consuming and distances are vast, you're usually better off with a doorstep-to-doorstep guided tour.

Consider Your Interests

Incorporating your special interests always makes travel more meaningful. An amateur genealogist talked for months about his exciting solo trip to study at the National Archives in Washington, DC, and seek out the tombstones of his Virginia ancestors. A couple traveling in the Orient made arrangements to visit the Hong Kong orphanage supported by their church, to which they'd been donating for half a lifetime. An artist inspected photographs of the areas she intended to see, so she knew in advance which would be the most interesting scenes to paint. These special interests later contributed to their travel stories.

Do you belong to a national or international organization? Write ahead to find out what's doing along your route. Not only Rotarians and University Women, but kite fliers, square dancers, model airplane builders, fishermen, ham radio operators, quilters, bridge players, and people tied together by practically any concern you can name, have associations with many branches. Get in touch ahead of time for a warm welcome. This kind of "getting ready" homework is not only personally rewarding—it often leads to a story.

Perhaps you'll want to join an organization especially for the trip. Depending upon your age and orientation, such groups as the American Association of Retired People, Parents Without Partners, the Union of Polish Women in America, the Society of Painters in Tempera, the Youth Hostels Association, the Sierra Club, the British-American Society, the Irish Georgian Society, as well as your professional or trade association, your alumni group, your church affiliation, and hundreds of other possibilities, can lead you to travel friendships, travel discounts, and stories with plus value. Plan far ahead and send for membership information.

If you explore the various sight-seeing possibilities, taking into consideration your personal tastes and desires, where you are going, and the type of sights you will be seeing, you can plan an ideal program within the framework of available time and money.

Whether it's your money or your editor's, you'll want to take advantage of financial considerations often given to those under twenty-five, over sixty-five, married, unmarried, teachers, students, doctors, patients, weekday travelers, weekend travelers, skiers, bowlers, joggers, and almost anyone alive and breathing. If it's the off-season, there's a special rate. If it's the right day you can go to the museum without paying. Days of the week and hours of the day can make a difference in the price of transportation, admission, and other travel writing needs. So look out ahead of time for whatever discounts or bonuses you're entitled to.

Line Up Your Informants

As you think about your upcoming trip and what you'll be writing about it, think first: Whom do I need to talk to for the stories I'll be working on? Then line up your interviews and appointments. In some countries you'll never get to interview anyone without a letter of introduction. Sometimes consulates and embassies can help you arrange business appointments; other times you can work through a company's branch offices. But it's imperative to search out the local customs and set all the wheels in motion early.

Will the person you need to see be available? Even if you're only traveling to the next town, check on the business days and hours, so you'll be able to do what you need to do while you're there. Does an annual May Day parade block downtown traffic and close most business establishments? Is Election Day a legal holiday in that town? Do you need to speak to somebody at the school board office during a week when all school functions are on half-day session? Will the store you need to research be closed for inventory? Have all the farmers you planned to interview taken off for the Apple Butter Festival?

The farther you travel, the more critical the problem becomes, because your actual transportation plans grow less flexible. One writer counted his single day in Buenos Aires a total loss because the taking of the census entailed a holiday that prevented him from finding the information to complete his story. Another travel writer, visiting Venice for an assigned photo essay on mosaics, found all the crucial people and places immersed in celebrating the Feast of the Redeemer. More than one surprised journalist has discovered that all of Australia races to a standstill on Melbourne Cup Day.

Both national and international holidays, like Papua New Guinea's Thanksgiving Day in August, Japan's Respect for the Aged Day in September, Hawaii's Aloha Week in October, and the "anything goes" Oktoberfest in La Crosse, Wisconsin, can be a plus or a minus for the travel writer. He has to work around the moveable feasts, too, like pre-Lenten Mardi Gras in New Orleans, Carnival in Rio, or Charro Days in Brownsville, Texas-Matamoros, Mexico; as well as Ramadan, observed in all Muslim countries with a month of daylight fasting, and Kurban-Bairam, when everything is closed for family festivities. Travel writers may avoid holidays or embrace holidays, but should always be aware of their existence.

If you're embracing the holiday—Good Friday in Seville, the Tournament of Roses in Pasadena, Queen Elizabeth's Jubilee visit to the South Pacific—and you want to go there at that time *because* that's the story you want, find out first what will be the best vantage point. Then beg, bribe, or buy your way into that vantage point. Consider, too, that you'll want to take pictures, so if there's a choice of vantage points, pick the one at a good height for picture taking, with the sun in the right direction. Try to ask friends who've been where you're going the best way to see the event. They may tell you that at Copenhagen's Tivoli Gardens you can rent a sort of periscope that lets you look over the crowd to see what's going on. Other friends may tell you to climb the steps to a rooftop restaurant overlooking the Djemaa-el-Fna Square in Marrakesh, where, for the price of a soft drink, you can see all the action. You can look down on and photograph the peddlers, the snake charmers, the storytellers, the water carriers with their tinkling bells and copper cups, and the mobs of fascinated bystanders.

The seasons of the year can be important to the travel writer. Naturally, if your story involves New England's fall color or the show of rhododendrons in San Francisco's Golden Gate Park, you'll take pains to be there at the critical moment. Sometimes, it's hard to second-guess nature. What week will the cherry trees bloom? What time will the fairy penguins parade up from the sea? Do your best to obtain accurate predictions from tourist offices, chambers of commerce, local residents and frequent travelers to the area. Human beings, on the other hand, are more predictable. In August, when the French take *their* vacations, most Parisian activities shut down or fold up; during the hot summer months many US East Coast businesses work a four-day week, or shorter hours some days, or different hours.

While off-season travel has many advantages, in cheaper prices, smaller crowds, warmer welcomes, it can have its disadvantages, too. The excursion boats don't travel up the Hudson to West Point or up the Thames to Greenwich; the famous restaurant may be closed; the planes, the trains, the buses will run on different, less frequent schedules. Twice a year the arrival and departure of daylight saving time can change your travel schedule. (Several November homecomings have found me waiting an hour at the airport for a relative to pick me up at the time it said on my daylight saving itinerary.) Nailing down these specifics is part of "getting ready."

Even days of the week make a difference. One travel writing team spent three Sunday hours restlessly pacing among the benches of a Paris train station after discovering the eleven a.m. train to Chartres didn't leave at eleven on *Sundays*. Another couple spent a long, hungry day aboard a Kuala Lumpur–Singapore train. Now they know—the dining car isn't always attached to the train on *Sundays*. In New Zealand and Australia you could starve on a weekend while the waiters and the dishwashers are out surfing and sailing, and if you insist on eating in a restaurant, you're going to pay extra for it. Your pretrip homework will reveal that in those countries and in many others, as well as many major US cities, sabbath laws regarding the serving of alcoholic beverages dictate what time the restaurants will be open.

What day *is* the sabbath? In Muslim countries it's Friday. In Israel it's Saturday, beginning at sundown Friday. Not only are all banks, business offices, stores, and restaurants closed, but transportation is limited as well. The wise travel writer confirms this information and takes it into consideration when getting ready to go.

Museums all over the world tend to be closed Mondays. Except some are closed Tuesdays. Or Wednesdays. Or Sundays. A California journalist making a trip to New York for the American Museum of Natural History's special show "Pompeii A.D. 79" heard the museum was open Mondays, but telephoned ahead to be sure. It was a good thing— the Museum *is* open Mondays, but not until after noon.

Will you be doing research at libraries, museums, archaeological digs? These often require letters of introduction before they let you through the gates. Ask the most eminent scholars you know to attest to the excellence of your character and the importance of your mission. (Then write ahead for a built-in welcome.)

The welcome extended to Alice Kennedy by the Shakespearean research area of San Marino's Huntington Library didn't include even her husband. When he started to accompany her into the special room, the receptionist stopped him. "I'm sorry, sir," she said firmly. "You'll have to wait here in the lobby. Only *Mrs.* Kennedy has permission to enter."

In some countries it's essential to have a "Reader's Ticket" to work at the National Library, the Public Record Office, the National Maritime Museum, or other research source. Save on-trip time by sending ahead for these permissions. An audience with the Pope? Write ahead to:

> Bishop's Office for United States Visitors to the Vatican
> Casa Santa Maria
> Vis dell'Umilità 30
> 00187 Rome, Italy

If you're a Roman Catholic, include a letter from your priest or bishop.

Whether it's for a story or just for fun, tickets to a special festival or event can add another dimension to your trip. But the Salzburg and Bayreuth festivals sell out a year in advance, and the every-ten-years Passion Play at Oberammergau is reserved long ahead of time. Whether you're going to the opera in Santa Fe, the Mozart Festival in Burlington, Vermont, or the Old Fiddlers' Convention in Galax, Virginia, write for tickets as soon as you know your plans. Enclose a self-addressed, stamped envelope or an international reply coupon to expedite the answer.

Do you want to review a Broadway show? Send a check and an SASE to the theater months in advance, to avoid paying scalpers' prices. (That's how we happened to have six seats in the first row of the first balcony for a hit musical. By the time we saw the show, the tickets were selling for a hundred dollars apiece.)

Your telephone can be your passport to efficiency and economy. In big countries like the United States, Canada, and Australia, an inexpensive early-morning call from west to east or an early-evening call from east to west still catches people during the business day. This often works for country-to-country calls, too, so the writer needing a telephone interview or wanting to make an appointment or check a fact with someone several time zones away can call at the cheapest rate. (I've found, incidentally, that an international phone call is well worth its price if you're trying to impress those at the other end with the seriousness of your intentions.)

If your itinerary isn't firmed up, you'll need mail arrangements. The traditional route, both within the United States and abroad, is "Care of American Express." Some Thomas Cook and Pan Am offices also hold mail for their customers. Another way, of course, is *poste restante* (general delivery). Find out how long the mail is likely to take and instruct your correspondents to mark "hold for arrival" on the envelope.

These offices are closed evenings, weekends, and holidays. So is the consulate, which will sometimes hold letters for you. But you can always get your mail at the best hotel in town. You don't have to stay there. Just give that as your address, then ask the concierge or mail clerk what is being held for *your arrival*; slip him a modest tip, and hint of more to come.

As for homebound mail, don't spend a huge hunk of trip time and money addressing postcards and letters to the folks back home. Always type out gummed address labels before you go, so you can just press them onto the postcard or envelope. Going a step further, you can buy the postcards themselves before you go. (Foreign Cards Ltd., Box 123, Guilford CT 06437, is one place—doubtless there are others.) Stick the gummed labels onto your prebought postcards and, if absolutely necessary, write your preplanned message. (I've never done this, but sometimes I've been tempted!)

Cross the "T" in "Document"

What kind of documents must you have to travel where you're going? Passport? Visa? Tourist card? Apply for whatever you need in plenty of time, and follow the directions carefully in filling out the forms. Check and recheck to be sure you have everything you need. Many times I've seen people at the airport prevented from boarding the plane because some "i" wasn't dotted or "t" wasn't crossed on their travel documents—or they had looked up requirements for the wrong country. (Incidentally, allow plenty of time at airports for inspection of those documents when you're traveling internationally.) Jot down the numbers of your travel papers, as well as those of your credit cards, traveler's checks, and airline tickets, and put them in a different place than the originals. If anything is lost or stolen, you'll have an easier time replacing it if you have the number.

Throughout your trip you'll often be required to identify yourself on various documents, and the phrasing of the information may be more significant than you think. In some countries, listing yourself as "Journalist" or "Travel Writer" is like waving a red flag. Consider the political situation. Perhaps it's better to stick with "Businessman," "Housewife," or "Retired." Sometimes this becomes a sexist matter. When we debarked from a ship in Chile a couple of years ago, the immigration people wanted to know all of the *men's* professions—even those who were retired had to come up with something to satisfy the questioners. But the *women* were never interrogated. On each woman's debarkation card, beside the Spanish word "Ocupacíon" was written the English word "Laborer"!

You may wish to describe yourself as a "Student" on your visa. Catherine Elwood did that when she was studying for her Ph.D. at Stanford University. One immigration inspector took a second look at her visa, then a second look at her forty-year-old face. "Student?" he muttered. Then he looked her straight in the eye. "*Still?*" he inquired.

If you can prove you have been a full-time student during the current academic year, apply for an International Student Identity Card. Send documentation, a small photograph, and a modest fee (currently three dollars) to a regional office of the Council on International Educational Exchange:

777 United Nations Plaza
New York NY 10017

236 N. Santa Cruz #314
Los Gatos CA 95030

Pershing Hall
49, rue Pierre Charron
Paris 75008, France

or apply at a student travel service or one of several hundred CIEE campus offices. Allow at least three weeks for processing.

Identified students become eligible for student-priced charter flights and discounted air, rail, boat, and bus fares, reduced-rate car rentals, museum entries, tours, accommodations at student hostels, welcome services, and special travel insurance, as well as a variety of helpful publications. In Los Angeles, for instance, students can stay at a desirable, centrally located hotel for seven to fifteen dollars a night. Even New York's venerable Waldorf-Astoria provides dormitory-style rooms at student rates. Many accommodations are under five dollars a night—some are free.

If you study only part-time and don't qualify for the CIEE card, you may still find that describing yourself as a student will open many doors. Mature researchers Norm and Rose Grabstein, while working for advanced degrees in archaeology, found that writing in advance for permission to see restricted sites, and beginning the letter, "We are students," usually led to the special permission they sought. When they asked to tour France's closed-off Lascaux caves, the French Conservation Service not only granted permission, but warned that visitors have to walk through disinfectant to protect the cave paintings, and suggested they wear shoes and clothing they didn't care too much about.

Your Clothes Can Be Important

As a travel writer you should *always* plan to wear clothing you don't care too much about. But the *type* of clothes can be important when you're searching for a story abroad. In many countries clothing customs require covering some specific part of the anatomy. In Saudi Arabia, women who do not conceal their arms and legs risk fine, imprisonment, or expulsion. In Jerusalem's ultra-Orthodox Mea Sherarim district they risk stoning and spitting. At the Vatican a Swiss Guard refuses admission to women considered immodestly dressed. (Formerly a nun posted at the main door to Saint Peter's lent plastic raincoats to women with bare arms and legs, but too many took the raincoats as souvenirs.)

It's all right for women to wear long pants at the Vatican, but at the Meteora, the cliff-top monasteries of Greece, they must wear skirts or dresses. To enter the African republic of Malawi, those skirts or dresses must cover the knees.

Malawi, incidentally, is one of the many countries that imposes its own grooming standards on the length of male visitors' hair and beards. If immigration officials consider them too long, the airport barber stands ready with the shears.

Golf courses and tennis clubs all over the world are becoming increasingly strict about players' apparel. If you show up in cutoff jeans and a tank top with an advertising message, they won't let you play.

Men must cover their heads at Jerusalem's Wailing Wall, as well as at any Orthodox synagogue, and paper skullcaps are usually provided. Women, however, should come prepared with scarves of their own. At the Wailing Wall married women of all faiths cover their heads, as do all women, married and single, in the churches of many other religions.

You should think ahead, too, to the parts of you that will be uncovered while traveling. At Muslim mosques and Buddhist temples all over the world, as well as at many other buildings in the Orient, you'll be required to remove your shoes.

You will, of course, inquire in advance about climate and activities that would influence your clothing choice. Try to take clothes that won't make you too conspicuous and outfits and separates that will do double or triple duty for many kinds of occasions.

Your pretrip research will not only help you conform to local dress customs, but will also alert you to differences in manners and mores you'll want to observe. Whether it's a matter of kissing the hand, kissing on both cheeks, arriving early, arriving late, eating with your fingers, or sending flowers to your hostess, you as a travel writer will want to blend into the local environment.

It shouldn't be necessary, but maybe it is, to remind the travel writer to try out *everything* at home. Break in your new shoes. Run a couple of rolls of film through your camera. Make sure your alarm clock works reliably.

If you plan to do any shopping on your trip, think about which brand of typewriter, photographic lens, binoculars, wristwatch, etc., is most easily serviced at home. Will you really know a good buy when you see one? How much duty will you have to pay? And what time do the shopkeepers take their siesta?

If you'll be driving in another country, get your International Driving Permit from either the American Automobile Association or the National Automobile Club. Valid for one year, the permit costs three dollars and requires two passport-size photos. They'll usually issue it while you wait. If you're an auto club member, inquire as to what membership privileges carry over to other countries: Emergency road service? Legal advice? Lists of club offices? Estimates of road conditions? In the British Isles, where US auto club memberships *are* honored, the British Automobile Association not only patrols the roads, but, if necessary, provides a key to unlock caches of petrol deposited for emergency use. Inquire of the auto club what time big buses and trucks jam narrow, winding roads, so you can avoid those times.

To guard against a possible fuel shortage, the travel writer at the wheel does all he can to ensure against an empty tank. Find out ahead of time: What days? What hours? Odd or even? One of the travel writer's most important research needs is the phone number of the gasoline hotline. Toll-free lines have been set up in most states to let you know what's happening up ahead, and some hotel chains have a special number to give out this information, too. If you know the answers, you won't linger watching the sunset while the last gas station is closing.

If you're driving your own car, of course you'll make sure it's in first-rate running condition before you take off.

If you're driving in another state or another country, look into speed limits, traffic rules, etc. Trucks, campers, motorcycles, bicycles (and probably burros) are also subject to certain regulations and restrictions, so find out what they are.

Check with your insurance carrier about what additional auto insurance you may need. Check, too, about health and accident insurance, trip cancellation insurance, baggage insurance, and perhaps a floater on your camera equipment.

At home or abroad, arrange for good maps. But don't be misled by them. Sometimes what appears to be an easy hundred-mile drive is really two hundred miles of winding mountain path. Learn the names of major towns along your route, and also your compass directions—your particular destination may not appear on the highway signs. Try to obtain (or photocopy from books) good city maps and site plans. Then you'll be able to mark the path you took down the mountain at Delphi, the sites of the different treasures, and exactly where you were standing when you took that dramatic picture with the wide-angle lens.

About Matters of Money

In addition to your purely professional planning, it's important to know, too, that local customs vary greatly as to when the banks are open. If you arrive in a foreign country when the banks are closed, you may have expensive dealings with a hotel cashier. Instead, buy in advance from your travel agent or foreign exchange broker enough currency to get you through the first few days, and spend some time memorizing what the different denominations look like.

Give thought to how you will handle your travel funds when you're getting ready to go. There are advantages to traveler's checks, and there are advantages to credit cards, which sometimes include automatic insurance, opportunities for securing emergency cash, easy car rental deposits, and other assistance.

If you're applying for a new credit card, allow plenty of time. Three trips in a row we applied three months in advance for a particular card, which never arrived until after we'd left. Leave some money in your checking account and take along your checkbook, too; certain establishments give discounts for cash.

You can often obtain traveler's checks at no charge from an institution that uses this service as a promotion, and they're a handy way of carrying cash, even if you're only traveling fifty miles. If you're staying more than a few days in a foreign country you may find it saves time and trouble to buy traveler's checks in *their* currency when you're getting ready to go. In any case, plan to take a handy selection of small-denomination bills. I've never had much sympathy for the travel writer who converted a five-hundred-dollar traveler's check into the currency of an Iron Curtain country where he was scheduled for two days. Since there were no souvenirs to buy, his trip was prepaid, and tipping was not permitted, by noon of the second day he was trying to trade the currency back into US dollars. He not only spent the entire afternoon at the bank, splitting and slicing red tape, but he missed his dinner and nearly missed his eight p.m. exit plane.

Can You Learn the Language?

If you're planning an overseas trip, you may want to learn, or brush up on, a foreign language. At least listen to records or tapes as you dress every day, and practice your pronunciation. While every travel advice writer emphasizes the importance of learning "Please" and "Thank you" and "Where is the bathroom?" in all the languages of your itinerary, it's also important to learn the directional words. Although non-English-speaking people may think they know the difference between "right" and "left," it's best to check the directions by repeating them in their language. How do you say "around the corner" in German? "Fourteen kilometers" in French? "Down the hill toward the sea" in Greek? "Back to the Imperial Hotel" in Japanese?

If you'll be interviewing somebody in a foreign country, even if that person speaks English, it's well to look up ahead of time translations for the key words you'll want. Look up words you'll be needing at the post office, at the camera repair shop, at the library.

English is a difficult language, and often people who have mastered a few words don't really speak or understand as much as we think they do. The *Eurail Guide* explains that even those who have mastered English sometimes hesitate to speak it—and when they do speak it, sometimes they're hard to understand. The Eurail Guide Travel Language System involves pointing to the appropriate question in French, Italian, German, or Spanish. The questions are arranged in the book to cover such emergencies as catching the wrong streetcar to the train station or finding yourself on the wrong train, *not* finding the porter who took your luggage or remarking to a fellow passenger, "You are sitting in the seat I reserved." The quotations are designed to enable a "yes" or "no" answer or an appropriate directional gesture or number.

Hal Gieseking suggests also learning the words in every language for "Is the service charge included?" Then you'll know whether to tip the waiter and the housemaid the traditional amount or just leave a little spare change.

You can talk to the waiter with a Berlitz *European Menu Reader* that not only translates and tells you how to pronounce the names of likely dishes, but indicates in many languages, from Danish to Serbo-Croatian, how to say: "That's not what I ordered"; "The meat is too tough"; "What's taking you so long?"; "You've made a mistake in this bill"; and a variety of other useful phrases.

Ellison Enterprises (2951 S. Bayshore Dr., Miami FL 33133) and Marling Menu-Masters (1330 Polk St., San Francisco CA 94109) have publications that provide clues in several languages as to what restaurant dishes actually contain and how they are prepared. After consulting Menu-Masters and with the aid of two bilingual nephews, the Italian owner of her local fish market, and a friend in a consulate, freelancer Frances Lilienthal prepared for each country she was visiting a neatly typed list of idiomatic phrases pertaining to food, including such phrases as "My husband is on a diet for his health"; "Low fat"; "Please serve the sauce on the side"; "Does the fruit juice have sugar added?"; "May we have unbuttered toast?" It not only worked, she says, but "responses were invariably pleasant and helpful."

While you're arranging for translations of menu information you may be thinking, "What if I eat *too* much? What if I get sick overseas? How will I tell the doctor what's the matter?" Send for *A Foreign Language Guide to Health Care*, distributed free by the Blue Cross Association (1950 Franklin St., Oakland CA 94659), which translates into French, German, Spanish, and Italian "I have a pain in my chest"; "I am allergic to novocaine"; "Where can I get this prescription filled?"; "I will need a detailed bill to collect my health insurance"; and, simply, "OUCH!"

How Healthy Are You?

It would be foolish not to candidly consider your physical condition as you get ready for your trip. Writers are often sedentary people. If you sit at a typewriter day after day you're likely to have overdeveloped hips and not much stamina in the legs and feet. (One travel writer, incidentally, considers a visit to her podiatrist an important pretrip ritual.) If you've hardly walked around the block all winter, your heart, lungs, and muscles will protest when you have to hurry between widely separated airline counters. There's a lot of walking involved in any trip—far more than the writer may be accustomed to—so you have to begin early to get ready. Start by walking five or six blocks a day at a good, brisk pace. Increase the distance daily until you've worked up to at least three miles a day for several weeks before you leave. If you intend to carry a heavy purse, camera case, or flight bag, haul it around at home, gradually adding items, so your arm and shoulder muscles won't be screaming with pain your first day of sight-seeing. If you'll be bicycling, dancing, or rock-climbing on your trip, practice before you go.

For really rigorous trips you need rigorous training. Martha Poppy, well-known mountain climber and ski instructor, who, at age fifty, climbs 19,000-foot ice-covered peaks and skis through the Alps and the Sierras with a pack on her back, thinks consistency is the most important factor in building stamina for rugged traveling. "Just running or biking once in awhile won't do it," she says. She runs five or six miles *every* day and bikes fifty or sixty miles *every* week, and feels she couldn't possibly make some of her difficult mountain crossings or undertake her mountaineering ski trips without the kind of stamina she's built up through consistent exercise.

Arrange for a complete physical examination, and obtain all required shots in time to recover by departure day. Have your yellow card entries validated by the local health department. See your dentist, too. But don't let him fill, extract, or work on a root canal within twelve hours of an air trip. As a midwestern dentist explains, "Whenever a tooth is opened, a small bubble may be included. Then that trapped gas expands as you're airborne. Changes in atmospheric pressure can leave you stifling screams of agony."

Do you worry that you may need a doctor while away from home? In the United States, just look in the phone book for the county medical society—the operator will provide you with the names of several qualified specialists. In foreign countries, American country clubs usually have lists of US-trained doctors and dentists.

If you're visiting a non-English-speaking country, your consulate or embassy may help you. But it's wise to be prepared with a list of well-trained English-speaking physicians on twenty-four-hour call. One method of obtaining such a list is a voluntary contribution to the International Association for Medical Assistance to Travelers:

736 Center Street
Lewiston NY 14092

1268 St. Clair Ave. W.
Toronto, Canada M6E 1B9

St. Vincent's Hospital
Victoria Parade
Melbourne 3065, Australia

17 Gotthardstr.
6300 Zug
Switzerland

IAMAT not only supplies lists of qualified physicians, but its twenty-four climate charts cover the globe, detailing specific climatic conditions throughout the year, advising on clothing, and outlining the state of sanitation in food, water, and milk in 1440 cities. Its "Traveler Clinical Record," completed by you and your doctor, belongs beside your passport.

Intermedic (777 Third Ave., New York NY 10017) also provides a list of qualified English-speaking doctors, who respond to emergency calls and charge reasonable fees. In addition, the National Travel Club's Mediguide Service (Travel Building, Floral Park NY 11001) supplies names of English-speaking doctors and dentists to its members.

Two organizations designed for a slightly different purpose—SOS Medical Service Program (1420 Walnut St., Philadelphia PA 19102) and Assist-Card Corporation of America (745 Fifth Ave., New York NY 10022)—will help you in major emergencies, if you need such services as an ambulance plane or a guarantee of your hospital costs. Assist-Card provides legal aid, too, and puts up bail, as well as hauling skiers off mountains and recovering lost luggage.

Two programs protect you by alerting others to information about your special conditions, medications, or allergies. Probe Medi-Guard Corporation (19 W. Forty-fourth St., New York NY 10036) converts your medical data to microfilm, which is read through a collapsible viewer the size of a credit card. Medic Alert (Box 1009, Turlock CA 95380) sells identification bracelets and necklaces that specify the wearer has a medical condition that might not be apparent, and provides a twenty-four-hour number to call for the patient's medical history.

While it's helpful to know about these services, one travel writer suggests, half-humorously, half-seriously, that the most important aid to the health of a pair of museum-hopping travelers is a wheelchair and a plaster cast. "One of you," directs Shepherd Mead, "pops the cast on one leg, sits in the chair and is propelled by the other past the ticket booth. Assume brave and cheerful expressions. . . . If you lean heavily on the chair it is easier and takes some of the weight off the feet. The other passenger is resting and gathering strength." He recommends a change of passengers every forty minutes or so, with the cast transferred to the other person's leg. "Alternately resting and pushing, you can last for hours," he guarantees.

On a more serious note, a traveling doctor contends that poison ivy, poison oak, and poison sumac have "ruined more vacations than the combined effects of bad weather, missed travel connections, and inconsiderate guests." Learning to recognize—and avoid—these is another precautionary pretrip preparation. Find out what some of the other botanical hazards may be in the area you'll be visiting. Are there animal and insect hazards, too? Those travel writers who are extremely allergic to the bites of bees, mosquitoes, sand fleas, or other common insects, will want to inquire carefully about the area's fauna.

While travel writers often require treatment for itchy eruptions, tired backs, overwalked feet, gastrointestinal disorders, respiratory complaints, heart and blood pressure problems, accidents, sunburn, insect bites, and heat exposure, the complaint you're most likely to have is jet lag.

Although there are many hints on how to prevent jet lag, nobody has really found the answer. If you cross more than two or three time zones, you'll feel it. Design an easy day after your jet lands, and don't plan anything too important; it takes three days to reset your internal clock. Arrange a stopover if it's a long trip. How long is a long trip? I don't know. But I do know that Johannesburg to San Francisco in one hop is *too long*.

One traveling family always begins changing time zones a week before going overseas, a half-hour each day. The day before they leave they eat breakfast at 4 a.m. and the children go to bed at 5:30 p.m., with the adults following shortly. Thus, they avoid wee hours' hunger pangs and general exhaustion.

Several scientific experiments are presently being conducted to determine the ideal diet for the "jet set," and it appears that particular combinations of foods and a change in eating habits may help.

Don't add boredom to fatigue. Ameliorate the effects of long airport waits and endless rides by bringing books to read, letters to write, work to organize. Survivors of many cases of jet lag and auto ennui advise the traveler to get up or get out and walk around as often as possible. If you're driving, plan to stop every couple of hours, whether anybody's tired or not, and take along some nutritious munchies and something to drink. Don't try to drive more than eight hours a day, and quit before your reactions begin to slow down.

Plan for Your Comfort

The travel writer should consider creature comfort in getting ready to go on a trip. Find out in advance how late your hotel will hold your reservation. Should you guarantee the charges on your credit card? And inquire about checkout time. Does the tropical beach resort shove you out at nine a.m., so you're sitting all day in your traveling clothes, waiting for your evening plane? Or will your room's previous occupants remain legally staked out until late in the afternoon, while you're arriving at dawn, exhausted by jet lag?

You may not have much choice in the selection of a hotel room, but if there is a choice, opt for the quiet one. Spurn the room with a door that connects it to the adjacent room (television and party sounds seep through the cracks) and the room that opens directly on the pool area (you'll hear the night owls swimming at midnight and the early birds trying to beat the dawn). The travel writer's greatest need (besides quiet) is enough light. If the room seems dim, ask for an additional lamp or larger bulbs, or carry along your own. If you're camping or youth hosteling your auxiliary light should be battery-operated.

If swimming and tennis are important to your story, make sure the pool and the courts will be in service while you're there.

Mealtimes are worth knowing. Is seven a normal dinner hour at your destination? In Ireland it's too late. In Spain it's too early. If you're the kind of writer who can't work on an empty stomach, important pretrip inquiries will be about food service on trains, motels with twenty-four-hour restaurants, and meals served on flights. If you have special food needs, find out in advance what kind of restaurants you should look for.

Let the airlines know your dietary requirements when you make your reservations, then double-check twenty-four hours before you leave. They'll provide you with an ulcer patient's meal, a low-calorie meal, a vegetarian or diabetic meal, hamburgers and hot dogs for your children, or whatever else you need.

Do you have a favorite airplane seat? Obtain the chart from the airline, and reserve your seat by telephone several weeks in advance. If you're a "frequent traveler," make that fact known to the airlines. Often they'll put you in the business section of the plane, where it's quiet and you have a little more room to spread out. The window seat is best if you'll be taking pictures. Try to avoid seats against the bulkhead that don't recline fully.

Most places you travel, a brigade of well-wishers stands ready to help the travel writer with personal or professional problems. But sometimes when people discover you're a travel writer, they want *you* to help *them*. They expect you to be expert in many fields and know something about anything they might ask you. Sometimes they have hard questions they've been waiting to ask somebody for months, and when you show up, they expect you to answer.

So one of the most important pretrip preparations is getting ready to answer the questions people will ask you. Whether it's in the next room or across nine time zones, the people you meet will be interested in what it's like where *you* come from. A little thought and a little homework will make it possible for you to present logical and informative answers.

Some questions, of course, like those about busing, fuel shortages, First Amendment rights, racial discrimination, inflation, strikes, unemployment, sometimes don't *have* any easy answers. But try to be prepared so you can present the facts without floundering.

Pondering answers to probable questions is part of getting ready for your trip. So is planning your sight-seeing program. And if you set up your business appointments in advance and arrange for your professional and personal comfort when you're getting ready, it will pay off in pleasure and productivity once you start traveling. Preplanning makes it possible for you to find plus values, and when all the pieces fit together for you as a traveler, you can begin to act like a travel writer. So think ahead, get ready, and go!

Basuto woman, South Africa

6

What to Take Along with You

et out everything you think you want to take along on your trip; then put half of it back." Experienced travelers have heard this truism so many times they're convinced it's true.

But there are four tools the travel writer must not put back; four tools every travel writer must carry—even if you have to leave behind your toothbrush and clean underwear.

The first necessity is **SOMETHING TO SHOW YOU'RE A WRITER**. Take along your letters of assignment from editors; go-aheads; tear sheets of your published articles; printed programs of travel lectures you've presented; newspaper stories and other publicity about you as a writer; membership cards in travel or writing organizations; a press card if you have one.

At the very least, arm yourself with a walletful of printed business cards. If you're going overseas, where business cards are an even more important appurtenance than in North America, have the blank side printed in the language of the country you're visiting. You'll be surprised how many doors those little pasteboards will open—everything from the press box at the horse races to a private tour of a government child-care center. With professional credentials you take on a professional air and encourage professional respect.

The second essential tool is your **CAMERA**. Now you may be thinking, "Oh, my camera really isn't very good—it doesn't have all those fancy gadgets," or "I'm not very good—I'm really not much of a photographer," or "I don't have time to take all those pictures—I need to see what's going on!" Carry your camera, anyway. Not only do photographs help you sell what you write, but even if they aren't of salable quality, they'll help you write your story. The very act of taking a pic-

California's "sequoia sempervirens" in Humboldt Redwoods

ture forces you to focus sharply, to concentrate on what you're looking at, to see it more clearly. And when you get home you'll discover details you'd half forgotten. I didn't remember, for instance, that Indonesian schoolchildren consider it an honor to sweep the schoolroom floor, and sweeping duties are always assigned to the best-behaved pupil of the day. I didn't remember, that is, until I saw my picture of the grinning Indonesian boy with the broom.

We've all heard jokes about the photographer who was afraid to look at the Alps with his naked eye, and the lady who took a Polaroid picture of the Pyramids so she'd get to see what they looked like right away. Pay no attention. While you don't want photography to overwhelm the trip experience, the advantages of taking pictures far outweigh the disadvantages.

You needn't be an expert photographer to strengthen your trip memories of a trip through photographs. Most modern cameras demand only the ability to focus on the subject and hold your breath for an instant to keep the camera still as you shoot. The cameras do the rest.

You don't have to invest thousands of dollars in photographic equipment. A medium-priced camera, operated by a moderately experienced photographer, will provide salable illustrations. And the cheapest Instamatic, operated by a stumblebum, will provide useful pictures to help you recapture the feeling of where you have been. Even an instant-processing camera, although it seldom produces publishable photographs, delivers valuable gifts for new-found friends in outlying areas, where picture taking is still a novelty.

While *National Geographic* sometimes sends out its staff photographers with 1,500 pounds of photographic gear, most travel writers settle for a good 35mm camera, perhaps an extra telephoto or wide-angle lens, a strobe light or flash gun, a filter or two (to protect the lens as well as to make the sky bluer or the flesh fleshier), and a cable release that enables you to shoot smoothly on a long exposure in dim light. If it's the type with a self-timer, a cable release also enables you to set the scene, then start the release and dash over to appear in the picture.

Take plenty of film. Although within the United States it's hard to visualize an area so remote that film isn't available, it's sometimes inconvenient to track down a supplier or to wait behind twenty others who also ran out. Overseas it may also be difficult to find your particular kind of film, and it will certainly be much more expensive than at home. So start out each day with at least twice as many packages as you think you might possibly need. We did that in Aegean Turkey—and still ran out by noon. We were delighted to find a peddler who had a single package of film, and eager to pay him three times the US price.

How much film is "plenty"? Eric Ergenbright, president of Thru the Lens Tours, says the average photographer on a photographic tour shoots thirty-five pictures a day. "If you habitually take more pictures than the average photographer of your acquaintance," he advises, "increase your film allowance accordingly." Whether you normally take more or fewer pictures than others gives you a clue to film needs, but you have to consider the time of year, the length of daylight, the weather, the character and interest of the sites, the number of different kinds of things you expect to see on your trip—and then double the maximum amount you think you'll want.

Sometimes it's possible to return unused film to the camera shop, if it's fresh-dated, has been kept cool, and the boxes are in perfect condition. If not, put the leftovers in the refrigerator or in the freezer, carefully wrapped. Eastman Kodak experts recommend thawing for half a day to bring the film up to room temperature before using. Several years after their expiration dates your rolls of film will be as good as new, if they have been correctly stored.

Although American airport X-rays are not considered dangerous to unprocessed film, there seems to be a *cumulative* fogging effect. So if you are passing through more than a couple of airports on your trip or traveling through overseas security, where they sometimes use stronger X-rays, either carry all your film in lead-laminated pouches (available at camera shops) or remove film from your carry-on bag and request a hand inspection at the airport.

Since US federal agencies are said to be the major purchasers of the lead film shields, apparently *they* don't believe the statement that airport X-rays are harmless. Even the lead pouches cannot completely protect against the very strong X-rays used at some foreign airports, as travelog producer Earl Dibble discovered. When all his film was destroyed in the Soviet Union he complained to the company that makes the film shield. The president of the company explained that "the X-ray device employed in Moscow emits a dose of X-rays some ten thousand times greater than 90 percent of the world's airports. To protect film under these circumstances, nothing less than three inches of lead would have sufficed."

If it's necessary to leave film in your checked baggage or mail it across international borders, be sure to mark the outside of the container "Unprocessed Photographic Film. Please Do Not X-ray." (See Chapter 15 for further discussion of photography.)

The third indispensable item in the travel writer's luggage is a small, lightweight **CASSETTE TAPE RECORDER**. Before the cassette era I once met a woman who told me she prepared for her around-the-world trip by writing in a diary every night to "cultivate the habit." For most of us, who write something every day anyway, that wouldn't be necessary. But no matter how sincerely we promise ourselves to keep extensive trip diaries, to record every detail in our notebooks, to send meaningful trip letters and write descriptive postcards, our willingness to tell the microphone more than we'd ever put on paper makes the cassette recorder very necessary. You're so *tired* when you return from a wonderful day of sightseeing, full of the thrilling adventures you've experienced, just finding the pen and paper seems like a formidable chore. You'll do it tomorrow; tomorrow, for sure, you'll write it all down. But with the tape recorder, you'll find it easy to talk a running diary-trip letter, and you'll include details you'd never bother with on paper.

Don't forget, though, to take brief, on-scene notes, so you'll remember what to tell the tape recorder. It's better yet to take the recorder along when you're sightseeing, and develop the habit of dictating into it everything you're seeing and everything you know about it. You'll never have to wonder later: How high are the foothills? Is the church on the same street as the school, or around the corner? Why did the ship founder on the rocks? How many people can play on the golf course? When did they serve the sherbet—before or after the meat?

Always tell your tape recorder the answers to the reporter's traditional five Ws—Who, What, When, Where, Why—and add the How. You can, of course, record the sightseeing guide's complete spiel, if you like, and if the guide has no objection. But keep in mind, voices in the open air do not carry as well as voices indoors, and voices with strong accents will reproduce with the accents exaggerated. So perhaps you'll want some written notes, too. Do take the time to label and date each side of the tape, jotting down a few words about the contents of each side.

Certainly you will use your cassette recorder to capture street sounds and native music. You'll probably also take it along to interviews you've scheduled along the way. Here, too, it will be easier to remember what the historian said, what the fisherman said, what the bank president said, what the lacemaker said, if you have it down on tape, rather than trying to unscramble it from scribbled notes.

One man used the tape recorder to great advantage when violence erupted on a Mediterranean island several years ago. He was caught in the gunfire and the bombings, which he was able to record. He also dictated a description of his plight, and later, of his dramatic rescue. Then he airmailed the cassette to a network newscaster, in exchange for a substantial sum.

Even if the information on the tape itself is not salable, it may provide you with deeper insights and endless enjoyment. My husband and I laugh again each time we listen to a tape made on an overnight train when the wife of one of our host country's high government officials invited us into her VIP compartment. She and her two children were traveling to join her husband on holiday, and she apologized profusely because he had already driven ahead with the hard liquor, so she had no "spirits" to offer us. She made up for it, though, by dipping generously into a case of sherry, which she had already sampled liberally. She enthusiastically agreed to our taping the conversation, but her humorous, pungent—and slightly tipsy—comments on the inner political workings of the United States and of her own country could never be printed. The tape, however, with its background noises of children playing and train wheels going clicketyclack against the tracks, provides enrichment for other stories.

If you're in a country where English is often garbled and directions are complex—a country like Thailand, for instance—have the hotel concierge or a knowledgeable guide dictate the directions for how to get where you're going in his own language. Then you can play the directions back for the cab driver or someone on the street who is trying to help you. Also be sure to have dictated the name of your hotel and how to find it.

Still another function of the tape recorder is to play music—cassettes of your choice that you've brought along. In addition to providing pleasant background for picnic lunches and predinner relaxation, your own music can drown out crashes and bangs from the street outside or uncongenial music, television programs, or loud voices from the hotel room next door.

Surprisingly, I once had the tape recorder, but not the cameras, confiscated for the duration of a Middle East flight during unsettled times. Generally, though, nobody has objected to the tapes or the recorder. Presumably X-rays don't hurt the cassettes, and often they're as easy to mail as trip letters. In sensitive countries, though, post office superintendents may insist on hearing what you've got on the tape before they let you mail it. Sometimes they're inquisitive about film, too. From some countries it's wiser not to mail at all—consider the political situation.

Mail also plays an important part in the travel writer's fourth essential tool, a supply of **BIG, BROWN MANUSCRIPT ENVELOPES**. These are especially important if you're traveling overseas by air, where luggage is weighed; or squeezed into a small car, six adults with suitcases between the knees; or traveling by bus, where baggage is limited; or making many connections, where each extra ounce is a nuisance. You save weight and bulk by mailing home at the book rate (every country has a less expensive book rate) all the guides, maps, theater programs, museum catalogs, statistics, historical data, hotel brochures, menus, newspapers, magazines, and other printed literature you find along the way.

Make an effort to pick up as much of this material as possible. Naturally you'll take everything that's free. And don't be too frugal about buying what isn't. You'll be amazed at the way this printed material fills in the gaps when you get home and can't remember how many people can be accommodated at Tree Tops, or when the first shrine was built in Córdoba.

You soon develop an inner sense about what to mail home to back up your impressions. You'll guess which materials not to bother with because they're likely to be in the vertical files of your local library, and you'll guess which ones your library would never have. Some materials you can borrow from a friend who made the same trip, or some you can easily send for later. But if in doubt, take it, and mail it in your big brown manuscript envelope. If your package is heavy, use two envelopes, one inside the other, to keep the corners from tearing through. If you're in a hurry, of course, you'll send your envelope airmail.

The envelopes themselves, while easy to buy in US drug and variety stores as well as in stationery shops, are often hard to find overseas. I wish I had a dollar for every time someone has stopped me in a foreign hotel lobby, as I was about to take my big brown envelope to the post office, to ask, "Where did you find that? I've looked everyplace for envelopes like that!" So tuck a supply into the bottom of your suitcase before you begin to pack.

With your big brown envelopes, your cassette recorder, your camera, and your printed business cards, you're ready to function as a travel writer, for these are the tools the *average* travel writer needs most.

But some of us are special. We've spent years experimenting and adding to our lists of unique needs and take-along requirements. Obviously, different travel writers traveling by different means, with different objectives, have their own individual "musts."

If your story is to grow out of your backpacking, mule riding, or wagon-training trip, you'll need to take along the appropriate equipment. If skateboarding, houseboating, motorcycling, or caravanning are your style, you'll need to be outfitted still differently. And if you're thinking of taking your four-wheel drive into the bush, you may want to follow the advice of Michael Bargo, Jr., who suggests in *Four Wheeler* that you carry along "all the spare parts you know how to repair."

Every travel writer must take the supplies he needs for his own distinct traveling interests as well as the more general items we all find essential. Here is a check list of things especially pertinent to the travel writer's trip:

1. *Assignment sheet.* Don't laugh! In the confusion of taking off, it's easy to forget which editors said "yes" to what, and which ones said "maybe." You probably have ideas of your own about what trip stories you'll surely write, and you'll want to keep an eye out for the stories in which editors expressed interest, but when it comes to arranging your travel time this sheet will ensure your allowing enough for the firm assignments.

2. *Address list.* Addresses and telephone numbers of those people you plan to call or see on your trip, and those you may need to call or write to at home.

3. *Tickets, vouchers, and confirmations.* Check, and check again, to be sure you have your tickets for transportation, theater, sports events, or whatever else you've arranged. Check on your vouchers for lodging, food, sightseeing tours or other items you may have prepaid, and your confirmed reservations for everything from the boat ride at Waterton Lake to the campsite at Yosemite.

4. *Documents.* Your identification and credit cards, as well as membership cards, essential health records, letters of introduction, and whatever else you need.

5. *Travel literature.* Condense all pertinent information into the margins of one guidebook. Then tear out and discard any parts of the guidebook that don't apply to where you're going. There's no use carting along *South America* when you're only visiting Chile and Peru. Don't forget, though, to take along those city and country maps you've been studying.

6. *Postcards and snapshots.* The people you meet enjoy seeing pictures of your town, neighborhood, house, family, pets, car, and holiday celebrations. Books about your area, as well as the postcards, become treasured gifts.

7. *Hardbacked writing surface*—a lap pillow or clipboard for taking notes, expanding notes, jotting down comments, writing letters, and other scribblers' tasks while riding in a car or bus or sailing on a boat or ship.

8. *Small change.* Regardless of the financial plans you make with letters of credit and traveler's checks, regardless of what country you're in, always begin each day with a pocketful of small change so you won't be paying ten prices for a newspaper, or have the cab driver tell you he can't change a twenty-dollar bill or have to choose between tipping five cents or five dollars for a fifty-cent service.

9. *Alarm clock*—especially if you distrust hotels' wake-up systems, or stay where they don't provide that service. Veteran travel writer Stanton Delaplane recommends a pocket alarm for air travelers: "Set it for a couple of hours before landing or you'll never get to the bathroom." He blames the bathroom bottleneck on women who consider it "a private dressing room." If you set your pocket alarm far enough ahead of the face fixers, you'll be sure to get your turn.

10. *Flashlight.* This is very important if you awaken in a strange hotel room or at a strange campground, disoriented, in the middle of the night. It's also important when you sightsee in caves, catacombs, and other dim areas, like Egypt's Valley of the Nobles, where the illumination—sunlight ricocheting off a pocket mirror—barely permits you to see the frescoes *with* your flashlight. Take along a pen flashlight, too, so you can jot down your thoughts in a darkened theater or write up your middle-of-the-night inspiration. Traveling by car in North America? Tuck a 100-watt bulb or tensor lamp in your suitcase. Motel rooms seldom provide enough light for a travel writer.

11. *Magnifying glass*—indispensable for reading maps and essential for buying jewelry, wonderful for viewing nature's or a museum's treasures. I usually remember to take one on long trips, but was furious with myself for forgetting when I traveled thirty-five miles to see the "Splendor of Dresden" exhibit in San Francisco.

12. *Batteries.* At least one complete set of extras for everything you're taking that requires batteries. If they are an unusual type, take *two* sets. Although small batteries can be found for sale nearly everywhere, they're rarely available at midnight, when you're telling the tape recorder what you saw today; or at noon, when you're shooting a flash picture inside the cavern, three miles from the

souvenir shop; or at five in the morning, when you're shaving before an early flight.

13. *Glasses.* While every traveler takes care of his eyes, the travel writer needs to be especially vigilant about possible eye-related problems. If you wear glasses or contact lenses, take along an extra pair and your prescription. Take sunglasses and a sun hat to keep your vision clear on bright days.

14. *Swiss Army knife.* It will tighten the screw in your sunglasses, loosen the cover to the battery compartment in your camera, and perform uncounted other tasks. Once our Swiss Army knife even cemented international relations. Driving through the Loire valley we stopped for lunch at a picnic area. We saw the French family at the next table searching desperately for something—under the tablecloth, in the corners of the picnic hamper, on the ground, back in the car. The six of them shouted at each other, pointing fingers. Then the father, a frantic look on his face, came over to us. It seemed they'd forgotten the corkscrew. When the attachment on our Swiss Army knife opened their wine, peace was restored, and all of them beamed at each other and at us for the rest of the meal.

The travel writer who goes abroad should also take along:

1. *International Certificate of Vaccination,* familiarly known as the "yellow card." Although many countries have relaxed their vaccination requirements, be sure you have the compulsory inoculations entered on your record, and take your yellow card along on your trip. (We know what happens to people who forget their yellow cards!)

2. *More documents.* Your passport, visas, tourist cards, International Drivers License, and whatever other foreign travel documents you need.

3. *Extra passport photographs*—for extra visas or other official documents.

4. *Currency converter,* pocket calculator, or slide rule for changing dollars to guilders or pesos.

5. *Foreign language phrase book,* if appropriate. Even more appropriate might be a fairly new device, the hand-held translator that, with different cartridges, converts some fifty English phrases and fifteen hundred English words into any of thirteen languages, and vice versa. In any case, don't forget your culinary translations.

6. *Extra notebooks,* carbon paper, typing paper, colored pens, paper

clips, pen refills, rubber bands, and that product of a thousand us-es—cellophane tape.

It's often hard to find what you need away from home, and the search uses up lots of travel time.

You'll notice I've said nothing about a typewriter. While it's handy for the travel writer to take one along—presumably the smallest and lightest available—you should consider how many times you are going to use that typewriter in relation to how many times you are going to carry it. If you'll be in one place long enough to make it worthwhile, you'll be happy to have it. Otherwise, the overweight charges of the airlines and the protests of your back and shoulders may nullify its advantages. An electric typewriter is too heavy to consider for anything but a long sea trip, when someone is driving you from your home to the dock. In that kind of situation, be sure to check the outlets aboard ship—are they the right kind or can they be adapted? Will your typewriter, electric or manual, be noisy enough to disturb those in the next cabin or in the next hotel room?

Sometimes you can borrow a portable typewriter from the ship's purser or the hotel desk clerk, or they'll let you use the one in the office after business hours. If, however, the keyboards are designed for a different language, they are often difficult for an English-speaking person to use. So you have to think carefully— would a typewriter be a big help to me on this trip? Do I really need it? Or would a combination of penmanship, tape recording, and borrowing answer my needs?

When you're thinking about clothes to take along, insist on com-fort. A travel writer's concentration should not be on his mirror. Naturally, if your trip will take you to the arctic, you'll pack a dif-ferent outfit than if you're going to the tropics. Will you need apres-ski clothes, or protection from mosquitoes and sunburn? If traveling to a variety of climates, dress in layers, so you can put on or take off without bother.

Unless you're going to watch the polar bears mating on the ice cap, take only a lightweight, all-weather coat or jacket. In over-heated airports, stuffy bus stations, airless hotel lobbies, unventi-lated vehicles, and warm rooms you'll carry your jacket more than you'll wear it. Outdoors, if necessary, snuggle into a sweater be-neath your coat. For every time you say to yourself, "My teeth are chattering—I wish I'd brought a heavier coat," there'll be ten times you'll say to yourself, "Why did I ever bring this coat at all—it feels like I've lugged it ten thousand miles!" The lighter the coat, the more muscle power you'll have left for other necessities.

Again—be comfortable! Don't let what you're wearing get in the way of what you're working on. Unless your trip is built around a posh event, like a coronation, a jet-set wedding, or an opera pre-miere, the travel writer has far less use for dress-up clothes than for casual everyday wear. So put your fanciest duds back in the closet. Your guidebooks may tell you the kind of clothes you'll need, but the best source is somebody who has traveled to that place or in that manner.

But when you're de-selecting what to take, do not remove from your suitcase two pairs of old, comfortable, well-broken-in shoes. The travel writer with the hurting feet won't be the travel writer with the prose that dances.

When deciding what kind of suitcase(s) will best contain your necessities, consider how you'll be getting where you're going. If it's by public transportation, check out in advance the luggage specifications of each carrier. If you're driving, test the limitations of your baggage space, and give some thought to this problem when ordering a rental car.

If you're going by air, avoid paying overweight. Have extra-large, extra-strong pockets sewed into your topcoat. In areas where luggage is weighed, carry all heavy items—the tape recorder, guidebook, razor, even a pair of shoes or a bottle of whiskey—in your pockets. In places where luggage is counted, rather than weighed, put the *heaviest* items in your suitcases and the *bulkiest* ones in your pockets.

Inquire how many and what size checked and carry-on pieces are permitted for each leg of your journey. Sometimes local airlines, used for brief hops, have more stringent restrictions on the amount of luggage allowed, but will relax the rules if you have an ongoing ticket for other destinations. Airlines often make special arrangements for such special items as skis, golf clubs, and fishing rods. (When natural hair wigs were in style, my wig case once rode with the diplomatic mail on an overseas flight.)

Even without camouflaging the weight or bulk of their possessions, women travel writers need pockets in jackets, shirts, skirts, and pants, and many men travel writers find that carrying a shoulder bag gives them a convenient container for all those extras, like maps and spare batteries and cassettes. Pockets and bags leave hands free to wield a pen, tune a recorder, or focus a camera.

On a long trip, start out with an additional small box or suitcase inside your luggage. Fill it as you go along, and send it home with everything you find you can spare. It's easier to unload a little way into your long trip as you discover what you aren't using. If you are a US citizen, mark the send-home package "American Goods Returned" or "Used Clothing and Effects" for duty-free passage.

Since porters are becoming increasingly rare, be sure your luggage has wheels. Never take more pieces or bigger pieces than you can manage yourself. Above all, be sure your carry-on case has wheels or rides on a dolly. This is the case into which you're always stuffing the heaviest, bulkiest items—the telephoto lens, the hiking boots, the bronze sculpture you bought Aunt Hattie, the duty-free perfume, and Gibbons's *Decline and Fall* to read on the plane; and this is the bag you're always having to carry yourself through the labyrinth of airport corridors and the jungle of arrival and departure lounges.

Travel writing doctor Burt Kebric points proudly to his seven-week trip around the world—and many subsequent trips—with his only luggage a bowling bag that fits beneath an airplane seat. Certainly there's much in favor of an arrangement that requires no wait for the baggage to be delivered from the transport vehicle or to the hotel room, but remains always in your possession.

In any event, always identify the outside of your luggage with your initials or your office business card. A home address tempts robbers, who now know you're away from home; but put full information on the inside of all baggage. For quick identification, tie two strands of colored ribbon or yarn, in identical combination, to the outside of each suitcase, carry-on bag, camera case, or coat. Keep a mental count of how many different parcels you should have with you at each stop, so a click in your brain will alert you— Something's missing! Remind yourself frequently, "I should be toting four things (why do I have only three?)."

When traveling overseas, find out the luggage and customs regulations of each country on your planned itinerary. Although most countries aren't too rigid about enforcement, it's expedient to know how many cameras, rolls of film, and other special items they officially permit you to carry in. Be sure to register all foreign-made cameras, tape recorders, watches, and other valuables with your own customs before you leave, so there will be no question about what you bought abroad this trip.

The travel writer is first of all a traveler. With each trip you become more adept at planning so you don't drag along too many things you rarely use, and you can manage without the things you left behind. The comfortable, well-equipped, but unencumbered traveler is the one likely to find the story with plus value.

7

What to Look for While You're Traveling

 ell equipped and well prepared, here you are—on the scene at last. You look around and wonder where to begin—there's so much to see, hear, smell, taste, touch, know, and enjoy.

Sometimes you start by looking for particular information, to flesh out specific ideas or to fit specific markets. Other times you approach the travel experience with an open mind, waiting for your story to find you.

In homes or palaces, temples or cemeteries, deserts or rain forests, the travel writer is always exploring, sampling the action, seeing for himself whether there's anything worth writing about.

You have to remain aware and alert, continually searching for ideas and information. Even "relaxed," on holiday, your mind is always working. One travel writer, who says 100 percent of his wanderings are related to writing and selling articles, admits that even short trips to attend weddings or visit his parents provide the basis for future travel pieces. That's because he's always on the lookout for the potential story.

When a story finds you, sometimes you immediately recognize its plus value. When we joined Japan's "Strangers into Friends" program, our visit to a Japanese home included a venerable grandmother who tore open her kimono to show us her gall bladder scar; a family argument about whether to buy a motor car, which the old lady vetoed as too dangerous; and a farewell with us standing in the doorway struggling into our shoes while the beautiful young daughter accompanied herself on her koto as she sang, "Oh, say can you see by the dawn's early light. . . ."

A glimpse of historic Charleston, South Carolina

Other times the story seems elusive and you have to *create* the plus value. On the Mediterranean island of Malta we saw what seemed like a jumble of prehistoric temples, Roman ruins, reminders of the Knights, beach resorts, British tourists, and bomb damage. It was hard to fuse them into an article. Then hospitable locals gave me a clue. Remembering that Saint Paul, shipwrecked on Malta, was also well treated by the native people, I emphasized Maltese hospitality over a period of thousands of years, which gave my story a focus.

Look for Other Stories, Too

Usually the best stories cover all the ordinary things as well as some special, unique angle. Search for that special angle while you're traveling. But don't neglect the "ordinary."

Search out the details of your story, but also remain on the lookout for additional stories. Often you'll see something more interesting than you expect.

I had intended, for instance, to include a paragraph or two about the museum of San Francisco's Presidio in an article about nearby Fort Point. Exploring the museum, however, I found there was much more than military history there. The diorama of the 1806 Presidio, with a Russian ship in the background and a Russian captain in the foreground, reminds viewers that the captain fell in love with "the prettiest girl in California," who waited many years for him, only to learn that he had died on his trip home seeking permission to marry her. The diorama of the San Francisco earthquake and fire is flanked by pictures of the city before the calamity, pictures of the city being rebuilt, of the 1915 Panama Pacific International Exposition, of the building of the bridges, and of Alcatraz and Angel Island. From an exhibit of Civil War clothing and antique medical equipment, to models of the early missions and a collection of John Wayne memorabilia, here was a fascinating museum, deserving a story of its own.

"Sometimes the best story ideas come from the little happenings that fall through the cracks in the itinerary floor," says Dee Henri. She tells of traveling to Nova Scotia in a forty-six person bus which stopped unexpectedly at a tiny roadside cafe. The single young waitress-cook was overwhelmed, simply unable to serve so many cold, hungry tourists; whereupon the passengers made themselves at home in the kitchen, opening cans of soup, brewing coffee, and serving each other. "The spirit of the lunch stop was more impressive than the sights we saw," says Henri.

Orientation Comes First

A brief sight-seeing tour is the best way to orient yourself to the important landmarks and obtain an overview of the topography. Sit or stand near the guide. Don't be bashful. Ask questions. If you're overflowing with questions—too many to ask—try to determine which answers you'll be able to find elsewhere—and ask the other ones. If the guide is a good one, write down his name and address, in case you have a question to ask later. (If you do write later, be sure to enclose a self-addressed, stamped envelope or, if he's in another country, an International Reply Coupon, purchased at the post office.) If the guide is a very good one, write a complimentary letter to his boss, to encourage excellence in tour guides.

Whether or not you take subsequent tours, do rely on public transportation for much of your sight-seeing. Procure a good map of the bus or subway system. If you're in a hurry in a big city, take the subway. But if you want to see the people and the neighborhoods, the kids walking home from school, the housewives pinching the fruit at the greengrocer's, the workers relaxing on front stoops, look for surface transportation. In addition to buses, trolley cars, and trams, consider the jitney, the shared taxi so popular in many areas; horse-drawn carriages; rickshaws. Bicycles and motorcycles give you still a different view, as you actually become part of the street scene. Riding a funicular or a cable railway or even on the top of a double-decker bus presents another perspective—farther removed, more telescopic.

Whenever you can, go by water. Practically all riverfront or lakefront areas offer waterborne transportation. From Westminster, for instance, you can take a water bus along the Thames, downstream as far as Greenwich, upstream as far as Hampton Court. Queen Elizabeth floats no more comfortably. The boat on Lake Geneva is a floating kaffeeklatsch. Mrs. A. embarks in Geneva, saving three seats for her friends; Mrs. B. comes aboard ten minutes later from the dock of a lakeside house; Mrs. C. boards at a small village five minutes away; then they order coffee and cakes, so they're all ready when Mrs. D. joins them at the next boat stop. The four chatter in rapid-fire French all the way to Montreux. The travel writer may not understand a word they say, but their appearance, their postures, their gestures, offer intimate insights that flesh out the story.

One of the world's biggest transportation bargains is a ride on a ferryboat. While on assignment in Turkey, we remained on deck as the ferry that leaves from Istanbul's Galata Bridge sailed past the elegant DolmaBaHçe Palace and the fowning fortifications of Rumeli Hisar and Anadolu Hisar. We zigzagged between European Turkey and Asiatic Turkey, letting off and taking on passengers and cargo at dozens of docks. Water traffic of all kinds crisscrossed the Bosporus around us. After debarking in Sariyer, where the restaurant sent a fisherman out front to catch our lunch, we took a bus back to Istanbul. The half-hour ride through fields, orchards, and peasant villages taught us much about rural Turkey. On-the-spot "research" aboard the bus and the ferry provided background for a number of stories.

It's not hard to find exotic transport. I've ridden a camel, an elephant, a mule, a donkey, and an ostrich, and I'm not very venturesome.

Camel rides across the Sahara or mule rides through the Alps can make for interesting articles focused on the method of transportation (See How), but usually such episodes are just one sentence of a story. Exotic conveyances can help you get the feel of a place, but overall, the most satisfactory type of transportation for a travel writer is shoe leather. On your own two feet is the best way to catch the most intimate glimpses of everyday life, as well as close-ups of parades, fiestas, and wedding processions.

To really know what a place is like you have to see its most important landmarks several times, at different hours of the day. Some sights, like the Taj Mahal or Ayers Rock, are always surrounded by rapt tourists at special times—sunrise, sunset, the light of the full moon; but even the modest plaza in a Mexican village looks different and feels different at dawn, at noon, and at twilight.

Notice what they call their plazas and squares and how they name their streets. Is the town laid out with First Street and Second Street intersecting A and B and C? Or are the streets, the squares, the gates, the areas named for famous people? What kinds of famous people? Politicians? Generals? Writers? Artists? Musicians? Entertainers? Millionaires? Sometimes it's the date that's important—Mexico City's Avenida 16 de Septiembre (named for the Mexican Independence Day), Buenos Aires's Avenida 9 de Julio (a crucial day in Argentina's struggle for liberty), Leningrad's Decembrists Square (the month of an early, unsuccessful version of the Russian revolution).

The place names give you the flavor of the community. California's San Jose and La Jolla, New Orleans's Bienville Street, Chartres Street, and Beauregard Square, evoke the areas' origins. Be sure to note interesting names to use later in stories or titles. Or to write an article about the names themselves. A newspaper story, datelined Norway, Maine, explains how such a true-blue Yankee state happens to have place names ranging from Madrid, Moscow, and Mexico to Paris, Poland, and Peru. Other travel writers have studied the history or patterns of street names or town names in certain areas, and have come up with salable stories.

Other clues to what the people of an area consider important can be found in their parks. Often there'll be trees planted by well-known people, noteworthy political or military figures. Prime ministers and rear admirals are invited to plant trees in parks all over the world. In whose honor were the fountains, statues, or other monuments erected? Are there more playing fields or hothouses? Has the city attempted to provide green space for its citizens?

The travel writer needs to look for the universal as well as the specific. Never be a mere name dropper, enumerating the airports and train stations you've waited in during your trip. Instead, cultivate the essence of the place so you can interpret it for others.

Meet the Local People

Visit a family at home if you possibly can. Practically every country has a program that encourages local families to extend hospitality to visitors with similar hobbies, professions, interests, or whatever.

Better still, take along the names of friends of friends, relatives of relatives, and even acquaintances of acquaintances. Any opportunity

Improve your travel stories by *noticing*. Observe the trees and shrubs and flowers. Are the gardens well-kept or weed-filled? Are there plants in the windowboxes? Trash on the sidewalk? Animals wandering in the streets? Iron bars on downstairs windows? Are there street peddlers? Hawking what? Lots of advertising signs? Promoting what? You learn a great deal when you *notice*.

We should notice with *all* of our senses. We need to remind ourselves later how it sounded—the clear chorus of church bells, the hoarse groans of the foghorns, the echoing footsteps of a solitary walker, the cascading of stream water over rocks, the shrill sound of a single bagpipe.

Do your feet notice cobbled streets or dusty roads? Will your fingers trace the pattern of a New Orleans balcony rail or an Arizona pueblo? How do they feel, the rough, unmortared stones of the seawall?

What do we smell? Fish frying? Damp wool? Incense? Cedar trees? Hot tar? The smells are part of the place—and part of the story.

Taste is important. Does clam chowder taste different in Boston than in San Francisco? Try the reindeer steak or shark's fin soup or the borscht. Taste commingles with the sights and sounds and smells when you eat sushi at a standup counter or tamales on a street corner or drink coconut milk on a palm-shaded beach, etching the scene on your brain.

Absorbing local color is not enough. *Record* it. If you don't have your tape recorder along, jot down reminders in your field notebook and amplify them on a cassette later.

to see how local people live provides the traveling writer with invaluable background material for stories: It's within the family circle that you really grasp the people's relationships with each other, their relationship to their government, and their relationship to the rest of the world, whether they live in august mansions crumbling in shabby gentility or in overcrowded apartments with wall-to-wall sleeping bags. The food they serve you is important in more ways than your observation of the kind of food it is. *How* it's served is a clue to the people's lifestyle. So is *who* is eating. Do the women do the serving, but don't serve themselves? Is the oldest person present served first? Are the children at the table?

Do the people speak freely about their government's shortcomings or parrot "everything's perfect" slogans? Sometimes when you dig a little deeper, long-held images are shattered. At a Moscow apartment the college professor's wife complained about the difficulty of obtaining eyeglasses in the Soviet Union. Since she was obviously wearing glasses, the American visitors wondered how she had managed to procure them. "Oh, *glasses* you can get," she said. "But it's impossible to find any designer frames."

Play where the local people play. One of my favorite memories of

Venice is a vaporetto ride to the Lido, where we bounced a beachball with a group of Italian children, and sipped red wine in paper cups with a visiting family from Naples. Of course, I wrote about it.

Eat where the locals eat. Sit and sip at a sidewalk cafe. Order the house specialty. Talk to the waiter. Don't rush. Observe. Eavesdrop. Stare.

Seek out old-timers to spin yarns about yesterday. You'll often find these people, who are, as John Wright says, "priceless" to the story, at the local mom-and-pop cafe. Search for a restaurant that's "a step above a greasy spoon, but a cut below fancy nonsense."

Picnic in the park. Let the sun caress your shoulders. Listen to the squeals of the children somersaulting on the grass. Watch the grandfathers pondering the next move in their eternal chess game. Taste the vanilla ice cream. Listen to the calls of the local birds. Throw back the errant ball that comes your way.

Go to the grocery store. Is it a supermarket, selling everything from laundry detergent to fresh fish, from shampoo to tennis shoes? Are the displays of canned goods veiled in layers of dust, their prices so high in relation to wages that the display is merely decorative?

Go to the outdoor markets, too. You have to start before dawn at Bangkok's Floating Market, where mangoes and bananas, coconuts and papayas are bargained for and bought from boat to boat, and you, drifting through the klongs and canals, are poled right into the center of the action. Start early, too, for Curacao's colorful Schooner Market, where dockside customers haggle with vendors in sailboats for fresh fish, exotic vegetables, and flashy fabrics. Go early, also, to Singapore's Chinatown, where customers dicker for snakes and lizards to brew into virility-producing broths; to North African suqs, where they sell spices and grape leaves and tiny cups of strong, sweet Turkish coffee; or to Pennsylvania Dutch markets selling pig stomachs, Amish pretzels and old-fashioned sweet bologna.

Stop in at the *boulangerie*, which lures you with the seductive smell of crusty bread and chocolate tarts, and the *charcuterie*, where the aging lamb is flanked by a pair of peacocks and a selection of wild hares.

You may be surprised at some of the places where food is sold. Ferryboats which cross international boundaries may cater to long lines of people who've taken the ride for the groceries. As soon as the boat's commissary opens, the passengers crowd around, eager to buy coffee, liquor, and whatever edibles and potables are scarce or expensive in their own country.

You will also get a realistic view of the people at the laundromat. Who's there? Career singles from the roominghouses in the next block? Camping families with muddy duffle? Senior citizens? I remember a stormy day in Southern California when the first mate of a small ketch commandeered all the dryers for her life jackets, cushions, bedding, foul weather gear, and dock lines. On another day, halfway around the world, in Alice Springs, Australia, an aborigine woman lugged into the laundromat bag after bag of blankets, towels, and clothing—enough for every washing machine in the place—as five children marched behind her, licking dripping ice cream cones that were getting their shirts into condition for next month's wash. Puerto Vallarta's main "laundromat" is on the edge of town—rocks for scrubbing, riverbank for drying. Immediately behind the washing area, at the city-built playground, the children of the laundresses sing as they scramble down the slides or swing out over the sharp stones. You can learn a lot at the laundromat. (Someday I'm going to write an article about conversations overheard in a cruise ship laundromat!)

Check out the department stores. Do they feature more dress patterns and sewing notions than ready-mades? More work shoes than ski boots? Electric orange juicers; manually operated orange juicers; or no juicers at all? What does all this tell you about the people in this community? How about the local shoppers in the department store? Are they queued up for a special bargain or because some household item, heretofore in short supply, has just been received by the store? Are people carrying string bags or elaborately decorated shopping bags? Do they look well dressed? Fashionable? Are they swathed in furs or shivering through threadbare wraps on a cold day?

Are most of the items in the store manufactured locally? If not, where are they from? What other services does the store offer? One huge Tokyo department store not only presents kimono fashion shows and demonstrates the art of flower arranging, but also provides lessons in the use of knives and forks—for chopstick users who want to learn Western ways.

Don't stop with the department stores. Visit the specialty shops, the bazaars, the suqs, the flea markets. "Shopping" is more than a frivolous pastime when you're searching for your story.

Even beauty parlors and barbershops abound in clues to an area's reality. My first time in Cairo, sixteen different people worked on my simple shampoo and set, from the young girl who handed me a plastic-bagged comb, brush, and towel, to the man who, two hours later, wielded the hairspray can. How to tip? Egyptian and European ladies were going around dispensing the equivalent of one cent to the teenager who brought the coffee, five cents to the shampoo girl, two cents to the young boy who removed the rollers, and ten cents to the maestro who set the hair, etc. That bit of local color found its way into one of my stories on Egypt.

Join the Congregation

While many of us are naturally reluctant to intrude upon the religious rites of others, I've often stumbled into a ceremony and been invited to stay: a prayer meeting in a Turkish mosque; a christening in a Greek church; a coming-of-age ceremony at Saint Peter's and another one, very different, at the Wailing Wall; a Buddhist funeral in Japan; a Presbyterian wedding in Brisbane. Religious ceremonies always provide special insights. Be sure to look up your own religious affiliates when you travel. You'll not only meet pleasant people, but you'll probably be invited to attend a coffee hour after the service, a congregational pot-luck supper, or the annual Sunday school picnic.

Look for Local Recreation

Do you feel you could never bear to see a bull fight? You might find it less gory and more interesting than you expect. And the real show is the people around you and how they act and react.

Ball games bore you? Don't be too sure. Whether it's sandlot or Super Bowl, with a little pregame explanation you'll understand enough of the action to understand the other spectators' enjoyment.

Too old for circuses? No, you're not. Applaud the elephant ballet and shiver in fear for the high-wire artists along with the rest of the audience.

The successful travel writer not only attends the event, he observes the crowd. Watching the people around you often leads to a story angle. My article about the Boxing Day race meeting in Auckland, New Zealand, focused on the women spectators' hats. In an era when women the world over practically never covered their heads, these stunningly dressed New Zealanders all wore their millinery proudly. I guessed there must be a reason, so I asked the woman in front of me in the buffet line. It's an annual contest, she explained, sponsored by Auckland's milliners, with a prize—a vacation in Australia for two—given for the most attractive hat at the meeting.

One of the most pleasant evenings I've ever spent was in Tampere, Finland, at the Pyynikki open-air revolving theater, where the audience is moved around to face the various changes of scene. We didn't need to understand a word of Finnish. The play was obviously the old story of the farmer's daughter and the traveling salesman. The audience laughed at all the right places. My readers enjoyed hearing about it, too.

The best part of participating in local entertainment is your opportunity to see the people of the area relaxed and having a good time. You learn from watching them, talking to them, joining them in joy, fear, amusement, grief, devotion, satisfaction, or anxiety.

Although *Sleeping Beauty* in Leningrad was one of the most beautiful ballets I've ever seen, what I wrote about was the young Russian girls in front of us who insisted, with gestures, that we share their chocolates, and the coat checkers who told us, in pantomime, that there was still another act, when we thought it was over.

Your readers will want to know how many people were present at any kind of public gathering—parade, concert, ballgame, political demonstration. This figure is not only important in gauging the popularity of the concert artist or the political candidate, but it lends meaning to the occasion. Are there a hundred people waiting in line for the art show to open—or only a dozen? Are there a hundred demonstrators waving signs—or a thousand? I've never forgotten my high school journalism instructor's directions to "count the house" first thing. For a quick estimate, if the crowd is seated, count the number of seats in a row, and multiply by the number of rows. If it's a restaurant, count the number of tables and the average number of seats at each table; then consider carefully the degree of fullness of the room. (If the number of seats is common knowledge, all you have to do is count those that are empty.)

Professor Herbert Jacobs of the University of California offered this formula for estimating standing crowds: First measure the length and width of the area in feet; then add the two figures together; if the people seem to be moving around fairly easily, multiply this sum by seven; if they're tightly packed, multiply by ten. Thus, an area 100 by 150 feet—a sum of 250 feet—contains approximately 1,750 freely moving people or 2,500 tightly packed people. Learn to "eyeball" an area measurement. Outdoors, is it bigger than a football field? Indoors, is it as long as three bathtubs or wider than two full-size beds?

Welcome Chance Meetings

While you're traveling, encourage chance encounters. Speak to the person sitting next to you on the plane, train, or bus. That person may turn out to be a pleasant traveling companion; and he may be the very person you need to alert you to an important story breaking along your route. Or he may be from a distant country, with ideas and insights that introduce you to that country in a way that years of reading never could.

Getting lost may be one of the very best ways to see an area. Local people love to show you the route, and the experience often leads the travel writer down interesting bypaths. While struggling with his high school French in France, John Pollack remembered Ben Franklin's advice to let others do you a favor if you want them to like you. He went around asking strangers to photograph him with his camera. This led to interesting conversations, vast amounts of inside information—and a huge collection of dull pictures.

While he was able to practice *his* French, in many countries people like to practice *their* English. When an English-speaking person asks for directions they're delighted to help. Never hesitate to ask questions. All over the world, people young and old like to show off their surroundings, and will often take an unbelievable amount of trouble to lead you to something they think you should see. Often the "something" is more charming, less crowded, richer in beauty and meaning than the well-known sight nearby. A stranger's description and a nudge in the right direction led us to the Roman ruins under the city of Barcelona. Other strangers have sent us to exquisite secluded beaches, exciting but little-known galleries, and hole-in-the-wall restaurants with tasty regional menus. Always listen to local people's recommendations. Pay attention when somebody says, "Don't miss seeing. . . ." or "Be sure to stop at. . . ."

Make use of every person-to-person opportunity. Sometimes you'll need special help while pursuing your on-trip research. But finding the individual who can give you the exact information you need isn't as hard as it sounds. Your at-home research provides a starting point. "Then it's easy," says Caryl Hansen. "Ask each source to suggest other sources." Jo Combs likens it to "unraveling a ball of string—find a starting person, and he will direct you to others, who will help you find still others."

While your embassy or consulate might assist in arranging interviews with people you need to see overseas, usually they won't do it until you actually arrive in the country. They've found too many people change plans at the last moment. (Remember, if you need the services of a translator, the interview will take twice as long, so budget your time accordingly.)

The hotel concierge prides himself on being able to answer practically any question or solve any problem. Ask him for advice and printed information as soon as you arrive. Lois Kirchner forgot to do this at the Park Lane Hotel in London. Only as she was leaving did she discover she could have walked through nearby Green Park to Buckingham Palace and witnessed a leisurely and uncrowded Changing of the Guard.

Others can help you, too. Question the saleslady, the flower seller, the cobbler, the proverbial man in the street. The more people you talk to, the better feel you get for the place, the more you know about it, and the better story you'll write. The dining room maitre d' led one writer to a French organization that dates back to the Druids and gave her the name of a book on the legends of Brittany that was exactly what she needed.

Go into a bookstore and ask if they have anything on local history. Listen for folk tales and stories of local heroes. Jot down the names of people and places you'll be able to look up at home.

Be sure to buy local newspapers and magazines (many foreign countries publish English editions, also) to find out more about the local scene, as well as events of interest. Read the want ads. Listen to local radio and television programs.

Even though you've done your library research in advance, you may want to pursue some special interest while traveling, and you'll find librarians everywhere glad to help you when you show sincere purpose.

When Winifred Johnson spent four months in Jackson, a town in California's gold country, she visited the museum so often that the curator set aside a special room for her to work in. On days when the museum and the library were closed, docents took her on tours, showing her memorabilia the more casual observer doesn't get to see, some of it from the time of the gold rush itself. She did her research in 1850s newspapers, and in private homes, whose owners heard about her project and invited her to visit.

James Winchester also found more help than he expected. Trying to complete a *Reader's Digest* assignment about Russian trawlers off Newfoundland, he was ready to give up when he heard on his rental car radio that the Russian oceanography ship working with the trawl-

In a later chapter we'll discuss photography and photo sources and how to send photographs. But let's say a word here about on-trip mailing of manuscripts, query letters, and research notes. If you're sending the original to an editor, put the carbon in another envelope and mail it to yourself at a different time. Even if you're sending it all to yourself, be sure you have two copies, mailed in different envelopes at different times. If you're traveling in a country notorious for the vagaries of its mail service, you may want to keep that second copy with you.

If you're overseas, special air letters are much less expensive to send than ordinary stationery. They work well for queries and editorial and personal correspondence, as long as you don't need an enclosure. Investigate, too, the different kinds of express mail, as well as alternatives to mail service, which seem to proliferate by the week.

The cheapest way to send files and publications is in Jiffy bags (available at post offices in many countries) at the book rate or printed papers rate.

Regardless of what type of mailing you're doing, visit the post office or other point of departure yourself. While bellboys and concierges will offer to send your material, their estimate of the charges is never in your favor, and sometimes, though you've paid for airmail postage, the material is accidentally sent by regular mail.

ers had put into port with a sick seaman. He hurried to the pier, though he didn't really expect to be allowed on the ship. He was, however, welcomed aboard. Many of the crew spoke English. The captain himself took Winchester on a complete tour. Whenever they came to a locked door the captain sent a seaman for the key. While they were waiting—and there were many such waits—they had a glass of vodka, bottoms up. Winchester was happy to report that he upheld the dignity of American journalism by remaining on his feet all day.

While you may often deal with less glamorous opportunities for imbibing, you'll still have to work out your own rules about alcohol. Will your hosts be insulted if you refuse? Will you be too sleepy to get your story if you accept? Should you stick to Perrier? A refreshing beer? Wine with lunch? There aren't any "standard" answers.

Alcohol Can Be a Problem

My own most difficult experience with alcohol ended at a Turkish waterfront cafe in Izmir, where I was the only woman. It had begun several hours earlier in the hotel bar, where our host had ordered a number of American-style drinks. When we arrived at the restaurant he said magnanimously, "We'll have another round." Turning to the waiter, he pointed to me and said, in English, "A screwdriver." I expected the tumblerful of orange juice with the jiggerful of vodka, diluted by ice cubes, that they'd been serving at the hotel bar. What arrived was a ten-ounce tumbler of vodka, with an orange juice chaser. I didn't want to insult our Turkish host; yet I knew there was no way I could add ten ounces of vodka to the drinks I'd already had and still walk out of the restaurant. I remembered I had in my purse, as I often do when I'm in foreign countries, a plastic flask of pure water. I asked the waiter for an empty glass and poured the water into it. By the time I moved the glasses around, poured some of the vodka into my flask, left some in the water glass, and otherwise juggled the liquid refreshments, my host never knew I was spurning his hospitality.

Individual circumstances and your own personality will dictate your response when alcohol is served. But do take into consideration the mores of the people you're with. Strict Muslims would be deeply offended by your invitation to "stop by the Hilton Bar for a drink." But if your Viennese hosts take you out to Grinzing to a *Heuriger*, a "new-wine" garden, they'll be insulted if you don't taste the new wine.

If you, yourself, are opposed to alcohol, don't make an issue of it. If everybody else is drinking, order fruit juice or a soft drink. Toasting is a very important activity in some countries, with rigid rules, but you can participate with an empty glass.

Check into alcohol-related etiquette and establish a pattern that seems comfortable to you. In general, I remind myself that *every day* is a working day for the travel writer, and a professional manner is imperative.

Knowing what to look for, what to listen for, what to think about, and how to use your other senses are the travel writer's "secret weapons." Take full advantage of your on-scene position as you gather material for the stories you've already planned—and the stories you didn't plan because you didn't know ahead of time what terrific stories they could be.

Jame Mosque, Kuala Lumpur, Malaysia

8

Put Yourself in Your Readers' Place

eaders—and editors—really appreciate that special information that comes from your personal research. Put yourself in your readers' place. Remember, you are their advance man. While you're there, get all the information your readers might need or want, and record it carefully, so you can pass it on.

Tell them, "Windy San Francisco street corners make the woman with the wraparound skirt wish she'd worn something else," or "If you're going on a houseboat and you like to work crossword puzzles, don't forget to take along a pencil," or "Theater ushers and restroom attendants in many countries expect to be tipped." Explain to first-time ship cruisers that glamorous evening clothes aren't really necessary and that *nobody* "dresses" the first and last nights or whenever the ship's in port. Mention the fifty-six-degree temperature at Carlsbad Caverns, and the fact that 11,400-foot Cuzco is apt to be cold in the evenings and early mornings, even if it's shirtsleeve weather at noon in nearby Machu Picchu.

Tell them the Portland, Oregon, Chamber of Commerce sells plastic raincoats all summer to surprised visitors unprepared for rain. Suggest they have birth certificates notarized for Mexico, observing that you had to cancel a trip when you couldn't find a notary at the airport. Give them the benefit of your experience by encouraging early reservations for camping space in California's state parks or for New Year's at the Williamsburg Inn.

Whenever possible, investigate different travel styles while you're in the area you'll be writing about. Your reader may opt for accommodations, recreation, or sight-seeing very different from what you, personally, would choose. You owe him the courtesy of checking out the

"Beefeater," Tower of London

entire scene. If you're staying at a youth hostel, go to the best hotel in town, stroll through the lobby, order a snack in the coffee shop, window-shop the boutiques. If you're staying at the plushiest hotel, check out the one-star around the corner, as well as the youth hostel, the YMCA, and the nearest campground.

Sample many types of transportation and travel experience. Author John Le Carré traveled through the war in Southeast Asia as he researched *The Honourable Schoolboy*. The *Washington Post* reporter who accompanied him tells of the giant bookkeeper's ledger in which he jotted every detail and anecdote as he drove to the front lines in Cambodia, flew on death-defying Cambodian planes, and "choked on the obligatory pipes of opium in one of Vientiane's more sordid dens."

Observe carefully, so you can warn your readers of the bad points, as well as extol the good ones. Is the restaurant near the dig so awful that they should return to their hotel for lunch or bring along a picnic? Is the pension around the corner the best buy in town?

The quality of service is very much the domain of a travel writer, so if your bus driver at Disney World is sour and the people in the hotel act as if they should be wearing Grumpy costumes, or if the restaurant service is "Caribbean casual" (you have to get up six times and pull your waiter out of the kitchen), let your readers in on it. If the restaurants turn out to be more expensive, the beaches more crowded, the tour operator less reliable, and the opportunities for recreation fewer than expected, take careful notes, so you can include these caveats in your story.

Today's travel writers are standing up to their obligation to tell the bad as well as the good. Some of them name names, while others make only vague references. (But you'd better *have* the names—in case your editor asks!) Write amusingly, but explicitly, about problems you've encountered.

If your own travel experience was truly terrible, can you write an exposé and get it published? Maybe. But don't try to write it while you're on the trip, still seething. Wait until you cool off at home. While you're having the bad experience—the humidity; the bugs; the filth; the noise; the lack of privacy; the miserably uncomfortable beds; the long walk to meals, where they are always out of everything; the long, long walk to the beach, where tar, seaweed, and undertow make swimming impossible and boating risky; the surly service and uncongenial clientele—note everything. Be very sure of your facts and don't exaggerate or distort as you record them. Then, when you go to write the story, you can tell all, in a calm and reasonable way, providing a well-documented article that will serve as a helpful warning to others.

Never use your typewriter to settle private scores, to get even with those who gave you a bad time. Both your praise and your complaint should be tempered by the knowledge that both the restaurant, or hotel, or wherever and you have good days and bad days. Before you write too bitterly about the atrocious lunch, take into consideration the circumstances that might affect your outlook: the fact that you're suffering from a heavy cold, the airlines lost your luggage, and an unseasonable rainstorm beat against your windshield the whole twenty miles to the restaurant; the fact that it's the chef's day off and the storm prevented delivery of fresh produce. Then, if you can be humorous, rather than grim—write explicitly, but amusingly—the result is often an entertaining, informative article. Tell your readers the truth—but be sure it *is* the truth.

Praise requires its own brand of caution. The perfect set of circumstances produces an enthusiasm that lends plus value to your article. Best be careful not to make it sound better than it is.

Sometimes local citizens may want you, the travel writer, to see only certain parts of their area. They try to hide some of the less desirable aspects—the slums and shantytowns, the polluting factories, the refuse heaps, the military checkpoints. Our hosts in Johannesburg were reluctant to take us to visit Soweto, the all-black suburb of a million people, but we insisted, and we learned a great deal about South Africa as a result.

On a press junket the travel writer is usually shown only the admirable and the advertisable. However, if you ask your hosts straight questions, you'll usually get straight answers. Be prepared to look beyond the facade and get a truer picture on your own.

Check Out the Details

In addition to absorbing the *feel* of the place, you'll need to find and record the *facts*. Be sure your information is complete and accurate and current and includes all the cogent details. Keep careful track of mileage and costs. Be ready to tell your readers which landmark signals the turnoff or what track they should stand on for their train. Find out, so you can say authoritatively, the best time of year to take this trip and how long to stay at each place.

Some publications prefer what they call "mentions"—the name and address of the hotel, the restaurant, the car rental agency, the sight-seeing company. Some only want you to "mention" when you're being complimentary. And some publications would never let you "mention." The wise travel writer, though, stows away the information, regardless. Your present editor may scorn "mentions," but the next time you sell a piece on this destination, a different editor may cover your manuscript margins with questions you can't answer.

The value of this is dramatized in Eleanor Bogart's article "Oh, Yes, I Remember It Well," in which she tells of her plans to write a story describing all the streets she's loved. She has just returned from four days in St. Paul, Minnesota, and she will begin with Summit Street. Or is it Summit Avenue? Or Boulevard? Or Drive? Are the trees elms or maples? Are the houses really Victorian? Or earlier or later? Well, at least the Hill mansion she remembers. But was it brown or red? Stone or brick? It was four stories, she thinks—or at any rate, three. Surrounded by a fence. Was it wrought iron? She ends up unable to recreate Summit Street (Avenue) because she didn't take five minutes to jot down the details.

We all do that—think we know a place very well, until we sit down to write about it. While we're traveling it's all so *memorable*, we think we'll never forget. But we do. Make it a firm rule to scribble or record those supporting details you'll need later.

With the details firmly in mind you can go ahead and write without stopping to look things up. If you have all the facts straight you can concentrate on plus value and won't have to keep asking yourself, "Was it on the corner or in the middle of the block? Were the children wearing their school uniforms or their play clothes? Was it a canoe or a rowboat?"

Once you're home, you'll discover it's very hard to track down some small, but colorful and enriching, fact. You may find yourself spending vast amounts of time and money searching for a nebulous tidbit that you should have written down on-scene—and never uncover it.

I try to organize my field notes by writing the solid information in order. The special little extras that I *might* want for something I either jot on a separate page or circle when they appear in the middle of more mundane information. When I tape my thoughts later I gather together all these colorful little extras and remark about them at the end of the more general information. Thus I'm reminded that the schoolgirls wore dark blue skirts with white shirts and blazers in a Black Watch plaid; and the red rowboat called *Erma* had yellow trim, a human eye carved on the bow, and shiny brass oarlocks.

It's the details that bring a place to life and make the reader eager to visit it. Robert Schiller must have been thinking of his readers when he wrote "Storybook Prague" for *Reader's Digest*. He must have marshalled all his senses and digested all the details to tell so much, so easily:

> Nestled below the castle is Mala Strana, the Little Town, Prague's loveliest section. Although most of its baroque palaces are now foreign embassies and government offices, the area has changed little since the eighteenth century. You must explore its winding alleys, exquisite little squares and courtyards on foot or you will miss the charming angels, eagles, chalices, keys and fiddles carved over the doorways, which told the postmen where to deliver mail in the days before houses were numbered.
>
> Cross the Vltava by the Charles Bridge, one of earth's most fascinating spans. Built in 1357, with elaborate Gothic guard towers at either end, it is lined with thirty sculptured groups of saints in ecstatic poses. Pious Czechs doff their hats as they pass the figure of Saint John Nepomuk, the "martyr of silence," who was tied in a sack and thrown into the river for refusing to reveal secrets of the confessional.
>
> The eastern end of the bridge leads into the Old Town. Here is the famous Carolinum, seat of. . . .

Do you, the reader, want to visit Prague?

Bill Peeples, of the *Los Angeles Times* travel section, is a hard taskmaster. He's always asking the writer, "How much was the tip you say won the guide's lifelong devotion? What do you mean by 'remarkably inexpensive'? How far is 'an easy day's drive'?" Peeples says, "It's amazing how many writers don't tell the reader what they saw. 'There was a beautiful panoramic view.' Period. Paragraph. Perhaps they never saw it because they didn't really look. But what the travel section needs are details, not adjectives."

Peeples, as a writer, tells about Nantucket's shops, restaurants, rental vehicles, boats, and sports, and where to get more information. He must have kept his eyes open to give his reader this vivid a picture of Nantucket:

> It has been said that the shape of the island, an accumulation of debris pushed off the mainland by the last glacier, is like a sailor's hammock. A full one, with a sailor in it. If that is the case, Nantucket town is right where the sailor's hands would be if he were folding them across his stomach while he slept.
>
> Nantucket town, safely inside the jetties at the west end of a long, narrow harbor, is a place mostly of asphalt streets, although three blocks of Main Street are cobblestoned. Main Street slopes up gently toward the north, a wide avenue framed by tall trees that shade shoppers but let the sun shine through, too. . . .
>
> Everyone watches as the moonglow becomes more golden. Then suddenly, as if someone held a ping-pong ball under the water and let it go, the moon pops up.

There's only one way you can write that way—know what you're talking about.

If your story is interesting and moves right along, but you still need to work in more details, try using a sidebar. Magazines and newspaper travel sections regularly carry sidebars to major stories, headed "If You Go . . ." or "If You're Going . . ." The sidebars, or boxes, are filled with straightforward facts on how to get to the place in your story, how long it will take, how much it will cost, and how to get more information. Because of its conciseness and prominence, the sidebar needs to be rich in facts that matter, so collect the details carefully. Naturally you'll be guided in sidebars you plan by the type your target market usually carries. You'll want to tell your readers which airlines fly there, how they can proceed from the airport, and where to make a reservation. Additional sidebars, or perhaps additional paragraphs in the same one, will cover accommodations, restaurants, recreation, and sight-seeing. Other publications will emphasize advice on shopping— what to buy, where to find it, how much to pay for it. Still others will seek something special, such as a historical vignette or an outstanding side trip. Brief roundups often work well for sidebars, too—assembling a group of arts and crafts or artists and craftsmen, special upcoming events or annual festivals, for instance. How something works, or how it got to be that way, or what happened when, sometimes fit a sidebar. So think about this format when you're gathering your on-the-scene information. Make the extra effort to follow through on something that doesn't seem to go with your story. You may be glad later.

Check and Recheck

Your reader will be quick to point out the slightest error. If you want to build a reputation as a travel writer, don't assume *anything*! Get the facts straight. Don't give him the chance to catch you in an error.

Once you have recorded a fact, don't mindlessly use it forever without rechecking. Constantly update your knowledge so you're presenting as current a picture as you possibly can. Although I always try to do this, I still remember with embarassment the time I, as an Enrichment Lecturer aboard a cruise ship, recommended to passengers a wonderful old hotel on the main street of Willemstad on the island of Curacao. "Sit on the veranda and sip a beer," I advised, "and watch the Queen Emma pontoon bridge open and close, as people walk over it or ships sail by." When our ship cruised into Willemstad, we discovered the old hotel had been torn down for a parking lot several months earlier.

Be sure you're recommending to your readers something that still exists. And be sure it's a travel experience the reader will be able to duplicate if he wishes.

━━

A sidebar is a block of information that runs adjacent to an article, often set off in a box or with a different color or typeface. It can come before or after the main body of the article, or in the middle or alongside. Solid facts are needed for the sidebar, where information is expressed concisely, not necessarily in sentences, sometimes even in chart form.

The sidebar has many advantages. It gives the editor leeway in layout, making it easier to schedule the piece. It helps the writer organize his material and tell his story in a readable manner, still confident that he's providing the necessary facts. It gives the reader in-depth information without slowing down the article itself. Many different kinds of material lend themselves to sidebars, and many pieces have more than one. To accompany a Nile cruise article for *Going Places*, a house magazine sent by travel agents to their best customers, I furnished three sidebars. One told of the many companies selling Egyptian travel, and how to get in touch; the second, of the various boats sailing up and down the Nile, their prices and accommodations, advantages and disadvantages; and the third delineated what to bring along—everything from binoculars and a strong flashlight to a warm jacket and an outfit suitable for camel riding.

The travel section in the *New York Times* and many other newspapers run similar sidebars which include this kind of information.

A story about threshing bees in *Chevron USA*, for instance, features a box explaining how a steam thresher works and another detailing where and when western threshing bees are held.

Odyssey's article on the arts and crafts of Mexico is followed by a Shopping Tips section set off in yellow that advises the reader what to look for in folk art and how to tell the good from the bad in copperware, silver, gold, weaving, onyx, and leather.

One issue of *Travel & Leisure* featured as a cover story a one-page "Mediterranean Miscellany," with a quote from Lawrence Durrell boxed in the middle of the page, followed by two pages of consecutive sidebars, which included a map. The sidebars dealt with such subjects as "Daredevil Drivers," "Worth a Major Detour," and a chronology, showing *what* happened *when* in the Mediterranean, from the Jewish exodus from Egypt in 1400 to 1200 B.C. to the death of Francisco Franco and the crowning of Juan Carlos in A.D. 1975. The boxes also gave the names and dates of Mediterranean-born VIPs, alphabetically, from Aeschylus to Vergil; a quick rundown on art museums in Mediterranean countries; an explanation of the "ill winds" of the Mediterranean such as the mistral, which Aubrey Menen calls the "cold displeasure of God"; and a definition of such terms as "Riviera," "Costa Brava," and "Côte d'Azur." As you can see, the sidebars were even more "miscellaneous" than the article.

In another issue of *Travel & Leisure* a six-page article on Philadelphia had five sidebars, one to a page. They dealt with the Liberty Bell's new home, where to find information at the Convention and Visitors Bureau, outstanding restaurants, a brief history of the old mansions and information on touring them, and a potpourri of scheduled special events.

Alongside "Nepal, a Trekker's Paradise," in *Adventure Travel*, is a box written by someone other than the author of the article, which is not too uncommon a device. In this case the sidebar was written by Jim Whittaker, the first American to reach the summit of Mount Everest. It describes trekking conditions in Nepal, comments philosophically on the environment and economic impact of the popularity of trekking, and advises the would-be trekker in such specifics as making arrangements through a reliable organization and planning the trek for some time other than peak season for the area.

Sometimes a travel writer asks an expert like Whittaker to write a sidebar to accompany his article; sometimes he discovers after he's interviewed an expert that the material lends itself especially well to a sidebar, and he designs one that's composed of quotes from the interview; and other times the editor makes an arrangement with the expert to write a short piece on the subject of the writer's story, and uses it as a sidebar.

Consider a sidebar, even if the publication doesn't normally use them, whenever it would help you round out your material without slowing down your story. If you wonder how to write and submit it— call it a sidebar, title it if you wish, and begin it on a separate sheet following the main part of your article.

The easiest way to write a travel article is to visualize your reader. Then say to yourself, "If *I* were that reader, what information would *I* want? Your writer's eye, writer's ear, and writer's nose will uncover what you need. Your most urgent task will be selecting from this mass of material the items you want to use in your story *this time.*

Springtime in central Switzerland

Wrap It Up When You Return

You may expect your story to write itself once you get home and listen to your tapes, look at your photographs, and review the printed material you've collected. But don't count on it.

You usually need a many-pronged assault to compile the research for any story. If you're alert to the possibilities before, during, and after your trip, you can combine the various sources so they reinforce each other.

As we've said, your pretrip research should include extensive reading—everything from brochures to the encyclopedia—and conversations with those who have been where you're going.

While traveling, you'll interview people—in person and on the telephone. You'll observe eveything with your careful writer's eye, ear, nose, taste, and touch. You'll record your impressions with camera, notebook, and tape recorder. You'll collect concrete details as well as register the overall feel of the place.

You may plan your story while you're traveling (target market and capsule sentence firmly in mind), or maybe you'll even write it on the road—and find the check in your mailbox when you return. But other articles you'll wait to write until after you're home.

Although I always try to gather the material I'll need on the trip itself, occasionally an editor wants a story I haven't prepared for.

I wish I'd known I was going to write about sheep dogs, for instance. When I returned from New Zealand I queried the *New York Times.* "I don't want a definitive piece," the travel editor replied. "Make specific proposals." A sentence in one of the eight proposals I wrote read, "You will be surprised how few commands the shepherd gives his flock-tending dog at a New Zealand sheep dog trial."

New Zealand farmer and his dogs round up sheep

The editor chose, "New Zealand sheep dogs, provided you go into their breeding, training, relationship with their masters, etc."

My total sheep dog experience was a one-hour trial demonstration for tourists. I hadn't intended to write more than a casual paragraph or two about the New Zealand sheep dog. My notes, tapes, and brown envelope materials yielded very little. My files and bookshelves seemed bare of sheep dog data.

So I headed for the public library. There, by chance, I met a friend who asked what I was working on. When I expressed disappointment at the library's lack of helpful material she suggested I call a veterinarian. Good idea! I made a dozen calls, most of them dead ends. But one call put me on the track of a veterinarian who had recently moved to Idaho. A letter to him elicited information on the breeding and training of sheep dogs and the name of a definitive book on the subject—now out of print.

Meanwhile, I called the New Zealand Tourist Office in San Francisco, and wrote the people at Taniwha Springs, New Zealand, where we had seen the sheep dog trial. After I mentioned the project in my writing class, a student from New Zealand gave me the name of someone else to write to there. I had lunch with a friend whose husband knew a lot about sheep dogs, but at that point I didn't know enough to ask the right questions. Each of these sources contributed a tidbit and the names of two or three other possible sources.

At the university library I discovered a New Zealand encyclopedia and a dog encyclopedia, both with helpful bibliographies. I wrote more letters and searched for more books. Even my typist contributed an anecdote about a childhood experience with sheep dogs.

But I still hadn't found a definitive book on breeding and training, and I knew I didn't have enough knowledge yet to start writing. Then I went to a California Writer's Club meeting, where the guest speaker was the head librarian from a nearby town, whom I had interviewed several years earlier. When I went up to greet him, he said, "If there's ever anything I can do for you, just ask."

"Well," I answered, "about the New Zealand sheep dog . . ."

Next morning a member of his staff phoned. She had not only located the out-of-print book, but had also found another useful volume, and sent both of them to my local library.

I soon received information from New Zealand about dog trial rules and requirements and several booklets on the training and breeding of sheep dogs. Some of this information was so complex I went to the Children's Library for assistance from reference books intended for third or fourth graders. It helped.

I was still sorting reference materials when I went to a dinner party and the man on my left said, "I hear you're a writer. What are you working on now?" So I told him. It turned out that he was a professor of plant ecology and had spent months on sheep ranches in New Zealand. By the time we got to dessert he was practically drawing pictures on the tablecloth to explain the finer points of sheep dog trials.

Another stroke of research luck occurred as I was beginning my final draft. When I went to the camera shop to pick up the black-and-white glossies made from my transparencies, the lady standing next to me admired my dog pictures. She raised dogs. She invited me to a local sheep dog trial and plied me with all kinds of useful information.

They all helped: the friend at the library, my student, the husband of my luncheon friend, my typist, the librarian who remembered me, the dinner partner, the lady at the camera shop—I needed them all.

That's the way it usually happens. Live research and library research; interviews and encounters; what's in the file and research by mail; who you know and what you know—all combine to fill in your story.

The Chinese Opera Story

Some time after the sheep dog story, one of my favorite editors requested a piece on the Chinese Opera School at Taipei, years after I'd spent a couple of hours visiting there. I didn't know much about Chinese opera, either.

But a student told me her parents lived in Taipei and would be delighted, she was sure, to send materials. Several months later eight thick books—in Mandarin Chinese—arrived.

My student had no time to translate the eight books, though she said she'd be glad to look up answers to specific questions. But I didn't know enough yet to ask questions. Back to the library!

I looked in the card catalog under "Chinese," and the cards jumped from "one-dish meals" to "Opium Wars." Under "Taiwan" the directions said "see Formosa," and under "Formosa" there were just a few books. Their indexes revealed nothing on Chinese opera. Under "Opera" there were many references—none of them any use. No help from *Reader's Guide*, either. "Maybe there's something under 'Music,' " I thought desperately. It didn't look too hopeful, but the catalog's "Music—Oriental" yielded two entries. Their indexes also didn't seem promising, but as I thumbed through *Music Cultures of the Pacific, the Near East, and Asia* I saw a photograph that looked exactly like a picture my husband had taken at the Chinese Opera School. They were, indeed, identical, and I learned a great deal about the *hu ch'in*, the bowed lute borrowed from the Mongols, and its place in Chinese opera.

Subsequent research was more informal.

A travel-writing couple I met on a press junket sent me an authoritative article on the facial expressions, makeup, and costumes of Chinese opera. Another piece of good luck followed: a newspaper story about Taiwan. When I wrote for more information, a former employer happened to see the letter, happened to be an authority on Chinese opera, and was kind enough to call me and renew our acquaintance. An actress friend lent me two books on drama that included articles on my subject, and a phone call to a nearby university for the names of several students from Taiwan resulted in a couple of helpful discussions. In time I knew the right questions to ask, and my student could find the right answers, and the article pleased my editor.

Talk About Your Subject

As you review your previous research, and return to the library, and expand your live investigations, don't forget to talk about your subject to anyone who will listen. You'll be surprised how many people will have something to add to your project, whether it's expertise in one facet of the subject or acquaintance with just the person you need to quote.

Notice I said *subject*—not *idea*. When people ask you what you're working on, or even if they don't ask, tell them in broad general terms about the subject you're researching. But don't go into detail about your concept and the clever words you'll use to implement it, especially if you haven't written them yet. There's danger you'll do such a good job in the telling, the freshness will be spoiled and you'll never get to the writing. So don't seek praise for your ability with words until those words are actually written and published. On the other hand, never be bashful about asking anybody—friend or stranger—"Do you know anything about Timbuktu? What have you heard about crossing Siberia by train? Do you know anybody who's had emergency surgery in Mexico? Have you heard of any families who decided on special vacations at home this year?"

Keep in touch with the people who helped you before and during the trip—tourist offices, travel agents, public relations people in the travel industry, superior tour guides, and interesting people you've met along the way.

In addition to consulting experts who've previously written about your area, search for experts of your own.

Finding the individual who can give you the exact information you need isn't as hard as it sounds. Newspaper and magazine bylines, library files, corporate public relations departments, and trade and professional associations often provide a starting point. Some universities publish press contact booklets, which list expert sources on the faculty. Even if your nearby university doesn't do this, it shouldn't be hard to uncover your own authority. (Why didn't I think of that when I was worrying about sheep dogs? I was lucky my faculty expert found me!)

Sometimes a quick phone call provides all the additional information necessary. For instance, a call to Pan American told me that the Around-the-World flight schedule for Istanbul had recently changed, and a call to the AAA confirmed my suspicion that Highway 80 had been closed due to heavy snow. It took two calls to elicit the information that the Wasa Museum had not yet been enlarged—one to the International Center at a nearby university for the name of a Swedish student who had recently been in Stockholm, and a second call to the student.

Sometimes a phone call will net more than your informant intends.

A new clerk in an airlines office, for instance, accidentally told me an anecdote which not only revealed that the airline seemingly participated in an illegal activity, but showed some of its employees as blithering idiots. Next day her superior called to ask me not to use the information, although he never denied its accuracy. I made no promises. But because the particular anecdote added nothing to the thrust of my story, and using it would have served only one purpose—to discredit the airline—I refrained from retelling it. Had it, however, fitted in with my story, or had my purpose been an exposé, I wouldn't have hesitated to include the unflattering anecdote.

Turn to Your Files

Use what's still valuable of the material in your files, but be sure to update for accuracy. When you come across an old quote from a good source, phone or write for an up-to-the-minute opinion. Reread the written materials you used in your original research, and visit libraries and bookstores to investigate new ones. If you began filling your file before you left on your trip, you'll have good resource materials to use when you return home. If you haven't done all the research you should have, now's the time to make up for it.

When you're wrapping it all up, consider the relative value of the research materials you're using. Take into consideration the author's qualifications, experience, education, and reputation, as well as the reputation of the publisher or sponsoring agency. Consider the range of the subject matter and the limitations. How up to date is the material? Does it seem accurate and unbiased? Is the book well indexed and well illustrated? Select carefully as you incorporate research material into your own story, so that you are giving your readers the most valuable information you can.

Compiling all your notes and references from before, during, and after the trip can seem like an overwhelming job. Sometimes you just don't know where to start. The easiest way is to make a carbon or photocopy of everything, then put one copy away as your master file. The other copy you can cut up, moving the pieces around like blocks to judge where they best fit into your story.

If the situation changes after you've written your piece, do your best to correct your copy before publication. If you inadvertently publish something no longer true, admit your error or defend your research.

Check and Recheck for Accuracy

As we've said, just *being there* is never enough—you have to flesh out your on-the-scene observations. You must check and recheck the information you've collected.

If you want your writing to inform and assist your readers, you must guard against errors. I've had readers question a single word or name in a four- or five-thousand-word article. I casually mentioned, in an *Aramco World* piece, the names of the sculptors who contributed to the ornamentation of the Temple to Artemis/Diana, one of the World's

Seven Wonders. A history professor wrote me a complimentary letter on the article, then commented cryptically, "Phidias would have been over 200 years old! Remarkable!" I found in my original notes a big red question mark after "Phidias" and then a scrawled "OK." The information came from a British Museum book written by the man who rediscovered the temple, and it obviously referred to a different Phidias than the one who ornamented Athens for Pericles. I was pleased to be able to send the history professor a photocopy of this impeccable source.

Another time a woman took exception to the hotel prices I gave in a *Los Angeles Times* travel article on Sri Lanka. She also objected to my statement that "first-class hotels there are like second-class hotels in Europe." The prices had been checked with the Sri Lanka Tourist Bureau the day I sent the article to the editor. The remark about the quality of the hotels was a matter of opinion. The travel writer has a right—actually a duty—to express an opinion in a bylined article. It's disconcerting, though, when you think how thoroughly your reader considers every word. A friend wrote "Collecting from Country to Country" for an art publication, and a mutual acquaintance called with compliments on the article's accuracy. "I couldn't find a single thing wrong in it," she said. "Not a thing! I looked up everything you said, and you didn't make a single mistake." While my friend and I chuckled, we both knew that she, like most readers, would have been quick to point out the smallest error.

The satisfaction of feeling you've done your best to provide accurate information for your audience cannot be matched. When a fan writes to tell you how much he or she enjoyed your travel article, you feel ten feet tall.

Asking Questions by Mail

During your post-trip research, or maybe at some earlier point, you'll often need to pursue another line of live research: questions by mail. Questionnaires are excellent for gathering a sampling from widely spread geographical areas. Usually they work best where you want brief answers to many questions but would also like the recipient to include an anecdote or two. Sometimes the very act of gathering a number of different answers to the same question—or no answers at all—forces the writer to rethink his approach, giving him a chance to refashion the story before it's written.

Questionnaires are of two types. When you want to obtain updated information or fresh quotes from the person whose initials follow the encyclopedia article or whose magazine piece interests you, you'll write a personal letter with personalized questions. Write care of the publication or get the address from *Who's Who*. This letter is usually brief, with few questions, and geared toward encouraging the recipient to spew forth a quotable quote.

Other times you'll compose a questionnaire to be sent to many people. (Always send your questionnaire to three times as many people as you need—about one-third will reply.) Often you'll need a geographic spread for a story on primitive campgrounds or theme amusement parks or commuter airlines. On that kind of questionnaire, formulate the questions so they can be answered yes or no or with a few brief words. But *leave room* for lengthier, more anecdotal answers—you'll be surprised how many recipients fill up the space you've left and add a couple of pages of their own. (It's *always* surprising how flattered people are at being asked their opinion and how eager they are to cooperate.) Aim for about thirty questions. If the topic is controversial or touchy, you'll have to decide whether it's better to intersperse hard questions with easy ones or whether to build up to harder and harder ones. Here, as in the face-to-face interview, let the last couple of questions be the pleasant, easy-to-answer type. Make your questionnaire itself as brief as possible. One page is better than two, and don't make it longer than two. Never query in broad, general terms like "How do you feel about rental houseboating?" or "What is your position on the increase of recreational waterways?" Such questions terrify the recipient, and he's likely to throw the whole thing in the wastebasket.

With either type of questionnaire, address your letter to an individual rather than an organization. Immediately explain your topic, your publication, how you got his address, and why you think he is the only person who can give you the information you need. (It is not necessary to mention that you're sending the same questions to fifty others!) Subtly indicate the publicity advantages of his reply with something like, "I'm sure *Blank Blank*'s million readers will be interested. . . ." Emphasize the urgency of a speedy response with reference to a "close deadline." Try to send your questionnaire at least a month before your actual deadline—further ahead if you can manage it.

Use informal language with easygoing contractions. As Max Gunther says, "Do your best to make the recipient *like* you." Avoid the stiff business phraseology of a bygone day: "The various endeavors of your erstwhile colleagues might seem to indicate that you would possibly be a potential candidate for assisting in achieving the objective of this communication, which is to formulate a compendium of replies to the questionnaire, so that we may ascertain. . . ." Avoid, also, the cutesy, the slangy, the ungrammatical, the marginal, like "lousy" and "hip."

One successful Western writer always asks her questions on a cassette recorder. Then she mails the cassette to the interviewee, who replies the same way. This method combines the advantages of the telephone interview (making it easy for the person to answer quickly) and the written questionnaire (giving the person an opportunity to think about the questions and come back to them). The only disadvantages to this type of research are the usual possibilities of stage fright on the part of the interviewee, and mechanical problems.

If you're addressing a private individual, be sure to enclose an SASE. If it's a big company or a government office, that's not necessary. It is necessary, though, to write a thank-you note to everybody who replies.

Sometimes you'll need a prequestionnaire. Where do you find the people to tell you about houseboating all over the United States? When I returned from my first houseboat adventure and found I needed to contact sources for a national magazine story, I went to the library. The *World Wide Chamber of Commerce Directory*, published by Johnson Publishing Company, gave the addresses I needed for my prequestionnaire. For other types of stories you might find the requisite addresses for geographic spread in the *Thomas Register of American Manufacturers*; Gale's *Encyclopedia of Associations*; *Poor's Register of Corporations, Directors and Executives*; Dun and Bradstreet's *Million Dollar Directory*; the *World Travel Directory*; or in several local telephone books. Here again, you'll find one source often leads to another. When I found the addresses of chambers of commerce in houseboating areas, I sent sixty copies of this letter:

> As a freelance writer with a *Better Homes and Gardens* assignment for a piece on rental houseboating, I would appreciate it very much if you could let me have all possible information about rental houseboating in your area. Perhaps you could include brochures and addresses of houseboat rental operators.
> Since my deadline is very close, I would especially appreciate it if you could let me have this information as soon as possible.
> Thank you in advance for your consideration.

With answers to these letters (about half the recipients replied), plus addresses from ads in a houseboating magazine and other boat-related publications, and information I had obtained at the boat show, I then sent several hundred copies of this letter:

> As a freelance writer with a *Better Homes and Gardens* assignment for an article on rental houseboating, I would appreciate it very much if you would send me all possible information about your houseboat rental operation. Mr. Blank Blank of the State Tourist Office recommended you as an excellent source of information.
> If you can take the time to reply to the following questions, I'm sure *Better Homes and Gardens* readers will be interested in your advice.

Then I wrote a dozen crucial questions: How many boats do you have for rent? How long is the average rental? How many people return to rent again the following year? etc. The next group of questions, a little more personal, but still easy to answer, inquired about clubs or families renting flotillas for a rendezvous; what special scenery or activities the area offers to houseboaters; famous people who have rented houseboats; handicapped people; people from far away; how neat the boats are left; what pets are permitted; and any unusual accidents. The third group of questions suggested the recipient might have anecdotes to add to the basic information, and inquired about weddings aboard, babies born aboard, "or other human interest material." I inquired if many people bring enough gear to be marooned for years, what rental houseboaters usually run out of, and what the rental operator advises them to bring along.

I concluded with:

> I know this is your busy season, but as my deadline is very close, I do hope you'll find time to send me as much information as you can, as soon as possible. Would any photographs be available? I'd certainly appreciate having some. I'd also appreciate a copy of your brochure and current price list. I'm looking forward to hearing from you, and I thank you in advance for your consideration.

About one-third of the rental operators replied, which was enough to flesh out my story. The replies included anecdotes: about the couple who rented a "ten-sleeper" for the two of them, their Labrador retriever, their Pekingese pup, and their Siamese cat; about the British doctor, his wife and eleven children who wanted to bring along their Saint Bernard; about the seventy-eight-year-old bridegroom and his seventy-five-year-old bride who honeymooned aboard a houseboat; about people in wheelchairs and iron lungs or accompanied by Seeing Eye dogs who enjoyed houseboat holidays; about the teenage girls who dragged along their entire wardrobes, then spent the week in bikinis; and about the couple celebrating their twentieth wedding anniversary who forgot they didn't have their six children with them and brought so much food they each gained ten pounds.

Although it's doubtless nicer, and perhaps more conducive to response, to type individual letters for each person you're questioning, I don't feel that a good-quality photocopy on bond paper is insulting. Word processing might be a good answer here if you have many questionnaires to send. Sometimes I type very brief individual letters to each person, and enclose a photocopied questionnaire. In situations where I've had few questionnaires to send, where the response to each was critical to my story, and where the publicity value to the recipient was dubious, so that anyone who replied was really doing me a big favor, I've typed individual letters. On the houseboat story, however, I combined the letter and questionnaire on one page, leaving blank space for the names in the first paragraph, and had it photocopied. I filled in the personalization (on the same typewriter) and signed each letter with blue ink.

As postage and paper costs escalate, this questionnaire-sending can be an expensive proposition. Too expensive, if you're only going to write one story from it. In the next chapter we'll discuss getting maximum mileage from your research. If you sell several articles from the same postage-paper-photocopy-and-time-for-signing costs, then it's just a matter of comparing this method of research with the price of and the time involved in telephone calls or transportation. A travel writer's business expenses are sometimes substantial. (Remember to keep careful records for the IRS.)

Either in your original questionnaire or in your thank-you note to the source, be sure to indicate you're interested in future developments on the subject. You may find yourself on a permanent mailing list that provides a wealth of good ideas for rewriting the same story or initiating new ones.

Whatever research methods you use, don't skimp or take shortcuts. So-called writer's block is invariably the result of too little research. If you know enough, you won't have any trouble putting it down on paper.

And never underestimate the intelligence of your reader. Don't depend on the forlorn hope that he won't know when you're bluffing. John Ball tells of a private screening of a two-million-dollar motion picture that showed a DC-8 taking off, and then, a few minutes later, a shot, presumably of the same aircraft in flight, "Only this time it was a 727-200, a very different plane, with the power plants in the rear, not under the wings." When Ball mentioned this to the producer, the reply was, "Who will know the difference?" At the formal premiere of the movie, when the wrong aircraft came on the screen, the entire audience burst into laughter.

Members of your reading audience are wiser than you think. Whether or not you've done the ideal amount of pretrip and on-trip research, be sure to do a good job on your post-trip research, so you can give your readers the most accurate, up-to-date information possible.

Royal Bank Building, Place Ville-Marie, Montreal

Getting Ready to Sell

ne of my students was vacationing on Maui, and her husband teased her about her writing class. The hotel owner, overhearing, teased her, too. "Let's see some of your writing." She showed him a photograph she'd taken of a Hawaiian sunset and a poem she'd written about it. He whipped out his checkbook and bought the photo and poem to use on his menu.

It's the unexpected sales that really spell success for the writer. You may not have many chances to sell a menu poem. But, if you're trying to sell an editor an article similar to those he's already using, STOP! Do something else! Sell him a piece he doesn't even know he wants.

When you try to sell stories on camping, national parks, or Greek Island cruises to a travel magazine; anti-burglary advice to a home and garden publication; or sunburn warnings to a health journal, your competition is keen. The secret of successful marketing is to analyze the readership of a publication and try to give those readers what they don't yet know they want.

Travel & Leisure covers exotic destinations and exciting activities, right? Yet Max Gunther published "Foil Your Local Burglar: How to Protect Your Home While You're Away," obviously a subject of great interest to *Travel & Leisure* readers. *Better Homes and Gardens* published an article on "Station Wagon Camping," a likely subject, when you stop to think about it, for home-loving readers. *Sea*, a magazine of recreational boating, warned its seagoing readers about "Sunburn," in an issue at the beginning of boating season.

Points, a company publication sent to General Motors truck owners that stresses family vacation and recreation activities, published "The

Park of 'Gentle' Volcanoes,'' about Kilauea's Park of the Volcanoes on the island of Hawaii.

Again and again we see travel articles in magazines that we wouldn't normally think of as travel markets. Somebody found an angle to appeal to the readers of that publication. "Greek Island Odyssey,'' for instance, sold to *Cosmopolitan*, not a huge purchaser of travel material. Harriet Heyman, the author, explains the rationale:

> I sailed on the *Viking of Kos*. . . . There were twenty-five in my group—most of us young and unattached, about half men, half women. Many were in interesting transition—between love affairs, jobs, marriages, countries—and eager to talk about our personal situations as well as our common goal of immersing ourselves in Greece.

You might think regional magazines and Sunday supplements would stick to their own areas, yet *Connecticut Magazine* ran an article on Florida for residents considering retirement there. *California Today*, the Sunday supplement of the *San Jose Mercury-News*, published Gary Hanauer's "Adventurers in Paradise" with the explanation that "many Californians dream of settling in Hawaii.''

Home economists and food writers continually find good markets in boating, bicycling, outdoor, and camping publications—everybody wants to know what to take along on a picnic lunch. One writer received a check for $250 from *Field & Stream*—for a pickled fish recipe.

"A Caretaker for All Seasons,'' an article exploring the profession of house sitting from both sides of the "sit,'' is a likely enough story for *TWA Ambassador*, but "The Tugs" at first seems a strange choice for Northwest Orient's in-flight, *Northwest Passages*. Think about it, though—air travelers are interested in sea travel, too, and it's an innocuous, time-passing kind of story, the kind the in-flights want.

What the in-flights do *not* want was described by Richard Cramer, former editor of United's *Mainliner*, in a *Writer's Digest* article that included examples that speak for themselves:

Dear Editor,

Did you know that in the past five years there have been fifty attempted skyjackings, and less than three have been successful?

Dear Editor,

My husband and I recently returned from two horrible weeks in Hawaii, complete with burgled hotel room, severe sunburn, and lost baggage. May I hear from you?

Dear Editor,

Do you think your readers would find fascinating some documented statistics on the number of plane crashes, with accompanying death and injury figures, over the past ten years?

When you're getting ready to sell, pore over marketing manuals and marketing information with the *unexpected* in mind. Don't try to compete with the hundreds of travel writers who are trying to sell destination pieces to *Travel & Leisure*—think, instead, of an offbeat feature that would appeal to *Travel & Leisure*'s readers. A tennis vacation to *Glamour*? Maybe. An Alaska cruise to *House Beautiful*? Perhaps. And if you have any unusual game recipes try an outdoor magazine!

You'll find, as you become more familiar with the field, market research will occupy a large part of your time. Try to do it as efficiently as possible.

The floor has always been my favorite place for heavy-duty market research. Although I might sometimes look up one market for one article while sitting properly at a desk, for assembly line methods I need the floor.

Years of freelancing, an agent who doesn't handle travel material, and an innate interest in marketing have helped me develop a system that seems to eventually get the right article to the right publication. First I gather from their various hiding places twenty or thirty letters from editors encouraging further discussion, a dozen marketing lists culled from various sources, a current *Writer's Market* and other marketing manuals, several scribbled and scribbled-over lists for possible future sales and what seems like a half ream of disorganized notes to myself: "Try H.B. on Corms. in 6 mos." or "New ed. at P.G. Try Bar. Rf.?"

Then, too, I have the forty-odd itinerary sheets for the forty-odd ideas I'm currently working on, and I spread these, alphabetically by country, in a sort of squared circle around me. These represent perhaps two or three articles for which I have only the vaguest glimmer of an idea, and four or five where I've focused the idea but I'm not ready to research and write it yet; as well as a dozen full-blown ideas waiting to be written. Then there are two or three articles already written—and rejected; and perhaps twenty recently published articles, for three-fourths of which I own the residual rights, so they can be resold for additional mileage. The five or six articles to which I've sold all rights still offer the possibility of being rewritten, using the leftover research, and submitted to some other publication.

On yellow legal sheets I write all the working titles, alphabetically by country, five to the page, with a hunk of space between each one. At the tops of two white legal sheets I write "query," for those publications that prefer it, and "send" for those that want to see the complete manuscript right away.

Then I go through the editorial correspondence, noting on the itineraries which ideas or articles have attracted an editor enough for him to say, "We're overstocked now, but try us again on this in six months," or "Have you anything else on Indonesia? We're running a

Bali piece this month, but we could use another Indonesia story in February," or "We're holding your Denmark article and the three transparencies. Do you have any black and whites?" If I have the black and whites or another Indonesia story or the six months is up, I get up from the floor, find the items and place them in a "send immediately" pile.

Next come the scribbled notes to myself. Sometimes I've commanded myself so firmly to "send" something that it, too, goes in the "immediately" pile. Other times, I transfer my directions to the itinerary sheet, or, if it's about something that hasn't yet materialized, like a rumor about a new travel publication whose premiere issue hasn't yet come out, I consolidate those notes on a new sheet of "futures."

Some of the markets on the old "futures" list are viable now. My latest marketing list says *Big Brass*, publishing its third edition, is looking for Caribbean cruise stories, and they prefer queries. So I write "*Big Brass*" at the top of the long white query sheet, "Carib. Cr." in parenthesis. On the long yellow sheet of working titles I jot under "Caribbean Cruise," "*Big Brass* (query)." If *Big Brass* is not listed in a marketing manual, I circle its address in red for easy recognition later.

Naturally, I give strong marketing preference to publications where I've sold previously, and even to those where I've had a near-miss.

Then I study the marketing lists and marketing manuals, juggling my forty ideas around in my mind and wiggling my cramped toes from time to time. When I come to a market I think suitable for one of my ideas, I write the name of the market under the working title on a yellow sheet, and the title of the idea under the name of the market on either the white "query" sheet or the white "send" sheet. Between times, I check against the itinerary sheets for markets already approached, and make sure I have the latest address for any I plan to try.

Two days later I have cramps in my legs, a cluttered floor, and a crossfile of markets for each idea and ideas for each market. Now comes the careful scrutiny. Here are twenty ideas suitable for *Paradise Magazine*—which three or four shall I select for the query? And here is that Caribbean cruise idea with twenty possible markets for it—where shall I send it or query on it first? I begin with the idea for which there are fewest possible markets and the market for which there are fewest ideas and continue matching and cross-matching from there. Taking into consideration pay, prestige, and likelihood in an indefinable combination, I end up, the following day, with orderly itineraries for each of my forty ideas. Any articles that have already been written I send immediately to the first market on the itinerary if that is suitable, or I query on it, if that's what the magazine requests. On the still-to-be-written articles I send queries, marking on the itineraries and in my "out" book (which tells what has gone where and when) what I'm doing.

Does this sound like a lot of trouble? It is at the time. But the information acquired on "Marketing Days" lasts many months. If the big brown envelope comes back, I know immediately where to send it next. If a query letter results in a negative response, I query the next market on the itinerary. Replies to all these queries usually result in enough go-aheads and assignments to keep me working full speed until next Marketing Day, which may be anywhere from six months to three years later, depending on how much traveling I do, how many other projects I have, and the usual variables of writing and marketing. Of course, I'm constantly updating, as I read marketing information and listen to the experiences of other writers, and adding to or subtracting from my idea list. But assembly line market research on the floor is a lot easier than looking up markets for each of forty ideas individually while sitting at a desk.

Get the Most Mileage from Your Research

Now that you've figured out where to sell your story, it's time to think of where to sell it next.

No travel writer can afford to take a trip and write only one story from it. If you do the research you should, you have made too great a time investment for a single story to suffice. So before you even leave on the trip, begin to think of what you will write and how you will get additional mileage from it. While you're traveling you'll see more mileage possibilities, and you'll find still more as you do your post-trip market research.

How can you sell your story more than once? There are a number of ways. Sometimes you'll use a combination of them and find that one article becomes almost an annuity for you as you go on selling the material again and again.

The most familiar method of collecting several checks for the same research is to sell only one-time rights to each story buyer. I haven't room here to go into a full discussion of copyright, but it's well to remember that the 1978 copyright law favors the author, making him the recognized copyright holder. (However, some publications today insist that the writer sign a "work for hire" agreement, thereby making the publisher the copyright owner, which is contrary to the spirit of the law.) Even before the new law, many publications had—and still have—no objection to simultaneous submissions or the submission of previously published material. Usually these are religious magazines (the Methodists don't know if the Catholics are reading the identical article in their publication), regional periodicals (Texans might be interested in taking a trip on the Mississippi Queen, and so might Floridians, and neither one cares what the other one is reading), trade journals, company publications and association magazines (where no individual is likely to encounter the same article twice, since he's not likely to be a hairstylist and also a fireman, and probably doesn't belong to both Elks and Lions). Newspaper and Sunday supplement editors don't mind if you submit to their colleagues in other parts of the country. When you send something to them, mark it "Exclusive Your Area," and don't send it to a competing newspaper. Nino La Bello, based in Europe, sometimes manages to sell the same story to three *hundred* newspapers around the globe. Even if you sell first rights to the first buyer, you'll still make money on additional sales of one-time rights.

Subsequent publication is the second way to get greater mileage out of a single article. When *Reader's Digest* condenses an article from another periodical, it pays the periodical *and* the author. Sometimes the *Digest* will help you place the article in another magazine so that they can later excerpt it, if they feel the story you originally submitted to them isn't strong enough for a *Digest* original. Other magazines also sometimes excerpt from each other, books are condensed or excerpted or serialized in periodicals, articles are collected in anthologies. International reprints and translations are an excellent mileage-maker for the author. One of my students published an article in a US magazine, and within a week an Australian magazine had contacted her for reprint rights. Another student's article in a US magazine was reprinted by *Reader's Digest*, and immediately a Canadian firm requested the right to reprint it in pamphlet form. Subsequent publication is not always author-instigated, but when the opportunity presents itself, seize it.

Syndication is a good answer to multiple sales, if you can interest a syndicate in your material. Sometimes sibling publications will share some of their nontechnical copy.

Sometimes a negative editorial decision extends your mileage. For instance, a publication may offer a "kill fee"—if the finished article does not turn out to be what they need. The kill fee is usually about one-fourth to one-third of the agreed-upon price, and the article, of course, then belongs to the writer and can be resold.

If an editor takes your story and pays for it on acceptance, and then many months go by and it isn't published, chances are there's been a change of editors and/or a change in editorial policy, and your piece will probably never run. If you ask if you can have it back the answer is usually yes, and then you're welcome to sell it again.

If editors keep your article and/or photographs for an unreasonably long time without making a decision, they sometimes pay a "holding fee" if they decide in the end they can't use them. Sometimes the holding fee is substantial.

Another mileage-maker is an outline. Some publications, as we've said, prefer an outline to a query. And sometimes they'll buy the outline—leaving the writer free to sell the actual story elsewhere, with the outline money as a bonus. When I sent an outline on Malta to *Aramco World*, the editor wrote that he was planning to travel to Malta, himself, and would write his own story. However, he said, he liked my outline so much he wanted to buy it. Then I was free to sell the story elsewhere—the outline money was pure bonus.

So far all the mileage-makers we've discussed are at least partially outside the writer's control. But how can you, alone, within the framework of integrity, get maximum mileage from your work?

Charlotte MacDonald begins her itinerary with a single subject, which she fragments into all the possible ways she can treat it for different markets. If the subject has several angles, it's easy to change the emphasis. Sigiriya, that gigantic rock rising from the plains of Sri Lanka, inspired me to write an article about the aerie-fortress occupied by a wicked king. So far it's been published by the *Los Angeles Times*, *Off Duty*, and the *San Jose Mercury-News*. That article mentioned in a sentence or two the picture gallery that's situated two-thirds of the way up, where soldiers on guard duty painted murals of beautiful ladies in diaphanous dresses, their colors still glowing today. An entirely different article, "The Painted Ladies of Sigiriya," concentrating on "the world's most unusual picture gallery" and barely mentioning the fortress, sold to *Réalités*.

I've written so many articles about Ephesus, over a period of seventeen years and four visits, I can hardly count them. The emphasis has been recreational (Aegean Turkey is a beautiful area with many inexpensive resorts); religious (Saint Paul and Saint John stayed here and so, perhaps, did the Virgin Mary); ecological (environmental disasters occurred long before men coined the term ecology, such as silting by the Maeander River); in some cases it's been strictly a travel piece (this is one stop on the cruise ship circuit and this is what you'll find there); and elsewhere the emphasis has been historical or archaeological or political. Each time some of the same basic facts, like location, are introduced somewhere in the story, but the various factors weigh differently, according to the emphasis.

Hal Schell did a piece on hot-air ballooning and then ballooned his research into the following sales: to *Motorhome Life*, a story of how a group of North Carolina balloonists use Winnebago motor homes for promotions; to *Feminine Fitness*, a story about prominent lady balloonist Andrea Floden and how the sport keeps her fit; to *LP-Gas*, two stories on the LP gas in balloons; to *PV4*, a story on how drivers of pickups can retrieve hot-air balloons in their vehicles; to *Relax*, a story about Dr. William Grabb, president of the Ballooning Federation of America; to *Four Seasons Trails*, a story about the fun recreational vehicle owners can have at ballooning events; to *Motorland*, a story on Brent Stockwell, a well-known California aeronaut; to *Highlights for Children*, a history of hot-air ballooning.

Sometimes you have a lot more material than you can possibly use in one article—unless your editor's willing to let you make the article 10,000 words long. Actually, if you have enough solid material for 10,000 words, you should be able to write at least five or six articles on that subject without plagiarizing yourself. Some of the basic facts you'll have to repeat in each one, of course, but if you make the beginnings and the endings all different, vary the emphasis and the anecdotes, and tack on new titles, you'll have five or six distinctly different articles. I've found this superfluity of material especially in subjects involving lots of live research, where I have an unlimited source of anecdotal material from interviewing a variety of people.

Using the overflow is another way to gain mileage. After you write the first article, gather up the bits and pieces you have left and concoct another story from them. Juvenile writer Mabel Watts says to be careful about doing this, though. After a trip to the British Isles, she sold one story with a Scottish background; then used her leftover research for another story. But the editor to whom she submitted it said, "You sound like the old Scottish lady who threw all the leftovers into the haggis!"

Often, though, you can get another story out of the overflow of material or with a spinoff from the one you're working on. Most of the spinoffs I've sold have been fillers or featurettes, such as the one to *Ladies' Home Journal* about how to avoid coming home from vacation to a houseful of dirty laundry, and the one to the *Denver Post* supplement on the origin of the English word *meander*.

Sometimes you'll expand your mileage years later, when you update and change a travel article written long ago.

Remember when John Fairfax and Sylvia Cook crossed the Pacific Ocean in a rowboat and landed at Hayman Island on Australia's Great Barrier Reef? Well, that was just about the time I was finishing my Barrier Reef story for the *San Francisco Examiner* travel section. So I wrote a new lead:

> John Fairfax and Sylvia Cook arrived at Hayman Island in a rowboat—one year, six thousand miles, and four cyclones after their departure from San Francisco.
>
> Most visitors arrive at Hayman via helicopter or motor launch. Unlike John and Sylvia, who rushed right off to publicize their Pacific rowboat safari, you'll probably want to relax at Hayman for days or weeks.

and a new ending:

> You can count on good weather any time of the year. And it's not absolutely necessary to *row* across the Pacific to land on Hayman. . . .

before I sent it off. Through an incredible comedy of errors, that article was accidentally "killed" in the composing room several months later. The *Examiner* paid me for it, but by then it was too late in the year for an article on Australia, where the seasons are reversed. A few months later, by the time I had queried *Relax* and had a go-ahead on the article, the world had long since forgotten John Fairfax and Sylvia Cook, so I snipped them out of the story and wrote a new beginning and ending. Another visit to Hayman Island expanded my information, and when airfares to Australia were sharply reduced, I used that as a peg for a newly expanded Barrier Reef story.

Often your mileage expands with the years. As you grow and change and become a better writer, you're inspired to re-treat ideas you now feel you didn't do justice by, and through your growing expertise an entirely new story emerges.

In your zealous quest for mileage, be careful, though, not to violate anybody else's rights. Sherman Grant says it's difficult to sell a story to an additional publication when the people you interviewed agreed to talk to you as the representative of the specific magazine that assigned you the story.

If that's no problem, other ways you can make mileage from your research are: rewriting an adult article as a juvenile, or vice versa; by using your travel background for a short story, a juvenile story, or a play, or taking the background from one of them for a travel article; by expanding a local story (usually by working out a "geographic spread" through additional research) into a national article; or converting a national article, such as my *Weight Watcher's* piece on travel charm bracelets, to a local one, using local people and local anecdotes for an additional sale to a Sunday supplement.

Larry Holden speaks of seasonal articles that can be used year after year, when that season rolls around again. He refers not only to holidays but also to special times, like tornado season, about which he frequently writes. Fanny-Maude Evans has done that with her research on lightning, which also has a "season."

Holden speaks of "blending" and "paring" for increased sales, too. Blending means taking bits and pieces from several stories you've previously written to make a new story. I snipped tidbits from several advice articles on how to save money and how to have a good time on your trip and added new material for an article on "How to Get the Most Pleasure from Your Travel Dollar." Paring is the opposite of blending. If you've written a definitive article, you can often slice out a specific section and sell it as a short separate article, once you've changed it around a little.

As you think about it you'll probably come up with additional ways for stretching mileage from your research. There simply aren't enough hours in the day for a travel writer to be continually researching new articles, and it's not necessary. Research thoroughly in the first place. Then write your story as well as you can each time. Willa Cather advised long ago, "Give your best every single time. Don't hold back and save anything out for 'next time.' 'Next time' will take care of itself."

If you put the best of everything you can think of into the story you're writing now, more good ideas will appear, ready for use in the next story.

One of the strongest examples of making one trip pay off is A.R. Roalman's three-week visit to Japan. He started off with assignments (resulting from queries) from *National Wildlife Magazine* for a story on Japan's loss of natural resources, from the *Chicago American* for an article on Japanese baseball, from the *National Observer* for a feature on the Mickey Mantle of Japanese baseball, from the *Lion* for a profile of an important Japanese who is a member of Lions International, from *Car Life* for a major story on the Japanese auto industry, from *Progress* for an article on cormorant fishing, and those two assignments from *American Forest* and *Popular Mechanics* for the oldest wooden building. (See Chapter 2.) His chance meetings with a Japanese garden expert and an American who was studying reading habits resulted in profitable stories. The Lion he interviewed told him about the Small Kindness Movement, which turned into another good assignment; his interviews for the auto industry uncovered a remarkable outboard motorboat, which led to still another assignment; and his baseball stories sold to about a dozen other major league cities' publications.

Sometimes you can spread your message internationally—and increase your profit, too—by selling to English-language publications in foreign countries. When you're overseas you'll naturally survey the kiosk displays of newspapers and magazines and select a few to send home in your big brown envelopes, along with the foreign in-flights and in-rooms you pick up. This is the best way to obtain foreign publications to analyze as possible markets; but you can also send for sample copies or buy an issue or two at a large bookstore or newsstand at home.

In *Writer's Market* you'll find an occasional foreign periodical amid the US and Canadian listings, such as *Glimpses of Micronesia* (a quarterly published on Guam), and *Baja California Bulletin* (a bimonthly published in La Paz). But the two major sources listing foreign periodicals are the *International Literary Marketplace* and *Ulrich's International Periodicals Directory*, both published by Bowker. The *International Literary Marketplace* is divided by countries, with information on periodicals, publishers, and related matters listed under each country. *Ulrich's* begins its fifteen pages of Travel and Tourism with *AAA Texas Motorist*, but continues with *AIM* (Adventures in Mexico Newsletter), *About London*, the *Abu Dhabi News*, and *Around Malaysia*. It continues through the alphabet to *World Travel/Tourisme Mondial* (with editions in English, French, and Spanish, published in Madrid), *Yatri* (published in New Delhi), giving editors' names, addresses and circulation figures.

Whether your special interest is jungle animals, international business, or Catholic shrines, scuba diving, black travelers, or Oriental art, you'll find an international magazine in the market for your work.

The *Australian Women's Weekly* buys material similar to that which appears in US and Canadian women's magazines, and often runs articles on international, as well as Australian, destinations. A sampling of other foreign publications that might make good travel markets for you includes the *Illustrated London News*, *Ireland of the Welcomes*, *Rhodesia Calls*, *Scottish Field*, *South African Panorama*, *Australian Photography*, Thailand's *Look East*, New Zealand's *Sea Spray*, and *Hemisphere*, an Asian-Australian monthly featuring travel and the arts.

For a list of Japanese publications accepting freelance material, send for *A Contributor's Guide to Free-Lancing In Japan:*

The Tokyo English Literature Society
T.E.L.S. "Tomeoki"
Koishikwawa Post Office
Bunkyo-ku, Tokyo (112)
Japan

There's a small charge.

Although payment from these periodicals is practically never as high as in the United States, they usually have no objection to previously published material. (The pay may be lower because the country—and therefore the circulation—is smaller than a North American magazine.) If you can sell the same piece over and over, that's mileage, and worth doing. Don't use up all the profits in the postage, though.

Usually it's best to first send a query or an outline to a foreign market. Then, if the editor wants to see the article, perhaps accompanied by photographs, find out from the post office the safest, cheapest, and fastest way to send the material. The rules change from time to time, and it may save money to wrap the pictures separately, leave the envelope flap unsealed, or observe some other regulation. If you want the article and/or illustrations returned if unused, enclose a self-addressed envelope and an International Reply Coupon. It costs less though, to send a photocopy of the article and tell the editor to destroy it if he can't use it.

What kinds of travel stories are likely to sell to foreign markets? Both foreign stories *and* North American stories. If you have something on the area the publication covers, wonderful. Many foreign editors would also welcome pieces about areas you know well.

Look your piece over carefully before you send it. Did you remove any references to typically American events or people that will be incomprehensible to a foreign reader? Try to de-Americanize the style, too, eliminating idioms, slang, and colloquial expressions. Most foreign publications tend toward British usage and spelling rather than American. Although they probably won't reject your excellent article just because you've called them *trucks* and *elevators* instead of *lorries* and *lifts*, or spelled what you expect them to send you as *check* instead of *cheque*, make it as easy for the editor as you can.

Countries likely to have English-language publications include:

Australia	Iceland	Norway
The Bahamas	India	Pakistan
Bangladesh	Indonesia	Panama
Bermuda	Ireland	Republic of South
Denmark	Israel	Africa
Egypt	Japan	Rhodesia
Fiji	Kenya	The Philippines
Finland	Korea	Singapore
Gibraltar	Malaysia	Sri Lanka
Greece	Malta	Sweden
Hong Kong	The Netherlands	United Kingdom
	New Zealand	Western Samoa

Explore the foreign markets as you plan your strategy for getting the most mileage out of your research.

The Back-of-the-Book Can Be Anyplace

Now let's look at a few market possibilities perhaps you haven't thought of. Some of them can be mileage markets, too. Have you wondered about those odd pages in many magazines—C70/1 and F70/6? And have you wondered why the stories on those pages never appear in the table of contents? Those are "back-of-the-book" stories. They may be located in the front of the book or the middle of the book, but they're still back-of-the-book stories. And this is a good market for the less experienced writer.

Nearly all national magazines accept regional advertising these days. That's the advertising on pages C70/1, C70/2, C70/3 and C70/4 in the August 1979 *Travel & Leisure*. It's also the advertising on pages W70/1 through W70/6. And it's the advertising on pages C12/1 through C12/4 and W12/1 through W12/6, which happen to be in the front of the book. You don't have to be Sherlock Holmes to figure that "C" stands for California and "W" stands for West. So what does this have to do with the travel writer? It's an entry level opportunity. The ads don't always entirely fill those regional pages, so editorial material is required.

The listing for *Travel & Leisure* in *Writer's Market* puts it tactfully. After "How to Break In" it says:

New writers might try to get something in one of our regional editions. They don't pay as much as our national articles ($300-$500), but it's a good way to start. We have a great need for these pieces and they run no more than 800-1,200 words. Regionals cover any number of possibilities, from rafting a river in a certain state to unusual new attractions.

Now this doesn't come right out and say, "Our regional editions are open to amateurs," but it does get across the point that slightly less polish is required. In other words, it's a good place for the less experienced writer to begin. This particular issue of *Travel & Leisure* has in its western sections an article about traveling in Colorado by train, jeep, or on foot; an article about river trips in Idaho; a nongeographic piece called "Auctions: A Grown-up Game"; and a brief quiz about international capitals.

Its California back-of-the-book material includes "Accessible Los Angeles: A Guide for the Handicapped" and "Endless Summer: By the Sea in Santa Cruz." *Better Homes and Gardens* has a special "Travel West" section in its western regional pages which covers such subjects as "Kite Festivals," a rundown on the what, where and when of flying kites in the West; "Surprising Solvang," which enumerates the attractions of the Danish hamlet near Santa Barbara; and "All Aboard for Money-Saving Travel By Rail" (traveling the West by Rail Pass). "*Good Housekeeping's* Travel Guide" appears in a back-of-the-book section, too, and includes areas like "Nevada's Stagecoach Country" and "Padre Island—Nature's Playground." *Redbook* published "California: Tourists' Treasure Chest" (a brief guide to San Francisco), *McCall's* used "Camping Out with the Kids," and *Ladies' Home Journal* ran "Traveling Safe" on an unnumbered page in the back of the book.

Sometimes, as you can see, the material in the western regional pages isn't particularly western. It's always short and on a subject that lends itself to short treatment because of its shallow scope.

How do you tell the editor you're sure your article isn't good enough for the national section so you're only asking him to consider it for the back of the book? Obviously, you don't. If the *Writer's Market* listing suggests you send regional material to a regional editor, then you'll do so. Otherwise, let the travel editor or the articles editor, or whoever is in charge of that kind of material, decide where your piece should go. (You'll follow instructions in the listing, of course, as to length, photographs, and whether or not to query.)

Other special magazine sections may be better markets than you'd think for different types of travel material. *Good Housekeeping's* "The Better Way," for instance, often features such subjects as trip and vacation insurance, better gas mileage, tips on packing a car for travel, and other loosely travel-related subjects. They want "just the facts, please," for this section—*they* adapt it to their format. *McCall's* "Right Now," which seeks "short pieces with a news or service angle . . . on any timely subject," ran a spread on "Offbeat Vacations for a Recession Year," a roundup of four dissimilar vacation ideas, written by four different people. "Close-to-Home Touring" tells about using guidebooks for various local sites; "Families on Campus" describes several types of college vacations; "Tennis Co op" explains the logistics of cooperating with other families to build tennis courts; and "Living on Wheels" discusses motor homes and other recreational vehicles.

What Are Your Other Markets?

Let's look at some different types of publications that use travel-related material of one sort or another.

Have you noticed the recent proliferation of travel newsletters? Mailed to subscribers, these purport to give the traveler the inside dope about hotels, transportation, restaurants, etc. A large percentage of this information is supplied by other travelers, who get paid for it. *Travel Smart*, for instance, says it's 60 percent freelance-written and pays $10 to $150 for candid advice on good travel values. There are several others of this type. They want the information to come from personal experience, but not always written in the first person. They need "mentions." If you've had a really good or really bad experience, you could detail it briefly, and consider one of these newsletters. Most of them prefer queries. They'll send report forms, if you like.

If you want to keep busy while traveling, but don't want to embark on a full-scale career as a travel writer, or you want something to supplement your career as a travel writer, consider working for Star Service, which puts out a manual for travel agencies. They need current hotel reports (you don't have to stay at the hotel—just talk to the manager and inspect the rooms), and they prefer that you do a number of them in one city, not merely an isolated example. They pay ten dollars and up per report and say they buy two thousand of them a year. Write:

The Star Service
Sloane Agency Travel Reports
Box 15610
Fort Lauderdale FL 33318

They also send you report forms.

Many newspapers publish some kind of "trip sharing" column. You tell about your trip in an informal manner and perhaps send a photograph. Some of them pay and some don't, so inquire first. Both newspapers and magazines occasionally run special contests for travel articles or photographs, and sometimes the prizes are substantial. Keep on the lookout for these. They often add mileage.

We've spoken of *Guest Informant*, which is one of the hardcover, four-color books placed in hotel rooms around the United States. Hotel rooms in foreign countries often have books of this type, too, in English. They use travel information only on the city in which they appear, and since it's such detailed information, you could work on one only for a city you're very familiar with. But they do use freelance material, so look into it further if you're interested.

Writing for *Guest Informant* is something you could do without leaving home. Let's look at a few other stay-at-home travel possibilities.

American Demographics magazine is interested only in statistics on where Americans take their vacations and what kinds of trends are evident; *Incentive Marketing* takes material on travel that firms use as a reward in motivational promotion.

Stay-at-Home Travel Writing

You can interview travel agents for travel trade journals. There are a number of travel trade journals, some monthly, some weekly, and they do use freelance material on various phases of the travel industry.

A Sacramento, California, woman, lamenting the fact that she doesn't get to travel much, contacts the Sacramento Convention Center to find out which groups, such as Rotarians, Presbyterians, etc., will be meeting there soon. Then she writes the editors of their publications with suggestions for travel stories on Sacramento.

Another possibility is writing brochure material advertising travel lecturers. The last brochure writer who interviewed me was producing such purple prose I asked him what qualifications a brochure writer needed. "Oh," he said, "you have to know how to lie a little."

Opportunities for writing publicity and advertising copy in travel-related fields increase every day. Whether you're writing about the objective of the travel—the restaurant, hotel, whatever—or the person who is going to tell others about those objectives, try not to lie more than "a little"!

Guidebooks, to your own area or elsewhere, or perhaps to something like "State Parks of Northern California," often provide good income for the travel writer. Travel puzzles and quizzes, as well as cookbooks, can be devised by the stay-at-home, too.

Travel lectures and radio and television programs, on the other hand, are the province of the active traveler. Juvenile and young adult audiovisual materials are another market for the returned traveler. In addition to the magazine and newspaper articles and adult and young people's books on travel, we mustn't overlook the value of the travel background for other types of fiction and nonfiction for all ages.

You can see the tremendous importance of market research, and what a variety of possible markets are available. But we keep coming back to the same precept: "There is no such thing as writing *generally*." Everything you write must be slanted to the reader for whom it's intended.

The same week as the Hawaiian poem-picture sale for the menu, another of my students made an unexpected "sale." An elderly gentleman, he was traveling on the highway when a Highway Patrol officer stopped him and fined him fifteen dollars, although he felt he wasn't guilty of the infraction charged. His letter to the officer's superior stated his case so clearly and was so well designed to appeal to the person who would be reading it, he immediately received a refund of the fine.

Look for the unexpected sale, but be sure you're selling to the right audience.

PART TWO

Fishing boats in harbor, Lisbon, Portugal

11

Sell Your Story Before You Write It

n Jaipur our Indian guide proudly mentioned his publications in *National Geographic* and *Vogue*. *National Geographic* I could understand—but *Vogue*?

"How did you happen to publish a travel article in *Vogue*?"

"Oh, I sent them a query letter," he replied. "They liked my idea and told me to send it along."

This man had guided a group of American travel writers working on a Jaipur story, and they advised him about his own work: "Always query first."

Good advice. Those travel writers believed—and I believe, too—that the query letter is the most important sales tool in the travel writer's repertoire. Although it looks like an extra step in the writing process, it's usually the quickest path to publication.

What is this magic tool, the query letter? It is, as it sounds, a letter of inquiry; a letter inviting the editor of a publication to express interest in your idea *before* you proceed to research and write the article.

Sometimes your query will sell your story before you write it; sometimes it will elicit the encouragement that indicates you're on the right track; and sometimes it will help you see that this particular idea isn't worth pursuing.

In this chapter we'll consider why the query is such an important tool, what elements it should contain, and what it can do for you. In Chapter 12 we'll take up the where and the when (and the when-not-to) of query letters, as well as different types of queries and possible editorial responses.

Why is the query such an important tool—what can it do for you?

First, it saves you time. It saves you the time spent researching and

Cypress trees at Carmel-by-the-sea, California

writing an article that is never going to sell. Although presumably you will study the *Reader's Guide to Periodical Literature* and the publications themselves to see what has been written on your subject lately, you have no way of knowing whether your target market is currently considering or has recently purchased an article on the same subject. While you're riding your mule to the bottom of the Grand Canyon, your editor may be buying a Grand Canyon piece from somebody else.

The query saves time, too, because it is read by a more important editor than the first reader, who plucks unsolicited manuscripts from the slush pile. Even if the first reader likes your complete story, it still must be approved by several others before reaching the decision-making editor, who is usually the one to consider your query immediately. And what busy editor wouldn't be tempted to rest his eyes on a short letter, as he postpones his attack on a long manuscript?

You can generally expect a reply to your query within a couple of weeks, except during the summer, when all editorial responses take longer. If your answer is delayed, after five or six weeks inquire if the staff will be considering your idea at the next editorial conference. You'll find that any time of year a "no" answer arrives sooner than a "yes" or a "maybe." When you see a "no," quickly query the next periodical on your marketing itinerary.

Preliminary inquiry also saves you postage. While you should include a self-addressed stamped envelope (SASE) with the query, as well as with the manuscript, you can send four or five letters for the same stamps as an average article. (If your article is accompanied by properly packed photographs, it will cost more than fifteen times as much as a query. See Chapter 8 for discussion of manuscript mailing.)

Another important reason for query writing is the chance it gives you to avoid the editor's taboos and to find his main interest. His objections to your subject matter or stance might make it pointless to send the completed article. But he may let you know that while he's not interested in the religious history of Aegean Turkey and won't permit you even to mention Saint Paul, Saint John, or the Virgin Mary, he's fascinated by the sixteenth-century Barbarossa brothers, pirates who pillaged Turkish beaches. He wants you to include every possible kernel of information about that era. Could you research and write your story in the direction he prefers? You'll never know *what* he prefers unless you send a query.

Too many writers, however, attempt to rely entirely on editorial preference, without making concrete suggestions of their own. I'm afraid I was much that way twenty years ago when I began writing about travel. I called or wrote every editor I knew with a "Guess what! We're spending the summer in Europe! What can I do for you over there?" While their answers were polite, they added up to, "If you don't know what you can do for me, how am I supposed to know? Give me some definite ideas, and I'll tell you what I like."

Recently visiting an editor's office while he fielded a phone call of a similar type from a writer spending the winter in Mexico, I heard him mutter, "What does he want—a nursemaid?" I cringed.

If your plans are firm enough to solicit sales several months before your trip, you increase your chances of traveling with go-aheads and assignments. As soon as your pretrip research reveals writing possibilities, suggest one or several ideas to your target market. Sometimes your insight will catalyze the editor into suggesting ideas of his own—assigning you to research them. This query, for instance, produced a favorable result:

When we revisit Australia this winter we plan to see a part of the country we missed on our last trip (Perth and Western Australia), stay longer in a city we enjoyed but didn't allow enough time for (Canberra), and repeat our wonderful experience at a favorite resort (Hayman Island on the Great Barrier Reef). Any of these destinations—or all of them—would make a good story for your readers.

Perth Americans remember as the City of Lights, its buildings illuminated for our space travelers. The gold-rush ghost towns and the working outback are very close. So are the beaches. Where else do residents rush to spend their leisure at a nearby island called "Rottnest"?

Canberra, Australia's capital, is so interesting it's too bad many Americans allow too little time for it. In addition to taking the launch ride around American Walter Burley Griffin's planned lakeside community, we'll visit the unique embassy buildings and the spectacular War Memorial Museum. We'll travel to the nearby Tidbinbilla Deep-Space Tracking Station, as well as Mount Stromlo Observatory and the Cotter River Recreation Area. We've been invited to visit the Snowy Mountains—both the complex engineering development and the excellent ski areas. We've also been invited to spend some time at Tralee Sheep Station, where we'll watch working dogs and sheepshearers, boomerang throwers and native fauna.

Hayman Island on Australia's Barrier Reef has always seemed like a dream come true, and I can hardly wait to return there. The hotel grounds and superb beach are so spacious, most of the time it's as though you, alone, have discovered paradise. Yet only a few yards away there is activity, conviviality, or any luxury you've a whim for. Fishing, snorkeling, fossicking on the reef, boat trips to Hook Island's underwater observatory, sailing, water skiing, and just plain dozing in the sun are some of the activities Hayman offers. You can enjoy tennis and badminton, lawn bowls and the biweekly Chinese New Years, where everybody eats with chopsticks.

May I write one of these stories for you while I'm in Australia or immediately after my return?

The editor replied:

Not the Barrier Reef. We already have too much Reef material on hand. But how about combining the other two? Would something like "Two Australian cities seldom visited by Americans— you'll learn to love them both" sound like a good theme for the combination? Compare and contrast the two cities.

Better tell how to get from Canberra to Perth and how long it takes and what's to see en route. Why don't more Americans visit Canberra or stay there longer? (I can see why they don't visit Perth!)

Is it better to see Australia via package tour or on your own? Be sure to include something about the cultural life of each city, as well as sports and recreation. How about prices? Everybody seems to be interested these days in just how much a US dollar buys. If the details get in your way, develop a sidebar and spell it out there.

You say you're going this winter, but I'm not sure when you'll be back from Australia. I wouldn't want to run the story much past May 1. (Doesn't it get too cold for tourists after that?) So let me know when you could have it ready. About 2,000 words. Ten or twelve black and white photos. Have a good trip!

An even more important plus value of the query is the way it makes a reservation for your story. If your subject intrigues the editor and he asks to take a look, he won't buy that subject from another writer, or encourage another proposer to work up a similar piece, until he at least sees what you produce providing you do it within a reasonable amount of time. While you're huffing and puffing up to the picture gallery at Sri Lanka's Sigiriya Rock, your pretrip query protects your story.

If the editor is in a hurry for your article, he'll tell you. He may suggest an approach, form, length, additional research sources, or other aids to enrich your piece. If you follow his suggestions, your manuscript will have a head start toward publication. Not only will you be able to mail it directly to the editor who encouraged you, but when he sees it he will recognize the idea as one he liked. If you've used your story lead in the query, he'll also recognize the words. Having encouraged you to send it, he's ready to praise your piece at the editorial conference. He has a stake in your success. To insure this recognition, many writers enclose a copy of the go-ahead or assignment when following a query with a manuscript.

The most important plus of the query letter is the opportunity it gives you to get organized. Obviously you can't write an appealing letter until you've thought through what your article will cover. Many times I've started to write a query and found I didn't know enough yet to make a strong presentation. Several times I've discovered that what I had at first thought so fascinating didn't really make a story after all.

On other occasions, trying to formulate the query proposal helped me find the focus for the finished piece.

While the focus should be clear in the query, it should be stated *briefly*. Without brevity, you lose your advantage. One page always attracts more favorable attention than many pages, so if necessary decrease your margins to avoid spilling over onto another sheet. In no case, write a query longer than two pages.

We've all heard writers say, "*My* idea is so wonderful, so unique, so exciting, so stupendous, there's no possible way I could confine its description to two pages." We've even heard writers say, "My idea is so wonderful, so unique, etc., there's no possible way I could describe it in writing—I have to *see* the editor and *tell* him about it."

Ridiculous! A writer is supposed to be able to write. If you can't describe your idea by putting words on a piece of paper or you can't describe it briefly enough to appear appetizing to an editor, you should enter some other profession.

The query letter is your showcase. To function as a sales tool it needs the aura of unmistakable excellence. It should sparkle with well-selected words and significant statements. The editor assumes that your finished work will be no better than your proposal. He takes it for granted that muddy thinking goes with mixed metaphors, and supposes that the person who wrote the following query would, if encouraged to send a complete article, turn in something unreadable:

Two women and three small children on a rainy day in Tahiti! We had excitedly, unbelievably figured for years on the freighter that took us across the Pacific along with five others only there were supposed to be 7 but one couldn't make it at the last minute because of I don't know what and the other said she was canceling reluctantly the captain said. Our freighter schedule was a delay in arrival necessitating an unplanned overnight as it seemed we would miss the boat when it left without us before breakfast.

Sad spirits were soon turned around by the warm and spontaneous generosity of a woman shopkeeper, Sue. After shutting up shop in case of burglars for 2 hours because she came from N.Y.— originally—though she's lived lots of places like Frisco, Alaska & Mexico, etc. In her car she drove us around Papeete, showing us houses, boats, plantations, answering our many questions of the businesses, imports that include oil and coffee, proposals for growing pineapple and Captain Bligh.

In 3500 words may I give your readers a fascinating and unplanned for travel account of four stranded lambs and how we conquered obstacles through circumstances and friendly feelings in "**SEE THE PACIFIC BEFORE YOU DIE.**"?

May I also interest you in other articles in my "Travels Around the World?" Which have spurred me to dream of writing especially as a career if I could be a travel writer which I do as good as some.

The professional travel writer plans and polishes the sales tool until he is proud to send it forth. Sometimes it's a good idea to begin the query with the hook you've devised for the finished piece. Designed to attract readers, it's also likely to attract an editor. Wouldn't the editor who received a letter like this want to read further?

> When the tour bus stopped near the Acropolis the tour leader pointed across the road. "Climb up and take a look," he commanded, mopping his brow. "But be back in ten minutes. We're leaving for Delphi." A middle-aged woman in sagging seersucker turned to her companion. "I've always dreamed of seeing the Acropolis," she said. "But how can I climb that hill in this heat and make it back before the bus leaves—even if I don't stop to look around?"
> Another lifelong dream punctured because of selecting the wrong sight-seeing plan.

Sometimes it seems more appropriate to encapsulate your idea in the first paragraph of your query, briefly summarizing what your proposed article is all about. This opening paragraph in a successful query was used by one California writer to woo the editor, although these exact words never appeared in the finished piece:

> Malta, one of the world's newest independent nations, encompasses one of the world's oldest civilizations. A dazzling gem to fifty centuries of would-be conquerors, this Mediterranean paradise today offers excellent climate, unspoiled beaches, and interesting landmarks.

Another type of query can begin with a startling statement:

> One out of every ten Americans will die in a transportation accident.
> An article I have in mind would help your readers protect themselves and their families against transportation accidents on their vacations.

There are many ways to launch your query, but be sure you begin with a grabber that induces the editor to read on. As you concentrate on keeping the "you" big and the "I" small, remember the editor isn't interested in what he can do for you—only in what you can do for him. Your success may depend on how well you can identify with his outlook.

Whichever way you begin, somewhere in your query, in one concise sentence, indicate the thrust of your message. Indicate also what your viewpoint will be. Are you writing a first-person experience, a second-person how-to, a concealed viewpoint destination piece? Are you the "devil's advocate" in a travel expos2e or a researcher/reporter gathering facts that a staff writer will use in his roundup article?

Give hints about how you will develop your story. If your message is, "South Carolina is the cheapest vacation spot in the United States today," show the editor how much it costs for a superior hotel room and a good dinner, and how much you tip the cab driver. If you say it's good, as well as cheap, show why.

Use examples that bolster the importance of your story and convince the editor that you are the only one to write it. Have you published in this periodical previously? In a sibling publication? In one or several big-name publications? Say so. Whether or not to include tear sheets with the query is an individual decision—you're balancing between showing off your best and burdening the editor with additional reading. The decision often depends on how appropriate the tear sheet is to your present query in terms of subject matter, style, and market.

What in your educational, vocational, or avocational background fits you to write this particular story? It may sound immodest to say:

> Several recent trips to Turkey and extensive library research make me well qualified to write this article for you. I have a master's degree in communication from Stanford, and my historically oriented travel articles have appeared in *House Beautiful*, *Modern Maturity*, *Bride's Magazine*, *Mankind*, the *Christian Science Monitor*, and many other publications of national circulation.

But this is no time to be modest. The editor is probably also interested in knowing if you are just leaving for the site of your story or just returning from there. Have you been there often? A long time ago, as well as recently? Do you have relatives there? Friends? Special connections?

If you have access to unusual research sources or unique skills as a researcher, mention them. Princess Grace invited you to the palace to see her favorite flower arrangements? Cairo University's dean of archaeology guided you through the Valley of the Nobles? You have an extensive bibliography of original sources? Don't keep these facts a secret.

While you're trying to think of everything you can in your favor, it's not necessary—or desirable—to include a five-page résumé. And don't include anything unrelated to the subject of the query. The editor is interested in you as a writer for this particular story. He's not interested in the fact that you are a widow with grandchildren or a divorced man with a girl friend. He is not interested in honors and achievements unrelated to the present business. Sending a list of your military decorations, details of your golf handicap, or recommendations from your mother-in-law will sway his decision in only one direction—a negative one.

The editor is also uninterested in your previous literary achievements if all they add up to is the assistant editorship of your high school yearbook or a sonnet published in a literary magazine long ago. On the other hand, it's foolish to confess in your query letter, "I have never written anything before." If you have nothing significant to say, say nothing.

Your relationship by marriage to the publisher's second cousin probably doesn't matter either, although I must admit that my own first job on a magazine, as a first reader, materialized because the publisher owed money to one of my relatives. (I highly recommend this type of summer vacation job if you are nineteen and as ignorant as I was.) The editor usually is not interested in your financial situation. Telling him how badly you need the money for the article is more likely to elicit antipathy than sympathy; and describing in your query the *reasons* you need the money is like talking yourself out of the assignment.

Attempting to ooze affluence, on the other hand, or embracing a "what's the difference?" attitude about finances, does nothing to gain editorial favor either. Never offer to work at a cut-rate price because you're "so anxious to break into print, I'll do anything—even give it to you for nothing." This not only indicates a low opinion of your own value, it exposes your amateur standing. The time to discuss money is *after* the editor says he wants your story. That's also the time to discuss editorial changes. Do not, as so many amateurs do, tell the editor in the query, "Feel free to change anything you want to." He already feels free.

Be truthful and don't exaggerate, but don't be falsely humble. If you start your query with something like:

> You probably won't be interested in my idea, but I just thought I'd ask you anyway, because now that I'm retired from my job as a bookkeeper I have lots of free time, and I used to think when I was a little boy I'd like to be a writer when I grew up. I just took a trip to Catalina Island, but lots of people have been to Catalina Island, so you probably won't want my story. My sixth-grade teacher used to say I was very clever at telling little stories, but you probably won't think my writing's good enough. . . .

The editor wonders why you bothered.

If you're not a regular reader of the target publication, don't say so. It's amazing how many would-be writers begin a query with "I never read your magazine, but. . . ." If, on the other hand, you've subscribed for thirty years, it's less important than a concrete demonstration of your familiarity with the magazine's contents.

If your selected market or a competitor has recently published something even slightly related to what you have in mind, it's wise to defend your originality and show how your approach, your idea, your information would be different—and therefore desirable. This letter addressed to the editor of *Better Homes and Gardens* begins with mention of similar material:

Although you published a houseboat piece last year, I would like to suggest a more practical, definitive article on rental houseboating vacations. My article would be addressed to the hesitant—to those who would like a houseboat holiday, but are afraid they can't afford it or that they don't have the necessary skills to run the boat.

While your previous article was helpful to the houseboater searching for destinations and activities, I had in mind something with more emphasis on life aboard the boat. Those who don't know much about outdoor recreation in general often wonder if they'll find comfort and enjoyment with a rented houseboat, and I would be prepared to answer their unasked questions with specific information.

A query addressed to the editor of TWA's in-flight magazine, *Ambassador*, begins:

Although you naturally encourage your readers to travel to Cairo by *air*, once they get to Egypt they can have a wonderful time cruising the Nile.

If your material is controversial, tell how you will show the other side, also. If you foresee objections to your idea, try to answer the objections before they arise. Be wary of sweeping generalizations and unverified facts—the editor may know more about your story than you do. Although it's all right to say, "I have never seen another article on this subject," do not say didactically, "Nothing has ever been published on this subject," or "Not much has been published about this subject recently."

If you have a catchy title for your article it helps the query (see Chapter 13 for discussion of titles). If your actual title, which you refer to in the body of the query, is "Go Where the Goodies Are," you might create a favorable impression by typing a banner across the top of your page: Proposed article on "How to Get the Best Possible Vacation Free." The words *new* and *free* are always attention getters. So is the word *you*. Remember, however, that the editor to whom you are sending the query is not the "you" to whom your article will be addressed. If you start your letter to the editor with "Are you hesitant about renting a houseboat or afraid you can't afford to?" you will give the wrong impression entirely. Editors say they are often offended by this type of query beginning.

Although a good writer should be able to shorten or lengthen any story according to directions, if your information is so limited or so extensive that the length of your manuscript is necessarily predetermined, suggest your projected length.

If you expect the publication to pay part of the expenses involved in obtaining your story, you'd better mention that in the query, too. If you're a newcomer to travel writing, the chances for expense money are slim. If you're an oldtimer, they're not much better. Sometimes, however, you can persuade an editor that although he cannot afford to send his personal representative halfway around the world on a story, he's getting a great bargain in providing you with a modest expense account. Explain that you'll also be using a combination of other expense accounts, travel perks, and your own vacation funds. Be sure all arrangements are spelled out on paper before you leave home.

If you have illustrations or you secure illustrations, say so. And help the editor to visualize them. Bert Goldrath thinks the key to his hundreds of magazine sales is the camera that is part of his *modus operandi*. "I research the picture possibilities first," he says. "Then in the query I always include details about the photographs I'm prepared to supply."

Some publications like you to include a couple of sample photographs with the query, and they so indicate in their market listings. Jim Shaw, *Off Duty*'s Pacific and Western editor, based in Hong Kong where art work is hard to obtain, sends out frequent letters reminding his contributors that "the cupboard is getting bare again." He asks for pictures plus a few sentences describing the story line. If he likes your photographs, he invites you to send your manuscript. Many other editors reply to preliminary suggestions with, "That might make a good story for us. Let me see your pictures and I'll let you know whether or not to go ahead with writing the piece."

Do try to offer the kind of illustrations your target market desires—color transparencies, black-and-white glossies, line drawings (see Chapter 15 for tips on taking salable pictures, advice on securing illustrations from other sources, and information on how to send photographs).

While the objective of your query is to arouse the editor's interest and cause him to ask for your article, don't oversell. Again and again my students have said, "You taught me to write such a good query letter, I keep receiving go-aheads. But I can't write well enough yet to come through with what I've promised in the query. So when I send the finished article, I get it right back."

In your query don't promise more than you can deliver. But *reach* in your query. *Reach* for an anticipation of excellence in your article. And within the article, *reach* for the best writing that's in you—and a little beyond.

Mayon volcano, Luzon, Philippines

Make Your Query Work for You

each for a better market than you think you'll hit. You have your marketing itinerary—compiled according to considerations of pay, prestige, and likelihood—so send your query first to the target market at the top of your list.

Once you've decided on the publication, how do you know which editor to address? The most important rule is to address *somebody*. A query directed to somebody by name and title, even if it's the wrong name or wrong title, has a better chance of landing on the right desk than the letter simply addressed to "Editor."

Your marketing book gives you the first clue as to who gets the query letter. You will find there the names of the editor, articles editor, features editor, travel editor, or someone especially assigned to deal with your type of material. Throughout the year, writers' magazines and yearbooks help you keep your marketing book up to date as they announce editorial changes. Another clue comes from the magazine itself. Which staff member listed on its masthead is the one most likely to be concerned with your idea?

Don't be too timid in your selection of a staff member. When a student sought my opinion of his query letter I asked why he had addressed it to Maribelle Simpson, first reader of *XYZ Magazine*.

"Well," he replied, "you said to address *somebody* on the staff. And I figured I'm such a new writer there was no use bothering the editor, the assistant editor, or even the editorial assistant. So I found out the name of the first reader."

While Ms. Simpson may be flattered by a query addressed to her, usually your query works harder for you if you aim higher.

But if you've had previous correspondence with anyone on the staff,

Shawnee National Forest, Illinois

you'll address your letter to that person. If you've had a recent nice rejection letter (we'll examine "nice" rejection letters in a minute), you may even want to refer to your previous idea in your present query.

This, for instance, went to an editor who had rejected three recent suggestions as sounding too "pedestrian"—an editor who had published many of the writer's articles, including one the previous month:

Dear Tim,

Thank you for your note full of nos. I see what you mean about "pedestrian."

The Travel Dollars piece looked great last month. As a matter of fact, that whole issue looked especially sharp.

Three other ideas I'd like to work out for you soon are:

1. Rental campers, from the angle of how to do it. Having just returned from a week's safari to the seashore, I'm compiling a list of things we should have taken, should have left at home, should have done differently, etc., to make this very pleasant excursion still more pleasant. I have rental information for nearby areas, and I had in mind a composite of where, when, how, and what, rather than a mere personal experience.

2. Travel charms. Did you know that. . . .

How well you know the editor and your previous relationship always determine the tone of your inquiry. A query to a stranger who has complied with the writer's request for sample copies and guidelines might read:

Dear Mr. Adams,

Thank you for your June 18 letter and the sample copies.

Your rural mailbox story made me feel you would be interested in a photo feature on laundry lines around the world. I have always felt nothing so unites the peoples of the world as the necessity for getting out the wash; so in all my travels I collect photographs of people washing, as well as mute testimonials to the fact that they have washed. Sometimes photographing the wash imperils the photographer. At a Spanish inn, for instance, where Cervantes is said to have written *Don Quixote*, when the innkeeper's wife saw me taking a picture of her laundry line she pinned up a soaking wet sheet and positioned it to drench me.

Even to a stranger, let your personality shine through. The editor is, after all, a human being. Be warm and friendly, rather than cold and impersonal. Don't be cutesy, though—that kind of personality is better concealed.

To an editor you know through previous letters you'll be even more informal and friendly. This query followed much cordial correspondence and several sales, although the writer had not yet met the editor, whose assistant had reported him ill:

> Dear Jack Smith,
>
> By now I hope you're up and feeling better. About all you can say to a rough break like that is, "Well, that's *it* for this year!" Soon, I'm sure, you'll be good as new and will settle back into your regular routine.
>
> When you are up to considering material for future issues, I hope you'll look favorably on an article about that marvelous engineering triumph, the Corinth Canal. During the half hour you're traveling through the canal you can almost reach out and touch the ice-smooth sides, while. . . .

This is a query to a longtime friend who has published many of the writer's stories:

> Dear Frank,
>
> Your trip to "The Top of the World" sounds fabulous. When I read your story about Iceland I could hardly restrain myself from calling a travel agent to make reservations. We missed you while you were away.
>
> As your travel pages grow more numerous you seem to be adding departments, and when I saw your "Destination for a Day" label on that Mendocino Skunk Train story last week I wondered if that is the beginning of a new department. Will you be running Destination for a Day pieces regularly? If so, I hope you'll consider an article on Buena Park, where there are activities to please every interest and every age group.
>
> Within five minutes you can ride. . . .

The late Mort Weisinger spoke of his "outrageous good luck" with much briefer queries to friendly editors during the years he was a regular contributor to the then-weekly *Saturday Evening Post*. When a picture on the New York *Times* financial page gave a tiny credit line, "Courtesy Chase National Bank's Collection on Moneys of the World," he sent the clipping with this sentence attached: "This collection contains over 75,000 specimens, representing every known medium of exchange. How about a story on its curator?"

A few months later, on a trip with his children to the Bronx Zoo, Weisinger was prompted by a couple of guidebook photographs showing keepers feeding fresh oxen blood to the vampire bats and ground-up bamboo shoots to the pandas to send the *Post* a one-line query:

"How about a piece on the problems of feeding everything that walks, flies, swims, or crawls at the Bronx Zoo?"

You have to be a very regular contributor to make such a capsule query work for you, and usually it's wiser not to send clippings.

When do you send a query and when do you just go ahead and send the whole piece? In general, you send a query whenever the research is more important than the style. Although the query letter is an excellent tool that can provide a strong plus value for the travel writer, there are times when it cannot be used.

Some publications prefer to see finished manuscripts, and if you try to send them a query letter they may send it back unread. At *Trip and Tour*, for instance, the editor says firmly:

> We receive manuscripts on speculation only, so there is no need to query first.

The *Retired Officer Magazine* indicates "submit complete ms." in its *Writer's Market* listing, and in case you forget, the editor will reply to a query with something like this:

> Unfortunately, we do not have the staff to answer all queries—we get thousands. Next time, submit the article itself. It's impossible for us to get a good idea from queries anyway.

There are times, too, when the material is so dependent upon the author's style, rather than upon the subject matter, that a query would be pointless. This is especially true of humorous, nostalgic, and personal-experience stories. Sometimes, too, the story is very short, especially if it's intended for a newspaper travel section or as a magazine back-of-the-book piece. If the finished story is shorter than the query, or only a little longer, send the story.

Also, if the time element is so limited that a query would jeopardize the sale, go ahead and send the story itself. I happened to be in London, for instance, one January when national strikes and fuel shortages were causing travelers to avoid London. I was surprised to find the situation less uncomfortable than anticipated. Although theater coat-check girls looked forlorn when muffled members of the audience refused to surrender outdoor gear, the hotels and restaurants were warm enough. Lights, food, and transportation were available, if sparse; and Londoners made cheerful jokes about fewer calories and more walking helping them slim down. It was a good thing I sent my "It's really not so bad" story off quickly, because within a few weeks the strikes ended, the fuel situation stabilized, and the weather turned warmer.

As a general rule, send a query first whenever the subject matter's significance eclipses the style, unless the editor says he doesn't want one or the length or timeliness of the story indicates otherwise.

When do you send the query? You send it as soon as you've done enough research to make an attractive sales presentation. "Enough" is hard to pinpoint. It might take one writer on one subject a couple of hours to research enough material for the query, while another writer, working on another subject, might spend six months gathering enough solid facts to put together a salable story idea.

An anticipated opportunity to sail through the soon-to-be-reopened Suez Canal sent one California writer to the history books for a pretrip query that began:

> We will be on one of the first ships to sail through the Suez Canal when it reopens later this month, and I'm planning to compare and contrast the 1975 reopening with the 1869 opening extravaganza. Then, as you know, fifty vessels bearing many of Europe's crowned heads sailed from Port Said to Suez, accompanied by blaring bands and fireworks. The celebration was climaxed by a $7‡ million banquet and a special performance of *Rigoletto* at Cairo's new opera house. (Guiseppe Verdi had been commissioned to write *Aida* for the occasion, but scenery and costumes were held up in Paris by the Franco-Prussian War.) This time *Aida* will be performed, all right, but it will have to be outdoors, since Cairo's Opera House burned down a few years ago. Doubtless the spectators' heads—both crowned and uncrowned—will be different, but I understand that fireworks and brass bands will proliferate once again.

A restaurant reviewer, on the other hand, says, "What research do I need before I send a query? Either the editor is interested in *poulet en croûte* at Lutéce, or he isn't. And whether the *poulet en croûte* is outstanding or merely adequate—that I can't know till I get there."

But a career army officer, who's sent three children through graduate school on editors' checks, says, "I've traveled so much—I have an instinct about where to look for the salable story. As soon as I smell it, I start researching. It takes me about half a day to get together enough for the query."

His wife interrupted to observe that he always seems to "smell" the story—and start researching it—the week they move to a new post, when there's the most to be done in the way of unpacking and getting organized.

In any case, you want to be sure to always do enough research so the editor knows you know what you're talking about. You have to have enough facts to instill a feeling of confidence, because every editor is haunted by the fear that he will accept a story by an inexperienced writer that later proves to be untrue or inaccurate.

It isn't only the inexperienced writer he worries about. Some publications now insist on written verification of facts and sources from everybody. One editor explains, "We've seen too many freelance stories reporting on interviews that never actually took place."

For another publication, an imaginative travel writer even described an island that never existed. The editor especially liked his story of a small Caribbean island that supposedly never appeared on charts because it had been a secret US Navy installation during World War II, and the Pentagon deleted it from all maps. The author described the island—discovered by him—as an Eden with a "happy native population virtually untouched by civilization."

Letters and phone calls from readers begged for directions to the island paradise. Only one protesting voice spoiled the climate of bliss. "It was Ernest Hemingway's brother," says the editor. "And he knew the Caribbean like the back of his hand. According to him, no such island existed or ever did exist."

When questioned about his sources, the writer, unabashed, replied, "I've always wanted to do a story about a mysterious, undiscovered island. But since there weren't any that I knew of, I just made the whole thing up."

Can you blame editors for being wary?

So in your query, allay the editor's fears with what is clearly well-researched information. If there's material you expect to use but haven't yet verified, call it unverified, so the editor knows you know the difference. A query like one of these works for you by building a feeling of confidence:

> All over the world parents, relatives, and friends spend millions of dollars (exact amount to be determined—maybe it's billions!) to. . . .

or

> Mr. Alex Chambers, Director of the Western Division of World Wide Travel, says tourism will increase by 27 percent this year, with 50 percent of that increase representing families who have never before traveled farther than fifty miles from home. (Mr. Chambers has promised me an interview next week, and he has indicated he will say something like this, since these are the approximate statistics, but I will quote him precisely in the article itself.)

Never take shortcuts with your research. But don't fall into the trap of endlessly researching something that may never sell. Many writers do this. The research itself becomes so attractive they postpone writing even the query until they spend "just another couple of days" and then "just a few more days" researching, and they somehow never get around to writing.

"That's my trouble," says an archaeologist-writer. "Although I've managed to sell two popular articles on Pompeii, I have a dozen more archaeologically oriented travel stories written in my head. But before I send the query I always check and recheck—and then check again—every single word. Did the original source find exactly the same thing I did? Perhaps I should look for just one more original source? Eventually the whole thing seems sort of stale. I begin to wonder whether any-body else would be interested, so I don't bother the editor by inquir-ing."

This writer is losing one of the great advantages of the query. A que-ry works best if you do only enough research to write the letter. Then if no one thinks your idea is as good as you do, you haven't wasted much time on something nobody's going to buy.

You will, of course, send some queries before you start on your trip. Others you may send while you're traveling. ("I often take *Writer's Market* along when I travel," reports Mary Jane Beck. "When I stumble over a story unexpectedly, I want to be sure to interest an editor imme-diately.") Still other queries you'll send upon your return home, and some you'll send long after your return.

The travel writer learns to think far ahead. Some writers use special calendars to remind them to plan the "Old-fashioned New England Christmas" story in March, to get ready for "Easter Week in Spain" the beginning of June, and to start querying in December on "Give the Kids a Treat at Disneyland Before They Go Back to School." If your target market says it needs material six months in advance, add to that how long it wil take you to write the finished piece, plus a couple of weeks for response to your query, and a couple of weeks in the mails. Then add a couple of weeks for unexpected delays. Do you have enough time? If it's already August and you don't have the story written, there's no point in sending a query about New England *this* Christmas. Begin, instead, to plan for next year.

If you have a travel story that's really *hot* news—something like a confirmed seat on the first space shuttle to the moon—you may want to telephone the editor for an early okay. Since telephone calls are sel-dom popular in editorial offices, try to find out when deadline times are, so you won't be calling at the worst possible moment, and always ask, "Is this a convenient time for you to talk to me?"

If the editor answers "yes" to your proposal, firm it up with a sup-porting letter, to protect yourself. Make it a pleasant, friendly letter, thanking him for the consideration and outlining your understanding of the arrangements.

Sometimes even a negative telephone call has value. As Mildred Martin, who often telephones proposals, points out, "If the editor tells you 'no,' he'll probably tell you *why*—which is important information for you to have."

If you are at the stage where you're making appointments with edi-tors, make those appointments productive. Plan ahead. Prepare to dis-cuss your specific ideas with the same care you'd put into a query let-ter. If you don't have enough facts yet to show the editor what you mean, do more research before you meet him. A social occasion, where you vaguely inquire, "Is there anything I can do for you," may be per-sonally pleasant, but professionally it's a waste of his time and yours.

Field & Stream editor Jack Samson says an oral query shouldn't be "so aggressive as to be obnoxious, but don't hesitate to ask." He reminds travel outdoor writers that once the editor has given the affirmative nod to an oral query, you're obligated to show the finished article to him first. He tells about a writer who discussed with him at great length a story about some lakes near his home. "The idea sounded good," he explains, "and I told him to send the article to me when it was done. I finally saw the story but it was in another magazine."

Don't play games with the editor. If he seems interested in your proposal, let him appear interested in the finished product before offering it to somebody else. Otherwise, don't expect him to even appear interested in your next proposal.

Face to face, you'll probably discuss a number of different ideas with your editor. But most inquiries will still be by letter. How many ideas should you propose in a single query letter? Many professional writers oppose presenting more than one idea at a time. "You only compete against yourself," they warn. "Send one idea, and if the editor likes it, then send another. If he doesn't like it, still send another. But send them separately, one idea at a time."

I disagree. If you have—as most of us do—more ideas than you'll ever use up in a lifetime, what difference does it make if you compete against yourself? I see no problem in proposing three ideas, and next time proposing three different ones. I often receive encouragement on the second or third idea, rather than the first one. Although I have occasionally proposed four or five stories in a single query, I usually find two or three make a more manageable letter.

I have several opening gambits for tying the ideas together:

Several articles I feel would interest your readers include: . . .

Two articles I have in mind for your readers are at opposite ends of the world. . . .

Three diverse articles I'd like to write for you emphasize unusual facets of the travel experience. . . .

Now that some of your readers will be traveling to more remote parts of the world, I have in mind a couple of travel pieces on areas far from the tourist circuit. . . .

Two very economical—but exciting—areas I'm sure would interest your readers are. . . .

I compose two hopefully irresistible paragraphs about each idea and link them with transitional phrases like, "Another article that would interest your readers," and "Still another idea for your publication." I add a paragraph about photographs, a paragraph encapsulating my qualifications if this is a new market for me, and end by promising prompt action in response to editorial encouragement. I try never to suggest that the editor has a choice of *either* this idea *or* that one, but to indicate I hope he likes *all* my proposals. Sometimes an editor will ask to see two or three of the articles I've suggested, and will occasionally buy more than one at a time.

I've even sold the *postscript* to a query letter. The first one accompanied a suggested article on Bangkok for *Coronet*, then a general magazine. After I finished extolling the beauties of Bangkok's rainbow world of rivers and klongs I discovered I hadn't spaced the letter very well on the page. There was too much white space beneath the signature. Should I retype the whole thing? No. I'd add a postscript. What could I propose in a postscript? I thought of the *Wasa*, that seventeenth-century Swedish battleship that sank before she'd sailed a mile, and was brought up in mint condition after three centuries of immersion at the bottom of Stockholm harbor. I really wasn't ready to write about the *Wasa* yet, but I hastily researched enough to add a postscript that said:

> Another article I'd like to write for you is about a ship that never went to sea—the *Wasa*. A seventeenth-century battleship intended for service in the Thirty Years' War, it sank in Stockholm harbor on its maiden voyage. Only recently recovered from the harbor, it was found with food still spread in the galley, carpenters' tools safe in their box, and coins jingling in the skeleton sailors' pockets. A museum has literally been built around the ship, and the *Wasa* story is one of the most fascinating in sea lore.

Coronet's editor replied, "We already have in inventory an article about Bangkok, but the *Wasa* sounds interesting. Could you send us 2,500 words?" I could and did. And they published it.

A postscript also triggered my first sale to *Off Duty*. After signing the query containing three of my current ideas, I remembered a story on taking our four teenagers to Russia that I'd sold to another magazine. Although I'd been paid, I was disappointed at not seeing the story in print. Recent inquiry had revealed a new editor's making a clean sweep, willing to return my rights. Would that story interest *Off Duty*? I inquired in the postscript. The editor's response included his reasons for rejecting my first three proposals. Then he said:

> I like your fourth idea, the reaction of your four teenagers to a trip to Russia. . . . This will not be an easy article to do. . . . If the reactions are of interest in themselves—not because "it's just what we in the family expected Janet or Frank to do"—the article will be of interest. Also, bear in mind that Russia . . . is no longer considered a daring or off-the-beaten-path vacation place.

He didn't know, of course, that the article was already written.

When I sent it, he wrote, "Just what I needed! What else do you have for me?"

Pretrip query letters often present several ideas. Then you can concentrate on the facets of your trip experience that interest your prospective editors.

Louise Boggess, whose travel writing is largely concerned with antiques, usually sends out a checklist of ideas before she starts on her trip. After her initial research, she composes three or four one-sentence ideas and sends the list to an editor on a page with extra-wide margins. On another page she outlines her travel itinerary, noting nearby antiques subjects. The editor usually comments in the margin, suggesting an approach to one or more of her ideas, or presents ideas of his own. As each editor makes selections, she substitutes other proposals before sending the checklist to the next publication on her preliminary marketing list. She continues doing this until she is ready to leave—with a dozen firm assignments in her attaché case.

Other writers save the checklist approach until they return from their travels. Then they compose a couple of fascinating paragraphs about each facet of the trip and arrange them on pages in such a way that, with the help of white correction fluid and good photocopy, they can endlessly add to, subtract from, or rearrange.

Still others feel idea sheets of that type work best for previously sold stories on which they own residual rights (see Chapter 10 for discussion of mileage). A friendly personal letter accompanies the list, which they offer to markets that accept previously published material.

Sometimes an editor will prefer one idea at a time, and will tell you so, either in his market listing, or in mailed guidelines, or in a personal letter responding to your multisubject query. Of course you will accede to his wishes. Usually, though, try to make your two-way postage on the query cover more than one idea.

With technical improvements in word processing and computerization, the writer is offered various shortcuts to sending query letters. Donna Dowdney plans her query letters to go out in batches—duplicating the paragraphs about her qualifications, her photographs, her recent trip, and changing only the addressee and the paragraph about her specific idea. She then uses word processing equipment and turns out many query letters in a single afternoon. With the help of technology, the writer's sales job becomes easier.

There are several types of commercially produced quick-query forms, where you merely indicate with a check mark whether your proposal is fiction or nonfiction, whether or not photographs are available, and how soon you can have it completed. The form gives the editor a chance to check anything from "Not interested" to "Send complete outline" to "Yes, let's have a look." I think these forms much too cold and impersonal to nurture the kind of editor-writer relationships that lead to repeated sales and assignments. Even the few seconds to make a check mark is a waste of editorial time, since these quick forms tell absolutely nothing about the questioner's writing ability or his integrity, and very little about his idea or how he would handle it.

Different writers use different formulas for presenting their queries. Anne Holmes makes hers look like a press release. "It has to begin with a grabber that's every bit as enticing as direct mail advertising," she says. "I want to lure the editor into reading on. So I type a banner headline across the top of the page and begin my letter with an aggressive '5 Ws' lead. This type of query seems to work best for me."

Other writers use other favorite forms. Hayes Jacobs believes in the outline query, beginning with the double-spaced lead of your article, then single-spacing the essential elements of the entire article in informal memo style.

Some editors say they prefer an outline, so that is what you give them. But it doesn't have to be the topic sentenced, Roman numeraled, lettered subhead type.

The outline could follow a chronological pattern, recounting events in historical order, or a geographical pattern, taking the reader on an orderly journey, or it could follow some other logical sequence, according to the material covered. For a sightseeing story on San Francisco (this was not a definitive destination piece, so I included no restaurants, shops, or entertainment) I tried to select the most important things to see according to the time available, keeping in mind the interests of the particular reader for whom this article was intended:

> When you have only one day in San Francisco, climb to the top of Telegraph Hill, see Golden Gate Park and its museums, Japanese Tea Garden, etc., include Fisherman's Wharf and Chinatown, . . .
>
> If you have two days, go out to the Cliff House, see the Japanese Cultural Center, the Opera House, the Cannery, . . .
>
> Four days is twice as good as two. Take a trip across the Golden Gate Bridge to Sausalito, Muir Woods, etc., visit the Palace of the Legion of Honor, the Museum of Modern Art, . . .
>
> With six days, ride BART or take a trip across the Bay Bridge to the University of California at Berkeley, the Oakland Museum, Lake Merritt; travel down the Peninsula, see Stanford University, Marine World, Great America, . . .
>
> If you're staying eight days, include Alcatraz, Aquatic Park, ethnic museums, . . .

I could as easily have chosen a historical or geographical pattern for this outline, but this one, based on the length of time the visitor might have available, seemed best for its purpose.

As you can see, there are many ways to make an outline. On subjects where you have access to unlimited information, offering a huge variety of approaches, the need to unscramble and classify this material for a query-outline makes it ultimately easier to write the travel article. It also makes it possible to write a stronger, more interesting, better organized and more accurate travel article.

I have from time to time sold the *outline*. Sometimes an editor will be about to take off for the destination I've suggested, planning to write his own story. He thinks my outline will save him time in getting all the elements together, and he's glad to pay me for it. Although I couldn't then send that identical outline to another editor, I'd be free to use the information in it.

Regardless of the form you use, put your best foot forward in the query. Neatness and care will never sell a poor idea; but smudges and typos will eclipse a good one. To make your query work for you, make sure its mechanics meet the highest standards of excellence—including the correct spelling of the editor's name. Remember, you have only one thirty-second chance to make a good first impression. The editor suspects your manuscript will be no better than your query.

Is a letterhead important? I think it is. It makes you look—and feel—*professional*. In the beginning you probably won't invest in four or five different sizes of stationery for different lengths of letters, so order either monarch size (7¼x10½ inch) or business size (8½x11), with matching envelopes. I have always felt black ink on white bond paper and a black typewriter ribbon were the only way to go. And I'm still convinced that red script on neon yellow or kelly green footprints on sheer sheets of hot pink will attract unfavorable attention. But when Ned Shapker showed me his letterhead—black ink on off-white paper—I liked the back of it as much as the front. He had arranged an attractive montage of the beginnings of sixteen of his published travel articles, some with photos, all with byline prominently displayed, then had it reduced to 8½x11 size for the *back* of his letterhead. It's eyecatching and interesting, without being intrusive.

Turning Rejections into Acceptances

Once you have gotten your query together, agonized over each word, typed it neatly, enclosed the SASE, and taken it to the mailbox, what kind of reply is it likely to elicit?

Unfortunately, the most common type in the beginning may be a small printed slip with a message something like this:

> Thank you for your proposal, which has received careful consideration. We regret that this material does not meet our needs at the present time, but we appreciate your interest.

Although these come in different colors, *Catholic Digest* says in *its* form rejection:

> Most rejection slips are blue, which is the way one usually feels. . . . This one, however, is green which is the symbol of hope and encouragement.

There's not much encouragement, however, in another basic rejection slip, the printed form whose only personal touch is the X marked beside one of these possibilities:

(   ) Subject matter not in line with our present needs
(   ) Similar material on hand

(   ) Idea too vague or too general for readership
(   ) Similar material recently published
(   ) Overstocked at present

Still worse is your own letter returned with something like "No thanks" scrawled across it.

Disheartening as these rejections are, overcome the temptation to throw them in the trash or burn them in the fireplace immediately. Save them. If later you take off some writers' expenses on your income tax (see Chapter 16 for discussion of tax deductions), rejection letters are good evidence for IRS that you're at least trying to be a writer. Eventually you'll have enough rejection letters to paper a wall. But as one writer says, "By the time I had enough rejection letters to paper the living room, I was also getting enough assignments so I could afford real wallpaper."

Learn to read between the lines of a rejection letter. The printed slip or checked form with somebody's indecipherable initials scrawled at the bottom or "sorry" scribbled across the top are a step above the lowest form of rejection. Across the miles you can picture the editor regretting, just a trifle wistfully, that he must turn down your masterpiece of an idea in so casual a manner. If "Try us again" is inked in the margin, that's definite encouragement.

A photocopied form letter may have the same message as the small printed slip. If your name is typed in and the title or capsule sentence of your idea is mentioned, it's a good sign. If there's a signature, a date, or any written message, you're moving up. The next step is also a form letter, but it's individually typed, addressed to you personally, with the name of your idea in the body of the letter and a signature at the bottom. A scribbled postscript explaining the rejection, such as, "We've already planned a Niagara Falls feature for next month," shows a definite glimmer of interest in you as a potential contributor.

A still better rejection letter is the one written especially to you by a specific editor detailing the reasons your idea(s) won't work for him right now.

Often you can turn a "nice" rejection letter into an acceptance by simply reading between the lines. Does the editor say your idea is too complex and would make too long an article for him to use? Amputate and requery. Does he say he has too much material on hand now, but "try again in six months"? Mark it on your calendar. Does he like the subject area but not your approach? Suggest a different one. Does he name another publication that he thinks would provide a better home for your idea? Try it. Does he say "no" because he feels your idea wouldn't suit his readers, while you know it would be perfect for them? Convince him.

Several years ago, when Hal Schell queried *Today's Health* on a European article, the editor didn't think most of his readers were affluent enough for European travel. Schell thought, "Well, I'm not very afflu-ent, and I've traveled in Europe." He rose to the challenge with a more convincing query: "How to see Europe without bending the budget." His article, "It's In to Camp Out in Europe," appeared as a beautiful center spread with four-color photographs.

Sometimes the editor explains why he doesn't like your proposal, but encourages you to try him with something else. Use care in select-ing another subject—either a similar one or one quite different, de-pending on what the letter said—and submit another query to that edi-tor immediately.

Keep good records of where and when you've queried on what, and don't accept a "no" as final. Often a new publication, a new editor at the same publication, or the same editor in a new mood, months or even years later will transform a no into a yes.

Not all answers to query letters are "yes" or "no." A great many of them are "maybe." That's what a go-ahead is—a "maybe." That's what the editor is saying when he indicates, "We'd like to see it on specula-tion." This is not an assignment. It makes no guarantee. All it promises is a careful reading. When you do send your manuscript, addressed to the editor who gave you the go-ahead, it won't land at the bottom of the slush pile of unsolicited manuscripts, but will be carefully read by someone who at least liked the idea in the first place.

Professionals are divided as to whether or not to send a photocopy of the go-ahead along with the completed article. Is it a handy reminder, or is it an insult to the editor to remind him? If you don't send the pho-tocopy, you should at least mention the go-ahead in your letter accom-panying the article.

> Here, in response to your May 14 go-ahead, is the article on Mount Rushmore you asked to see. I hope you'll like "Four Faces for the Future" for your readers, and I look forward to hearing from you.

A go-ahead does give you the advantage of being able to say to an information source, "XYZ Magazine is interested in having me write an article on Mount Rushmore. Can you help me with my research?"

How long dare you wait to send your manuscript after the editor's expression of interest? That depends. It depends on the timeliness, both seasonal and topical, of the material. It depends, if you've queried before your trip, on how long you'll be away. It depends on the diffi-culty of the research. And it depends on the enthusiasm of the editor, which may or may not be related to a particular hole he has to fill, a special edition he plans, or the possibility of securing an accompany-ing advertisement.

What if the article is already written, having been rejected by some-body else? Should you send it as soon as you receive the go-ahead, thereby alerting the editor to his second-choice status? Or should you wait four or five weeks and pretend you're writing it just for him? A variety of circumstances will dictate your decision in this situation. Is the subject matter so timely it will soon be obsolete? Are there enough other possible markets for you to adopt a casual attitude toward rejection? Is the research so complex and time-consuming that this sale is all-important? There's no single "right" answer.

Always, though, reply to a go-ahead with a thank-you for the invitation to send your article. Indicate how long it will take you to complete the manuscript. In your estimate allow for all possible detours and distractions, and if in doubt, say, "I'll send it soon." Consider six months an outside limit, and aim for four to eight weeks.

If the writing takes longer than you anticipate, send progress reports, so the editor doesn't lose interest or assign the idea to somebody else. Dr. William Rivers, professor of communications at Stanford University, feels the writer puts himself at a disadvantage by sending only the query and then the manuscript. "There is reason to believe," he says, "that a freelancer should undertake much more correspondence." He goes on to tell of writers who have greatly improved their percentage of sales after sending subsequent letters indicating progress of their research and asking for the editor's reaction to the shape the article was beginning to take, which was sometimes quite different from the shape originally suggested. Dr. Rivers says:

> The value of this process should be apparent. Correspondence helped the writer involve the editor. . . . After two or three letters, the editor had a stake in the writer's success. Sometimes the idea became more the editor's than the writer's; [it] . . . evolved into an even better idea—at least from the editor's point of view.

How likely is the beginner to receive any kind of positive response to his query? The statistics on receiving a go-ahead are one in ten when you're just starting out. And then you may consider the article half-sold. That doesn't mean some other editor won't encourage your idea or buy your piece eventually—the statistics only mean it may take twenty queries to sell an article.

More than twenty queries and no bites? Perhaps it wasn't such a good idea after all. Or perhaps your query isn't enticing enough, or your marketing itinerary was not astutely selected. Five go-aheads in a row—followed by prompt rejections? Either you haven't lived up to what you promised in the query or the five editors who gave you go-aheads have all died, retired, resigned, or been fired.

But don't be discouraged. As you learn to write better query letters, as you study markets and read between the lines of your rejections so that you're matching ideas and target markets more accurately, the statistics improve. An experienced freelancer expects a go-ahead or an assignment to result from one query letter in three. And then the statistics zoom. Instead of selling five out of every ten articles the first time out, you'll be selling nine out of ten or better.

Add the skills of a salesman to your skills as a writer for an unbeatable combination. You'll sell your travel stories as fast as you write them when you learn to make your query letters work for you.

Hurricane Ridge, Olympic National Park, Washington

13

Writing for Others to Read

riting, it is said, cannot be taught—it can only be learned. "But what about talent?" is a question potential travel writers frequently ask. "How can I tell if I have what it takes?" If you like to write and you like to travel, you can learn to write well enough to succeed. If you are writing for others rather than merely to please yourself, you'll have to follow the principles of effective travel writing, so let's pinpoint some of the fundamentals.

One basic precept we encounter again and again—and travel writers need to be reminded of it again and again—is that there's no such thing as "writing generally." Writing has to be *for* somebody—a particular publication, a particular reader. Remember, that reader is always asking "Why are you telling me this now?" Can you answer your reader's question?

Study your target markets carefully, as we've said before. Then slant accordingly. "Slant" is not a dirty word. Slant is a means of insuring that your material is read by those for whom it is intended. If you're writing for the *New York Times*, slant it for *Times* readers. The well-written travel article is filled with general information and enough slanted specifics to appeal to a particular reader.

In "Favorite Fly-Outs: To Penn's Cave and the Luray Caverns," Jack Elliott tells *Aero* readers about interesting journeys they can take in their small private planes. In addition to describing the great natural wonders of the sites and the pleasures of spelunking, he inserts such flier-oriented specifics as:

Caves are wonderful places for one-day flying trips. Luray Cav-

Keystone State Park, Oklahoma

erns Airport has a beautiful, 3500-foot paved strip with runway lights and VASI on both ends. The field is about a mile away from the Caverns and there is a courtesy car. . . .

Intrinsic to the travel article is the *message*. You must be able to express the idea behind your article—your message—in a single pithy capsule sentence. The capsule sentence should appear early on, and it should remain in your mind (and your reader's mind) from the first word to the final period.

What is your message? What are you trying to say?

The Kona Coast is a beautiful place to vacation.

Take your children to the Circus World Museum in Baraboo, Wisconsin—you'll enjoy it, too.

New York in summer is very different from New York in winter.

At Club Med the young at heart welcome new adventures.

Once you've settled on a clear-cut capsule sentence, tack it above your typewriter or write it on each page of first-draft paper, as an ongoing reminder. Then everything in your article will relate to or confirm or amplify the message you've selected. Don't make that message too broad and general: "Wisconsin"; "New York." And don't make it too narrow: "My little boy liked the unloading of the circus wagons at the Circus World Museum in Baraboo, Wisconsin," or "Take the Staten Island Ferry on July 14 at two p.m." Once you've decided what you want to convey in the completed article, it's easy to fit the pieces of information into the mosaic of the whole.

The length of your article can be controlled by manipulating the capsule sentence. If you need a longer article, broaden its scope: "Hawaii has many beautiful spots," or "Investigate the Club Med." If you need a shorter article, narrow the scope: "The fishing's good at Kona," or "I learned to snorkel at Tahiti's Club Med."

Unless all segments of your story relate to the capsule sentence they form what editors call "a string of pearls"—a series of unrelated incidents. No matter how interesting the individual anecdotes, unless they're skillfully slanted and connected to each other and to the capsule sentence, they will not hold the reader's interest. I've had students write of fascinating experiences in Chile, Portugal, Tahiti, and Ethiopia, with no commonality, no single thread or theme that united them. Until we could agree on a capsule sentence that expressed the student's reason for writing about these particular experiences, and could tie each incident to that sentence, there was no story.

Another fundamental is *viewpoint*: the identity from which you're telling the story. Every piece of writing is told from *some* point of view, so decide in the beginning which you will use. You have several choices. First-person travel articles (I, or we, saw this and did that) of all types are becoming increasingly popular:

My favorite experience in Japan was watching the cormorant fishing and seeing the merrymaking aboard adjacent boats.

Although most personal-experience stories are written in *first person major character*, don't feel this is the only possible viewpoint for travel articles.

First person minor character, while less common, sometimes works out best:

On the boat next to ours they were setting off firecrackers. "Soon the cormorant fishermen will come," said the geisha girl. "I hope they never come!" I heard the man beside her say. "Or at least not for a long time. After the fishing boats have come and gone, then I'll have to go home to my wife." He spoke in English, which surprised me. . . .

Will Stanton frequently presents himself as the minor-character observer when he travels with his children. He tells the story through the major characters, the children, giving their reactions to New York or Disneyland.

Third-person viewpoint, either major or minor character, is used less often in travel articles, since it lacks the warmth and on-the-scene feeling of the more personal "I" or "you."

Third person minor character is like this:

Yoshi watched the geisha girl. She looked like she was getting tired, but she was still smiling. "The fishermen will be here soon," she said. He wondered if she. . . .

Third person major character is like this:

The Japanese worker looks forward to cormorant season, not only for the spectacle itself, but also for the fun aboard the chartered boat.

Sometimes a third-person travel article is unavoidable, as I discovered when I wrote about the travels of my daughter's Girl Scout troop. Since I did not accompany the girls on their trip, I tried to make up for the once-removed viewpoint with quotes from the girls, substantial amounts of dialogue, and liberal use of anecdotes that showed the Brownies and the Girl Scouts during the nine years they prepared for the trip as well as while they were traveling.

Second-person viewpoint is popular in travel articles, usually used in combination with first person or third person:

I enjoyed the train trip.
You'll find the trains comfortable. . . .

Their room overlooked the river.
If you ask for a riverfront room. . . .

When second-person articles are structured like recipes or how-to-do-its, commanding peremptorily, "Take the nine o'clock ferry" or "Buy the tickets in advance," it's still obvious that I, the writer, am telling you, the reader, what to do, even if neither the "I" nor the "you" is mentioned. For example:

> In Japan be sure to take the excursion to see the cormorant fishing.

Another viewpoint without personal pronouns is the *implied*. Although the person telling the story is not identified, the reader is aware of someone providing the information. Through word pictures, active verbs, and strong emotional responses, the writer projects a "you are there" feeling. Implied viewpoint usually requires greater skill and more writing experience, so it often develops a stronger story.

> Acting much like a Big Game busload of convivial old grads, a boatload of Japanese co-workers makes merry while waiting for the cormorants. Men and women, comfortable in kimonos, sing and dance as they cook supper over hibachis, pass the saki bottle, and shoot off sky-brightening fireworks.

The objective viewpoint appears only in such straightforward travel writing as the encyclopedia:

> Cormorants can stay under water a long time when they dive for fish. They swim with their webbed feet.

The *omniscient* viewpoint, where the author enters the minds of all the characters—the Japanese worker, the geisha girl, the fisherman (and possibly the cormorant)—is presently eschewed by most writers, since it produces a weak and wordy article.

Must the entire article remain in one viewpoint? Generally, yes. Since the reader identifies with the viewpoint, switching complicates the story and requires extra wordage to prevent confusion. The transition from first or second person to implied can sometimes be accomplished smoothly, but make sure that every time you switch viewpoints, you gain more than you lose.

Your narrator won't operate in a vacuum. A good travel piece has a beginning, a middle, and an end. Unlike the traditional inverted pyramid of a newspaper story, where the most important facts are told in the first paragraph, with decreasingly important facts spelled out in succeeding paragraphs to allow for hasty cutting from the end, the travel feature story is a unified entity, and can only be shortened through paragraph-by-paragraph or sentence-by-sentence or word-by-word deletions.

A travel article's beginning should be sparkling, exciting, compelling: a *hook* that induces the reader—and the editor—to *read on*. Considering you have only sixty seconds to nab a busy editor or page-flip-ping reader and involve him in your story, the importance of your opening cannot be overemphasized. Some writers say they spend half their writing time on the hook. Yet it's hard to describe what makes a good hook, although many writing teachers have tried.

I group travel article hooks into these three categories:

The **you** approach tells the reader why the information in this article will be especially valuable for him.

The **compare-and-contrast** hook builds tensions, arouses the reader's curiosity, and stimulates him to learn more.

The **scene-setting** hook hints, in an almost fictional manner, about a fascinating story to come.

These "you" examples plunge right in and tell the reader how he will benefit from this article. Notice how many of the benefits concern money, such as:

If you want a vacation spot where your dollars buy full measure of sunshine and sport, culture and cuisine, history and hospitali-ty, head for southern Spain.

If you bemoan the fact that your travel dollars never seem to take you where you want to go, if you return from vacation feel-ing frustrated because you spent more for less fun than anticipat-ed, it's time to analyze exactly what you want your vacation dol-lars to buy.

And notice how many of them are concerned with providing plea-sure or alleviating discomfort, such as:

For vacation activities to please every member of your family, try Buena Park in Southern California. There, you can ride an Old West stagecoach, inspect a $250,000 Rolls-Royce, or pet a lion cub. . . .

If winter rains and post-holiday letdown are sending your thoughts toward a warm-weather vacation, remember it's sum-mer in Lima and Buenos Aires.

In the compare-and-contrast type of hook, sometimes the tension that forces the reader to continue is provided by a surprise element.

Thanks to Prohibition, juvenile delinquency, a crippling acci-dent, drunken brawlers, and Johnnie Holzwarth, Rocky Moun-tain National Park opened its first living-history exhibit in 1974.

This hook compares and contrasts us and them:

Ask a Texan his nationality, and he'll tell you he's American. Ask a citizen of Germany's southernmost state the same question, and chances are he'll answer, "I'm a Bavarian."

Sometimes hooks compare and contrast now and then:

> The fastest transportation available to man in the year 2000 B.C. was the camel caravan, which averaged approximately 3.5 miles an hour. Invention of the horse-drawn chariot raised the maximum speed for short distances to roughly 20 miles per hour. Little over a century ago this was still a record. It took 3500 years to get man's travel speed up to 100 miles an hour. Yet in the past century it has soared from the railroads' 100 miles to the Concorde's designed speed of 1350 miles per hour.

Some hooks compare and contrast here and there:

> How does it feel to suddenly find yourself hospitalized six thousand miles from home in a strange land, worse yet in a Communist country with whom your own America had severed all ties more than a generation ago?

Comparing and contrasting seasons leads to a good hook:

> It's summer. All the skis, toboggans, boots, sweaters, mittens, and snow shovels are gladly packed away. It's time to load up the kids and the dog, the golf clubs, tennis rackets, swimsuits, sunglasses, sunburn ointment, and picnic basket, and head for the nearest ski resort.
> SKI RESORT????
> That's right. Ski resorts are fast becoming the hottest summer vacation spots in New England. . . .

When the travel writer paints an enticing scene, he lures the reader into continuing the story. Conflict provides a big part of the enticement. All three kinds of conflict—man against nature, man against man, and man against himself—can be used to good advantage. Man against nature:

> He stands an instant, poised at the cliff's edge, then springs. His flying body plunges through the air, hurtling down more than 130 feet toward a narrow chasm of churning tidewater. . . .

Man against man:

> Anyone who has traveled abroad without knowing the local language has worried about being able to communicate. I thought I'd learned enough French in high school to get me from Paris to

Marseilles, but a waiterin Lyons taught me differently. He not
only brought me cream of watercress soup instead of créme cara-
mel, he overcharged me ten francs.

Man against himself:

After practicing six months in preparation for the canoe trip, I
didn't believe the doctor when he said I wasn't strong enough to
go. "I intend to go anyway," I told him. "Even if I have another
heart attack, it's worth it.",g43but a waiter in Lyons taught me diff
only brought me cream of watercress soup instead of créme cara-
mel, he overcharged me ten francs.

Man against himself:

After practicing six months in preparation for the canoe trip, I
didn't believe the doctor when he said I wasn't strong enough to
go. "I intend to go anyway," I told him. "Even if I have another
heart attack, it's worth it."

Notice how many of these hooks don't begin at the beginning—just
as Homer didn't start with the day Helen of Troy was born. Like Homer, learn to begin in the middle of the action, then occasionally flash
back to those parts of the beginning the reader needs to know. Whether
it's an adventure tale or a nuts-and-bolts travel article, begin at the
"mattering moment." That's the moment immediately preceding the
action. Although the story may flash back and tell us about his first
heart attack and his canoe trip preparations, the moment he decides to
defy the doctor is, for this story, the mattering moment. We may later
learn about the Acapulco diver's training and practice and even something of the history of diving, but the story begins with the diver poised
at the cliff's edge, about to start the action. Draw the reader into your
story with something exciting, then later give him, as briefly and unobtrusively as possible, the background he needs.

The travel article, like its cousin the short story, is plotted. Although
you should never distort the facts to improve the story, you can, by
careful selection and arrangement, through screening and emphasis,
create a plot.

Theodore Vogel begins at the mattering moment in his *Réalités* story
"Where It's Still Fair Whaling." While the subject matter is controversial, and the actions very graphic, it's a good piece for analyzing the
use of flashbacks and flashforwards:

A harpooned sperm whale had turned and was coming back toward us with monstrous ease. Twenty-five tons of fat and muscle, and a tail four yards wide capable of disintegrating our frail
boat with a single blow. . . .
The gigantic snout rose slightly, then slipped below the boat.

There are about thirty teeth in a sperm whale's mouth. A tooth can weigh ten pounds. No one had expected those teeth to surge from the water and clamp onto the *Claudina*'s rim—but there they were, just a yard away. . . .

Then Vogel flashes back two centuries:

Azorians hunt whales the way it was done two hundred years ago, when American companies recruited oarsmen in the islands and introduced the whaler's ways. . . .

Back to the present:

Today Azorians still hunt whales better than anyone else. . . .

A brief flashback:

Four years ago the *Maria da Conceição . . . harpooned an enormous sperm whale which turned and attacked the boat . . . the whale boat . . . smashed in three places . . . two men . . . dead.*

He then flashes to his own pretrip agreement to "accept all the responsibilities that would result from my death. I signed quickly," he says, "and handed it to the captain. . . ." He explains that lookouts in a whale-hunting village fire flares and radio the tugs when they see a white spout. Then he takes us back to his own whale hunt:

The sperm whales seemed monstrous to me in their surges and dives . . .
   At a yard's distance, Almerindo flung his harpoon, hitting the whale just below the hump of its back. Everything happened so fast that I had trouble registering it.

Vogel discusses the danger and tells of whalers who have been hurt. Then he flashes to the present, where their boat is being towed by the whale. They move in for the kill, hunters and whale fighting, the water growing red. An hour and a half and twelve spears later, the whale is dead.
   Vogel introduces philosophical remarks about the whaling industry, international protection of whales, and the future of whaling. Then back to the present:

It was two p.m. I felt as if years had passed.

A storm comes up and the eight men huddle together in the stern, but they are in good spirits:

And for a moment, I really understood what it was . . . that had sent men out to sea in ships, for centuries, to hunt.

Had Vogel begun with the history of whaling, mentioned his own adventure in the middle, where it comes chronologically, then ended with the outlook for whaling in the future, the story would have lacked the drama, excitement, and emotional impact it imparts. When you write for others you soon learn to seduce your reader by presenting the most spectacular item in the beginning and adapting the chronology to your own plotting purposes.

My *Wasa* article in *Coronet* involved an additional problem, since the here-and-now aspects—the discovery and recovery of the ship—were already some ten to fifteen years in the past, too long ago for a news peg. So I started with an earlier mattering moment, the day the *Wasa* sank:

> As the seventeenth-century battleship *Wasa* raised sail to begin her maiden voyage, holiday crowds lining Stockholm's Royal Quay waved cheerfully and shouted good wishes. Sweden's naval pride moved majestically into mid-channel. . . .

an earlier mattering moment, the day the
Wasa sank:

> As the seventeenth-century battleship *Wasa* raised sail to begin her maiden voyage, holiday crowds lining Stockholm's Royal Quay waved cheerfully and shouted good wishes. Sweden's naval pride moved majestically into mid-channel. . . .
>
> And then the *Wasa*, sails billowing and flags flying, heeled over and vanished without making even the harbor exit.
>
> Three centuries later the ship returned from her eighteen-fathom grave . . . her figurehead still glittering with gilt and her captain's tankard still filled with schnapps.

Then the capsule sentence, appropriate for *Coronet*'s general readership:

> The story of the *Wasa*'s downfall, her subsequent resistance to decay during three centuries of submersion, and her ultimate recovery is, indeed, stranger than fiction.

Next I tell about present efforts to preserve the *Wasa*, flash back to events leading up to the mattering moment of the hook, then explain subsequent attempts to raise the ship, extending over several hundred years. Then:

> . . the *Wasa*, denuded of her most valuable accessories, was left to rot at the bottom of Stockholm harbor. . . . But the Baltic is the only shipping sea in the world that has too little salt to support teredos, which are wood-eating shipworms.
>
> In a way the teredo led to eventual rediscovery of the *Wasa* three centuries later.

I explain about Anders Franzen's thinking a ship sunk in teredo-free waters would be well preserved and his years of efforts to discover the *Wasa*. The flashback takes place in his mind:

> Surely, he reasoned, someone must have informed the king of the disaster. . . . After months of searching . . . the message. "Off Beckholmen."

Back to the immediate past, with divers discovering an old ship with two rows of gunports:

> . . . Franzen was sure. It *had* to be the *Wasa*! But . . . What does one do with 1400 tons of seventeenth-century warship anchored in mud, 110 feet beneath a busy harbor?

I continue with the salvaging and recovery of the ship and its contents. This leads to a discussion of seventeenth-century shipboard life. Then back to the present with a description of the museum where the *Wasa* and the finds are housed. Then more about seventeenth-century life aboard ship, tied in with the present museum exhibits. I next cover the steps being taken for the *Wasa*'s preservation, and her probable future. Then:

> Visitors can stand on the museum's catwalks and look down through the chemical fog to the heart of the ship. . . . They can, with a little imagination, see the *Wasa* as she looked on the day of her debut, sails billowing and flags flying . . . sailed less than a mile in her lifetime . . . reincarnated to live forever.

Ten years later, when I wrote a completely different *Wasa* story for *Off Duty*, I was able to tie the hook to the 350th anniversary observance of the ship's sailing (and sinking). Because *Off Duty*'s European edition is published for US servicemen who might visit Stockholm on leave, the capsule sentence of that story is:

> Today the *Wasa* occupies a museum, complete with skeleton sailors, seventeenth-century schnapps, and slightly rancid butter.

After mentioning the guns being fired with a false charge for the anniversary celebration, I go on to the sailing day disaster, then return to what you, a Wasa Museum visitor, can see today, interspersed with explanations of why everything is in such good condition. Then a chronological report of salvage efforts, the recovery of the *Wasa*, the building of the museum, and a forecast for the future, ending with:

> . . . this ship now lives to carry tourists and scientists . . . back into history.

A sidebar tells when the museum is open, how much it costs, etc.

It's easier to write a story like this when you have an anniversary peg to tie it to, but a heavily historical article written for a popular audience always requires many flashbacks and flash-forwards.

What else goes into your travel article? Ideally, your substance will sing with active verbs and precise nouns that appeal to the reader's five senses. Salt sparsely with adjectives and adverbs; avoid clichés, today's slang expressions, and anything that dates the piece or sounds "cutesy." On the other hand, utilize all the tricks of the fiction writer's craft. Anecdotes, scenes, dialogue, characterization, and dramatic action belong in the travel story. Write with the breathless excitement of the best travel brochures—but only within the framework of truth and accuracy.

A *New York Times* travel editor summarizes the *Times* formula for good travel writing:

> You must use all the devices of the writer's skill to keep readers interested—a hook beginning; a "billboard" to tell them what the article is about near the beginning; word pictures, which is what travel writing is all about; what it looks, smells, tastes like. Amateurs use adjectives instead of word pictures. They write, "It was a lovely scene," instead of telling us what kind of scene it was. Was the sun slanting in from the west? Was there ice on the ground? Were there leaves on the trees? What kind of scene was it? Show, don't tell.

When you hear a writer or an editor say Show, don't tell, it means you should sharpen it up, by getting rid of all the nonworking words, all the deadweight, and, at the same time, flesh it out with details that count. For instance:

> **Telling:** Many medieval people were convinced that the dust from the tomb of Saint John held extra special curative powers, and many ailing pilgrims climbed up Ayasuluk Hill.

> **Showing:** Medieval Christians on three continents whispered to each other that dust from Saint John's tomb held special curative qualities. Thousands of them plodded up Ayasuluk Hill carrying blind babies or lugging lame relatives on donkey-drawn stretchers.

Or

> **Telling:** One night during the cruise there is a passenger costume competition where everybody dresses up like a sheik or a dancing girl or a mummy. Then passengers adjourn to the dining room for a spectacular Mideast buffet—everything from a sculptured lamb to baklava and grape pudding.

Showing: When the pseudo-sheik with the bath towel turban beckoned to the black-veiled harem "girls" they thrust out their stomachs and belly-danced around the passenger salon. . . . They adjourned to the dining room. Earlier that day our guide had gathered us together and spelled out procedure. "Use your elbows and your shoulders," he advised. "This buffet is really *something*—and everyone rushes to be first in the dining room line. Don't stand back politely—push like everybody else!" Actually, there was plenty to eat, even for latecomers. But at first sight, that buffet table was worth a little elbowing. The artists of the galley had even sculptured the meat into the shape of a lamb, kneeling on a bed of rice that had been browned to simulate the desert. Roasted pheasants and game hens climbed an ornamental superstructure and a half-dozen varieties of fresh fish surrounded the "desert." Purple half shells of savory eggplant alternated with stuffed green peppers and tomato-topped Oriental salads. Dishes of olives and plates of cheeses adjoined the platters of grape leaves rolled into dolmas, which encircled a huge bowl of yogurt. Steam rose from the couscous and the kabobs. Melons, grapes, oranges, and a dozen unfamiliar but delicious fruits and a garden of miniature decorated cakes accompanied the baklava and grape pudding, and were followed by demitasses of strong, sweet coffee.

Good writing is always good rewriting. When you feel your article is finished, put it away for at least a week and try not to think about it. You'll return to it with fresh insights and a renewed ability to recognize its faults and to set about correcting them. Many times you'll find ways to cut constructively; practically all writing is improved by cutting. Consider these examples:

If you are a passenger on board a cruise ship, you will know whether or not to buy the ship's shore excursions. (22 words)

Aboard ship, you'll know whether or not to buy the shore excursions. (12 words)

Houseboat operators usually require a $50 to $100 deposit when you make your reservation. This becomes your damage deposit, which is refunded when you return the boat intact. (28 words)

The $50 to $100 that accompanies your reservation becomes your damage deposit—refunded when you return the boat intact. (19 words)

You'll find the more times you go over your finished piece, the more words you'll discover you can cut. Don't skimp on rewriting time. In college I asked a favorite professor who had published many books and articles if he thought there was something wrong with me because it always took me five or six drafts to write an article. "If there is," he replied, "there must be something wrong with *me*, too, because it always takes *me* five or six drafts."

Read your article aloud when you're working on it. A word of caution, though: If you put enough vigor into your voice and your posture and your facial expression, *anything* sounds good; the editor, unable to see or hear your performance, will be limited to the words on the paper. So read it in a monotone, so that you recognize words carelessly repeated, "fat" that could and should be cut, inactive verbs that need active substitutes, abrupt transitions that should be smoothed, and complex, dense, or convoluted sentences that need recasting.

A transition is like a road sign that points your reader toward the next paragraph. We're all familiar with the standard "ongoing" words and phrases, such as *and*; *furthermore*; *similarly*; and the "backup" transitions; *however*; *on the contrary*; *despite*. We know, too, the cause-and-effect relationships: *as a result*; *because*; *consequently*. These are often overworked, though, so look for additional types of transitions to guide your reader to the next phase of your story. Time is a good transition; *the next morning*; *the following year*; *by six o'clock*. More subtle time transitions might be; *my coffee grew cold*; *the daffodils were blooming*; *when our ship sailed in*. Repeating a word from the previous paragraph, repeating the rhythm of the last sentence, comparing and contrasting—are all good transitional devices. You'll find ways to smooth out your forward motion as you revise.

Your reader will consider your ending almost as important as your beginning. An article's ending should grow out of the article itself, to provide a finale that seems logical and inescapable, leaving the reader satisfied. Many travel writers write the end at the same time as the hook. This not only brings you full circle, with beginning and ending written in the same mood, but defines the boundaries of where you're going. It's easier to stay on the track when you know where you will finish. The ending should usually not be a summary of what you've said in the article, nor should it be what Professor William Rivers calls "a crashing conclusion"—an ending with more force than the story itself, an ending that "tells all" and then tells it again. Instead, it should be a convincing culmination that leaves your reader either smiling or frowning, but definitely thinking about what you have just said. Notice how these endings grow inevitably out of the article beginnings:

Beginning: Sigiriya bursts upon you. As you round the bend of a jungle road in central Sri Lanka, the gigantic red rock "fortress in the sky" looms six hundred feet above its surrounding pleasure gardens. Visiting this preserve of a fifth-century royal murderer is a memorable experience. . . .

Ending: When you leave Sigiriya the red rock disappears as suddenly as it appeared. Then you see only the lime-green plain where Kassapa met Moggallana, and the ever-encroaching jungle.

Beginning: The wonderful thing about oysters is that they taste the way the ocean looks and smells.

After describing a day's boating on Tomales Bay, which included fresh oysters for lunch, author Robertson Pease concludes:

Ending: The wonderful thing about Tomales Bay is that it looks and smells just the way oysters taste.

Margaret Bennett's excellent article "A Japanese Orientation to Travel" in *Bon Voyage* extols the excellence of the Japan Travel Bureau and the arrangements it made for her and her friend. She begins with a compare-and-contrast question:

When is a tour more of a tour by being less of a tour? Although this question may seem to resemble one of those unanswerable Zen problems, like "What is the sound of one hand clapping?" it can be easily answered by anyone who has taken an "independent tour" of Japan arranged by JTB, the Japan Travel Bureau.

The story continues in first person, then switches to second in the last paragraph:

So if you're considering a trip to Japan, you should also consider that considerate organization, JTB. If you do travel with them, when you get back home, although you still may not know the answer to the eternal Zen question "What is the sound of one hand clapping?" there will be no doubt in your mind as to what the sound of *two* hands clapping is—it will be you applauding the services and the personnel of the Japan Travel Bureau.

You wonder perhaps how I've brought you to the end of this chapter without saying anything yet about titles. There are two reasons: First, the best titles often grow out of the article itself—sometimes I don't decide on the final title until I'm putting the manuscript in the envelope—and second, the title should be influenced by the kind your target market routinely uses. Are they usually mere labels (The Alcan Highway) or questions (Where Can You Find the Cheapest Airfare?) or direct orders (See Europe This Winter!) or how-tos (How to Travel with Teenagers) or cutesy (Portugese Climate, Customs and Madeira, M'Dear)?

If a wonderful title occurs to you early on, of course you'll use it, regardless. If you can't think of a thing, try some of these possibilities: Everybody likes a title that talks about saving money or time; a title that promises improvement in health, creativity, or prestige; a title that hints of the newest, the latest, the most up to date; a title that tells you the article will tell you how to do something. *You*—either spelled out or implied—is a very important word. The title should be intriguing, startling, or thought-provoking, and usually no longer than six words. Its sales pitch becomes increasingly important as magazines turn more and more to newsstand sales rather than mailed subscriptions. More titles are used on the cover, to lure the potential buyer, and the titles themselves have more punch.

Even if the editor changes your title, and he often does, its value as a sales tool cannot be overestimated. Some of the best titles combine the familiar with the unfamiliar: "Lewis and Clark Were Name Droppers" tells of their mapmaking activities; "Rooting Around in the Gambia" discusses the *Roots*-inspired desire of black Americans to find their own roots in Africa.

Alliteration in the title is a plus: "Shannon is Super for Shoppers" or "Patriots in Petticoats." Hyphenation can be used to advantage: "Charm-ed, I'm Sure" (about travel charm bracelets) or "Turkish Delight-ful." The best titles use reversal: "All Is Good in the Badlands" or "Wild Horses Could Drag You There" (about untamed stallions in Wyoming) or "Don't Come In Out of the Rain" (about taking travel photos in bad weather). A play on words is always welcome: "How to Operate a Den of Antiquity" (about flea markets), "Virginia City's Silver Lining" (silver mining in the Old West), "They're Forever Blowing Bubbles" (a tour of champagne wineries) or "The Last Resort" (Canada's northernmost fishing lodge) are all alluring.

The title should always, of course, give honest hints about what's in the story. Don't mislead your reader. Have you heard the legend of the old *Liberty* magazine's cover story from 1940, "My Sex Life" by Mahatma Gandhi? Well, the story begins, "In 1906 I took the vow of celibacy." And that's the end of the story. Don't try to fool your reader that way.

Do remember your reader as you're writing your travel article. Give that reader the best, most interesting copy you can write. Remember, a dull story from Istanbul or Bombay is just as boring as a dull story from Podunk.

14

Asking Questions—The Interview

"W here were you?" my daughter asked as I slipped into a seat beside her in the ship's lounge. "Where did you disappear to after dessert?"

Dessert had been flaming baked alaska carried around the darkened dining room by a platoon of waiters and kitchen helpers. The baked alaskas not only looked spectacular, they tasted delicious. As soon as we finished eating, I went to interview the chef.

When you have an assignment to write a cruise article, the chef is one of the principal characters. Other principal characters—such as the purser or the deck steward—may have something to say for your story, too.

When you need information, what do you do? You interview the people who can supply it. How many dozen eggs are whipped to froth in the ship's galley each day? What is the ratio of crew members to passengers? Do many people get seasick or need treatment for other ailments? How many hundreds of sheets, towels, etc., are washed in the ship's laundry every week? When celebrities sail aboard this ship do they sit on deck with the hoi polloi, or is special provision made for their privacy? What percentage of passengers turn out for the various shipboard activities?

If it's statistics you want, ask the head man, the purser. The deck steward is more likely to tell you an anecdote about the famous actress whose string of Oriental pearls broke while she was swimming in the pool. He might even whisper the name of the aging politician whose tinted hair turned green in the sunlight. And don't forget the ship's doctor, the head housekeeper, and the cruise director.

The Sphinx, Egypt

The face-to-face interview is one of the travel writer's most important tools. Interviews translate abstract ideas into human terms, and they're indispensable for many types of stories. You, the interviewer, are not only asking questions you expect the subject to answer, you're acting as a sounding board, listening to the subject's message and interpreting his stance.

Your purpose in interviewing may be to know more about an individual for a profile, but in travel writing it's more likely to be the *topic* that interests you. You're trying to draw out the person's expertise so you can write an authoritative story for your readers. It's very important to know your objectives. What are you searching for? Insights into personality, basic background, oral history, personal anecdotes, enriching secondary facts, pithy quotes—or do you have a variety of objectives?

You should, before you even arrange an interview, have in mind the *focus* of the piece you intend to write, or, in some cases, several different thrusts for several different pieces. Then you can successfully steer the interview toward the specific information you need.

Don't ever hesitate to ask for an interview. Most people *like* to be sought out. As a noted interviewer says, "No one objects to questions about the measure of his own accomplishment." You are not imposing on him or invading his privacy.

Sometimes beginning travel writers are timid about requesting interview time. "I don't represent anybody," one complained. "I'm a nobody, myself, and I can't even say I'm writing the article for a particular publication. How do I know if I can ever sell it?"

This *is* a problem. If you do have an assignment, of course you'll mention it when you ask for the interview. But even if you have just a go-ahead answer to a query, you can say, "*Blank Blank* magazine has expressed an interest in this story." Or you can say, "I'm writing this for *Blank Blank* magazine," as long as you're careful not to imply an assignment that doesn't exist. Surely you'll have in mind the publication you'd like to be writing it for before you begin interviewing.

Generally even the busiest, most prominent people are cordial and cooperative to an interviewer. But even such experienced reporters as Joan Didion speak of experiencing "sweaty palms" and "knocking knees" when trying to make the arrangements.

If you can, telephone or write for an appointment, indicating the length of time you'll need—usually an hour—and whether or not you'll be photographing at the same time. If, however, an interview becomes important during your travels, and you've had no opportunity to plan it in advance, try to get it anyway. You'd be surprised how often such spur-of-the-moment attempts succeed.

Do as much homework as you can before the interview. If you're at home, search the library for general background about the person and the subject. If an opportunity presents itself while you're traveling, perhaps the local library can provide clues, or the secretary or assistant to the person you're interviewing can give you some information before the interview itself. Aboard ship, reread the biographical material in the brochure and the ship's newspaper. If you can, ask in advance for printed materials, scrapbooks, excerpts from speeches or other interviews—anything to help you get acquainted beforehand and prevent you from wasting your time and the interviewee's with "Where did you go to school?" or "How long have you been with the company?" Already knowing the answers to questions like these saves time, and you get off to a good start when you can say, "How do you like it here in Texas? I understand you grew up in Wisconsin and went to college in Minnesota—this must seem quite different to you."

Some interviewers like to send the interviewee an advance list of possible questions or outline of areas they want to discuss. This gives the subject an opportunity to think about the focus before the interview and perhaps collect enriching information. These questions should be broad and open-ended, not the kind that can be answered yes or no.

You may not want to ask these specific questions when the time comes, but you'll want to at least jot down a few starter questions that will move the interviewee in the right direction. An interview should not be an exercise in "Q&A" but should give the subject an opportunity to speak freely about the topic, with the interviewer only occasionally inserting another question or deftly moving him back onto the track. Starter questions should be designed to encourage colorful, anecdotal, quotable answers. Again, you'll want to avoid questions that can be answered with yes or no or a date or statistic. The open-ended question is fine for stirring up the interviewee ahead of time, but when you're actually talking to him, avoid this kind of question. Where there's no precise answer, sometimes the subject just talks on and on, without saying anything quotable. Try to get specific answers. From the specific you can generalize, but not the other way around.

The ability to frame effective interview questions is the mark of the professional.

Jessica Mitford says she prepares for an interview by asking an expert in the field what questions to ask. "If I were going to interview a prosecuting attorney I'd . . . ask [a defense lawyer] if he were a reporter what would he ask the prosecutor."

This is good advice when the subject matter is controversial. However, you're not always meeting your subject in an adversary relationship. When you ask the chef to identify the most difficult, or the most popular, dish he prepares for the passengers, there's no need to be aggressive in your questioning.

The main thing to remember is: Put yourself in the place of your reader. What questions would he like answered? What part of your proposed article could be better explained through a quote from the interviewee? Often you, the travel writer, are merely the middleman interpreting your subject for your reader. Again the framing of the questions insures the accuracy and completeness of that information.

Sometimes your editor, wanting the interview to follow a particular format, will suggest the questions. When I wrote up a series of interviews with travel agents for the trade journal *Travel Age West*, the stories were for a regular feature called "Counter Intelligence." The directions were to "focus on the travel agency's staff, rather than the manager, and make it light and gossipy. We want to hear about unusual travel experiences, difficult or funny clients, worst or best travel experiences, interesting or strange hobbies," the directions continued, then went on with what *not* to do. The editor suggested that a question about how long the travel agent had been in his position or where he had worked before was okay to start him talking, but "it does not make very interesting reading. Neither does how much they like the travel business. . . ." Instead, she suggested, "Be warm and light and, if possible, be funny. What we are after is the personality of the agent, not the stuffy professional image that some may wish to give."

Following directions, I made up a list of warm-up questions about the person's hobbies and interests, family, unusual trips, difficult customers, etc. I also designed a few broad questions to lead into what I hoped would be quotable material, such as "What special service do you feel you and your agency have to offer? Are most of your customers realizing a lifelong dream or are they traveling because they think it's the thing to do? What changes do you think should be made in the travel industry?" As soon as the travel agents began talking, I listened for opportunities to elicit "light and gossipy" material. That's how I found out about the travel agent whose attempt to bring back swords from Taiwan as gifts for her husband and son resulted in a confrontation with the Taiwanese authorities who refused to let her board the plane, shouting "No! No! Weapons!" while she shouted back "Yes! Yes! Souvenirs!" And about the client who left his traveler's checks in the pocket of a shirt left on the beach while he went for a swim—forgetting that the tide was coming in. Others mentioned complex itineraries that eventually "jelled," unusual services performed for unusual clients, and personal hobbies that led them to far-out places.

When you have a list of interview questions, always number them so you can refer to those numbers as the questions are answered. How will you record the replies? Will you use a tape recorder, take notes or rely on memory? Perhaps all three.

You must ask permission to use a tape recorder. This permission will usually be granted by people who are accustomed to being interviewed and who feel comfortable with mechanical devices. Sometimes they prefer it: They're sure of being quoted correctly. The tape, of course, gives you a perfect record of the conversation, and on sensitive subjects might provide a valuable reference for direct quotes. Try to use a tape recorder with a built-in microphone, as small and inconspicuous as possible. Be sure it's working properly, has fresh batteries, and that the "record" button is depressed. Watch for the end of the tape, and change it unobtrusively. Remember, also, that music or loud background noise of any kind, such as the clatter of dishes in a restaurant, may prevent a clear reproduction.

Even if you use a tape recorder, take careful notes anyway. There are two reasons for this: first, the danger of mechanical failure. I never completely trust a tape recorder—I've seen too many chagrined expressions after interviews, as the interviewer unwinds a twisted mass of tape or plays what turns out to be a blank cassette. The second reason for taking notes is the way it makes you focus on what the person is saying. Too often the interviewer relies on the tape and doesn't listen attentively because he thinks "It's all there—I can replay it any time," thereby losing the essence of the interrelationship with the subject.

"What do you use for taking notes?" is a question students frequently ask.

I, as well as every other interviewer I know, use a stenographer's notebook, the kind issued to newspaper reporters. It's not only a good size—large enough to get lots of thoughts down, but small enough to handle comfortably—it also features easy-to-turn pages and a firm cover. It has an additional advantage, too: Many interviewees, accustomed to dictating to secretaries, are psychologically receptive to the steno pad.

Two note-taking rules every interviewer should commit to heart:

1. It is possible to take notes without looking down at them (thus losing eye contact with your subject). Practice. Keep your eyes on a person or a TV screen as you write what is being said.
2. Transcribe all notes before you go to bed that night. Regardless of what kind of personal shorthand you use, regardless of how well you think you'll remember every word that was said, "cold" notes lose about half their value in forty-eight hours and three-fourths of it within the week. A month later your notes, unless you've immediately clarified and amplified them, are practically worthless.

Some interviewers, of whom Truman Capote is perhaps the most notable example, spurn the tape-recording, note-taking process, claiming total recall without memory aids. That may be. But if you don't take any notes it makes the interviewee nervous.

I recently spent an evening with a friend who had been interviewed at noon by a writer who took no notes. "How can she possibly remember what I said?" my friend muttered. "There she was, eating her shrimp salad and acting like it was just an ordinary conversation—and all the time asking me questions that could get me fired if she misquotes me." He was very apprehensive until the interview—which did not misquote him—appeared in print. It's usually reassuring to the subject when the interviewer jots down answers—especially to critical questions or those involving facts and figures.

Gay Talese says he gets information by "just hanging around." But every once in a while he takes out his notebook and asks a question like, "What year did you say your uncle was born?" just to remind subjects that he is, after all, a reporter, and is not trying to conceal that fact.

Sometimes, though, tape recorders, and even notebooks, are prohibited, and the travel writer *must* rely entirely on memory. Such was the case in Cairo when we attended a briefing at the US Embassy during a critical period in Middle East affairs. Although questions were permitted, writing and recording the answers was not, and the material discussed was to be used for background only.

While we're all familiar with movies where the cub reporter violates a confidence to scoop his competitor, and everybody cheers his ingenuity, real life is different. The travel writer who accepts an invitation to a briefing at the embassy with the understanding that no direct or indirect quotes will result from it had better not violate that confidence—if he expects his sources to continue to help him.

The *Washington Post's* Sally Quinn feels it's very important to wear the same kind of clothes and behave in the same manner as your interview subject. "Create an atmosphere of sympathy. Don't scream, 'I am different from you!' as soon as you enter the room," she says. She relates it to Method acting—actually becoming the person you're interviewing.

Every interviewer has a special way of warming up the subject with preliminary small talk. Alice Phillips, who has done hundreds of interviews, says she always asks a male subject who gave him his necktie, and this usually produces a good anecdote and leads into the questions she wants to ask. I thought of her technique last year when I interviewed the manager of Waikiki's military hotel, the Hale Koa, about changes Congress was imposing that affected the administration of the hotel and the admission of retired military personnel. Because the entire operation was in the midst of a congressional investigation, the manager asked the colonel who was deputy chief of staff for the US Army's Western Command to sit in on the interview. But I was unable to follow Phillips's advice. Both men wore open-necked Aloha shirts.

Usually the interviewer begins with a simple question like "Have you enjoyed your tour of duty here?" This is to get the subject in the habit of responding. Be sure to keep the focus on him. Do not permit him to turn the conversation to you for any length of time. If he asks how you became a travel writer, say something like "I've always liked to write and I've always liked to travel." Then turn it back to him with, "I know you've done a lot of traveling, too. What's your favorite part of the world?"

Keep in mind why you're there, and don't let the conversation ramble off in all directions. If the subject expounds on a technical matter in technical phrases, ask "How shall I explain that to my readers in layman's language?" If he makes a controversial statement, don't pounce gleefully and hurry to scribble it down. Be casual. Ask another question while you're writing the controversial answer. Don't bulldoze your way into the conversation: Use gentle tactics, beginning your controversial questions with "I imagine that . . ." or "It appears that . . ." If you can't seem to pin the interviewee down to specifics, give him a misquote, like, "Others are saying the airline is losing two million dollars a year." This encourages him to reply indignantly, "That's not true. It's less than a million! Only about $875,000!"

Some travel writers believe in interspersing the "hard" questions with the "easy" questions, while others favor an easy beginning, getting progressively harder and more controversial. With either method, make your last two questions soft and innocuous, to end the interview with pleasant feelings on both sides.

If you want a reluctant subject to explain something, say, "Nobody seems to understand about this situation," implying that the interviewee is the only one who might be able to set your readers straight.

Silence is sometimes an excellent interview technique. Don't rush in to fill the void as soon as the conversation flags. Observe a moment of silence, and let the interviewee be the one to break it.

When you don't know anything about the topic under discussion, try to relate it to something you *do* know. When I was freelancing for my local newspaper, the city editor sent me, on ten minutes notice, to interview a missionary visiting from her post in Korea. I had never been to Korea and didn't know much about missionaries in general or her denomination in particular. But I soon discovered she was an English teacher at a college. *That* I knew about—English and colleges. We progressed from discussing the architecture of the college to the architecture of the surrounding city of Seoul, from the teaching of English to Koreans to Korea's place in the world today, from a woman's adventures teaching in a faraway land to her travel adventures and experiences in other places.

If your subject doesn't say what you want him to, sometimes you can persuade him by putting phrases in his mouth. Begin "In other words . . ." and then frame the sentence you want, asking only for an affirmative nod. If you tell him about the Greek Island jeweler who almost managed to get you arrested, he may respond with his story of a weekend in Guatamala under "house arrest" in his hotel. One mistaken identity story leads to another mistaken identity story.

Although you can't very well say, "Tell me an anecdote," sometimes you can encourage the interviewee to open up by telling him one of your own.

Give the reader the feeling he's met the person you're interviewing. Provide insight into character through selected details. Don't just note "He's a big man," but be prepared to write, "He gingerly lowered his muscular six-foot frame." Don't be satisfied with, "He's fair," but fill your tape recorder or notes with details: "afternoon sunlight," "picture window," "straight brown hair," "appears almost white."

When you see an office with a picture window, a rosewood desk, an Oriental rug, you're seeing a man of substance. Observe how he sits at his desk—ramrod straight, leaning back with feet on the desk top, or simply relaxed? Is music playing? What kind of music? Is the desk cluttered or bare? What books are in evidence? Family photos? What is the subject wearing? A necktie? Desert boots? A gold bracelet? If you're interviewing a woman, did she have her hair set for the occasion? Is she wearing Earth Shoes? A diamond wristwatch? Are her fingernails short or long? Be a sponge. Absorb everything.

When Alex Haley was still traveling around collecting material for *Roots*, I heard him say at a writers' conference, "When you interview a man, if his wife is present, watch the expression on *her* face. It can tell you a lot." That evening, as I listened to another big-name writer present a rather boring speech, I glanced back a couple of rows to check out *his* wife. She was sound asleep.

Some interviewers have trouble with "off the record," and it's very important to clearly settle that matter at the start. Always set guidelines: Anything that is said will be on the record unless agreed to be off at the time it's said. This prevents the interviewee from remarking at the end of the interview, "Oh, you know, that whole bit I told you about the State Department investigation of the travel industry—that was off the record, of course." Whether or not to listen to off-the-record material depends on how badly you need it for background and whether or not you'll be able to get it on the record from somebody else. Once having promised it's "off," you must keep your promise. Then it's awkward if the same information comes to you on the record in another manner, so consider the overall situation and the various people involved before you decide yes or no.

When your subject says "Not for attribution," you can use the content, but must not name your informant. You must attribute the statement to some shadowy source, such as "a West Coast travel agent," or "an American traveling in Italy." While it's all right to use such quotes occasionally, too many of them destroy the writer's credibility. Be sure your article has fewer "blind" quotes than direct ones.

You may want to ask your subject's permission to refine the quotes, since spoken language, full of extraneous sounds and words, often looks silly in print. It's usually all right, though, to go ahead and edit clumsy or unclear words, if you're careful not to change the sense or the color of the statement.

At the interview, don't overstay your allotted time unless it's apparent that the subject wants you to. If you notice him glancing at a clock or an engagement calendar or if he says something like "Well, I guess that's about all I have to say," it's time for you to leave. On the other hand, your interviewee will sometimes tell you more than you really care to know. One of the traits of a good interviewer is the ability to keep the subject on the desired track and not let the interview take up more time than is productive for the writer. In any case, at the end be sure to say, "Is there anything I *should* have asked you about that I've overlooked?" Request permission to call back for any additions or clarifications you might need. Then listen carefully for the casual remark, the gem of an anecdote, the perfect quote that is nearly always uttered as you stand with your hand on the doorknob, glasses off, notebook put away.

Do be aware of libel laws and write your article accordingly. But never promise you'll submit the finished article for the interviewee's approval. You are under no obligation to do so. You may, as a favor to him and as an insurance policy for yourself, submit facts and figures or direct quotes to verify their accuracy. But under no circumstances permit the subject to delete something he told you "for the record" or to alter in any way the thrust of the article.

As the instructions to writers from the St. Petersburg Times say, "We like to think that editors are editors and writers are writers, and the subject of the interview cannot assume those responsibilities."

Always follow up the interview with a thank-you note on your letterhead. This is not only common courtesy, but it also reminds the subject of where he can reach you should he think of any additions or corrections, and it paves the way for you to go back if you need to. If you promise to send a photograph, or copies of the published article, be sure to do so. Taking good care of your sources is future-story insurance.

If a face-to-face interview is impossible, try for a telephone interview. For this, too, make an appointment and indicate how much time you'll need. You might want to suggest, "Call me collect, Tuesday at two, or let me know if there's a more convenient time." Some writers find it best to conduct telephone interviews in the evening. The subject is more relaxed at home than at the office. Again, you may want to presubmit a list of questions, giving the person a chance to prepare the answers before the interview. If the subject is willing, you can hook up your tape recorder to the telephone. Sometimes a telephone interview turns out to be more chatty and unstructured than a face-to-face situation; other times, it's more formal and punctilious.

One East Coast writer attributes his successful telephone interviews to his habit of calling long distance from a pay telephone. "When the person you're interviewing hears the clink-clank of all those dimes and quarters," he says, "he knows it's your own money you're using, not a publisher's expense account credit card. So he's especially helpful and informative."

What kind of interviews do you need? That depends on the story.

A here and now story about a new tour being featured at San Simeon might materialize from the tour itself, some PR handouts, a few questions to the tour guide, and a phone call to the state official in charge of San Simeon tours.

A definitive destination piece would include interviews with a city official, with somebody from the chamber of commerce or tourist bureau, with a spokesman for each of several attractions, and probably with a hotel executive and several restaurant owners.

An in-depth analysis of a foreign country's new approach to tourism would probably require interviews with the director of tourism, someone in the public relations department of the country's chief airline, and the manager of the leading hotel. It should include scattered quotes from restaurateurs, on-the-spot tourists, spokesmen for car rental agencies, and other hotel managers. Several owners of sightseeing companies and tourist attractions, the mayors of principal cities, a museum director, and a representative of a wholesale tour that in-cludes the country, would make good additions.

When a travel story requires interviews with more than one person, it's especially important to remember your theme, and base all the in-terviews around it. That's what makes the piece hold together.

In covering an *event* you'll usually have several people to interview: the fans, who are participating in the activity; the sponsors, who make the time and space available to enhance their public image; the ex-perts, who excel at this particular talent; the public relations people, who are eager to catch your ear and often come laden with handout sheets; and the spokesman—usually the master of ceremonies or guest of honor.

Introduce yourself to the spokesman first, presenting your business card, of course. Ask about taking photographs. (See Chapter 15 for more on photography.) Discuss the problems involved in this particu-lar field. Then later, when you interview the expert, you'll impress him with your knowledge of his problems. At the same time you're get-ting information from his viewpoint.

A good example of *roundup* interviewing (see the appendixes for more on roundups) is "Living with Others in a Small Boat" by Pa-tience B. Wales in *Sail*. Telling of a four-year world cruise she and her husband and another couple took in a forty-two-foot ketch, she says the number one question people always ask is "How did you all stand each other for so long in such close quarters?" That's probably what gave her the idea for this article, because she not only analyzes some of the factors that made this relationship possible, but tells of other peo-ple she's interviewed whose relationships foundered in close quarters at sea. She did much of her interviewing in Tahiti, where, she says, "the waterfront seethes with the remains of friendships."

In researching *my* roundup story about what causes traveling cou-ples to argue, many of those I interviewed protested at first that they had nothing to say. "We *never* argue when we're traveling," both Sally and John assured me. Then she remembered: "Of course, there was the time you got us lost looking for that old country inn in the Berkshires, and it got to be midnight and we hadn't had dinner and. . . ."

"*I* got us lost!" John interrupted. "*You* were the one that looked at the directions and told me to go north when you meant south!"

"What's there to argue about?" asked Tim and Ellen. "When we're on vacation we always have a great time."

"There's just one thing," Tim said hesitantly. "I wish Ellen wouldn't always take so long getting ready. When you're trying to make a plane—gee, I hate always racing to the gate as they're calling our flight."

"*Tim!*" Ellen almost shouted. "How can you talk that way! *You're* the one who always leaves everything scattered all over the place. If you'd be neater it wouldn't take me so long to get ready. And besides, if you'd. . . ."

The face-to-face interview can be revealing. It can also be amusing, informative, and controversial. It's one of the travel writer's most valuable tools, and using it with professional skill can make the difference between a good, publishable travel article and a batch of meaningless, indecipherable notations.

15

Bring Back Your Story in Pictures

The traveling photographer on San Francisco's Chinese Heritage Walk stopped to take a picture.

Half a roll later he looked around for his twenty-odd tour companions. They had disappeared. He walked up to the Alley of the Balconies. Down to Grant Avenue. Back to the Chinese Cultural Center. No, nobody knew where the tour was. The Chinese Heritage Walk he'd reserved and paid for ended, for him, in the first ten minutes. He hadn't realized he was taking such a long time with lens switching, light meter reading, and picture taking.

Another eager picture taker took a step backward to get a better view of his wife walking down the steps to the Dreaming Room at the Aesklepeion in Pergamum. He tumbled into the Sacred Spring.

Other traveling photographers have become so engrossed they've fallen into the Grand Canal while trying to frame the pigeons of Saint Mark's Square, plunged over a cliff while getting a light reading on Lincoln's nose at Mount Rushmore, and been arrested taking pictures of Iranian pilgrims on their way to Mecca. Many have missed seeing or hearing or understanding some significant facet of the travel experience because they've been concentrating on taking pictures of some other facet.

It's exciting to feel you can capture a memorable moment and recreate it for your readers through a combination of your words and your pictures.

While photography *is* important, don't let it become the only significant activity of your trip. Instead, use all your senses and expose yourself to a variety of travel impressions.

It's exciting, though, to feel you can capture a memorable moment

Steer wrestling, Oklahoma

and recreate it for your readers. And whether they're active or arm-chair travelers, you move them on-scene and add to their knowledge and enjoyment through a combination of your words and your pictures.

The successful travel writer knows illustrations help sell his story, because they enhance and enrich his words, giving the editor—and subsequently the reader—the entire picture. He understands how more and more publications break up their blocks of type with photographs; and more and more editors prefer to receive manuscript and illustrations in one package, rather than having to make separate arrangements for photographs.

As we've noted earlier, even an inexperienced photographer can take pictures useful for recreating the travel experience, and a travel writer with modest shutter talents can illustrate his own stories. While it's impossible to "cover" photography in these few pages, we hope to improve whatever skills you now have. This discussion of planned and unplanned photos, the kinds of pictures editors need, using props, composing, shooting on the move, picturing people, avoiding legal problems, equipment and film needs, overcoming bad weather, selling and sending photographs, and obtaining pictures from others when you don't have what you need, should help you illustrate your articles.

Can You Shoot Both the Planned and the Unplanned?

In taking travel pictures, sometimes you plan in advance the pictures you want, something to illustrate a story already designed or already written. Other times the photography is spontaneous—you see something interesting and you shoot it.

To portray a geographic area so your reader can really know it, you'll want pictures of people of all ages and occupations in all types of situations; wildlife and domestic animals; landscapes and gardens. You'll also want markets and restaurants, hotels and historical sites, clothing and costumes, handcrafts and souvenirs, art and architecture, signs and flags.

What will you do with all these pictures after they're processed? Some you'll send along with the first article you write about the area—color or black and white, as the editor has indicated. Send more than you think he'll need—to give him a choice and perhaps to persuade him to use more photographs (and send you a larger check) than he had originally intended. Even in situations where the photos are part of the article "package," for which there's no extra payment, I've often found editors send a bonus for a large selection of good pictures. File your leftovers carefully, to use with future articles. Some of them might prove useful for roundup stories or roundup photo essays, where you have around-the-world variations on a single theme.

Just as some people collect rare gems or antique scimitars, I collect laundry lines. For years I've collected photographs of people washing along with the lines of clothes they have washed. I also collect pictures of schools and colleges, uniformed schoolchildren, shoeshine boys, and several other universal themes. These make great international roundups—"Wash and Wear around the World"; "School Days from Country to Country"—as well as illustrating individual aspects of a specific area.

Shoot lots of pictures. Film is cheap, compared to the cost of getting there. In color, it's even cheap in comparison to the cost of having duplicates made. It's always more desirable and less expensive to take several pictures of the same scene than it is to duplicate later.

Don't forget to bracket your exposures. Take one picture at the shutter speed and lens opening you think correct. Then take one an f-stop smaller and one an f-stop larger. One of them will be perfect.

Shoot both horizontals and verticals of each scene. You change the feeling of the picture when you turn the camera, and this gives the editor a choice. If you're hoping for a magazine cover, of course you'll shoot verticals, keeping in mind the need for a "loose" area where the logo will be. Compose all your pictures on the loose side, giving the editor opportunity for creative cropping.

Vary the distance shots and the close-ups. Get the overall scene and then the particulars. Be sure to make those close-ups close enough to capture the emotion and detail you need. The best photographers remember this rule: Move in until you think you're close enough—then step three feet closer. Try unusual angles on cliche scenes. Kneel down and shoot up or climb on something and shoot down.

Try not to date your picture by its background. Sometimes the people's clothing and hairstyles, cars, and advertisements for trendy items spell out the year the picture was taken. Clothing styles change less often for men, middle-aged women, and small children, so use them as models when possible. And perhaps you can block out parked cars incriminating advertising. Make your picture usable for years to come.

If the person is the most important part of the picture, try to also include a recognizable landmark. A beach is a beach is a beach; but if Diamond Head is in the top left corner, we know where we are. Titles and road signs are useful, too, when selected thoughtfully, so that they aren't distracting. Take pictures of the Continental Divide, the state line, the Mexican border, the highest point in the Sierras. If the sign says, "Elephants have the right-of-way" or "Golf balls in hippo footprints may be lifted without penalty," think how to pose somebody looking at the sign. Even if you don't have anybody to pose, you can take poignant pictures, as Tom Biema did for Rider magazine. His photographs of the Australian Outback include one of a road sign depicting a black wombat on a yellow background and the legend "Wombats next 26 km." His riderless bike stands beside it, a white helmet decorated with an American flag resting on the seat. Another picture shows the motorcycle in the foreground, the emptiness of the outback stretching in front and on both sides, the mirrors reflecting the emptiness behind.

Sometimes, when you don't have any particular illustrations in mind, you'll be taking travel pictures as you see them.

Henri Cartier-Bresson, one of the most respected photographers of all time, tells us what to look for:

> To me, photography is the simultaneous recognition, in a fraction of a second, of the significance of an event as well as of a precise organization of forms which give that event its proper expression.

Cartier-Bresson speaks often of the "decisive moment," that instant when it's about to happen: the hiker finding himself at the edge of the crevasse; the child about to begin dancing; the young man ready to take off on his motorbike; the tourist deciding which necklace she's going to buy. That "decisive moment" is the instant we try to capture.

How Will Your Pictures Be Used?

Certainly shoot whatever appeals to you. But if you're thinking primarily in terms of illustrations, it helps to think of how the photographs will be used. In a *picture story*, the photos do most of the telling, and need little, if any, explanatory caption material. For instance, in Christchurch, New Zealand, where they have big red city buses with hooks on the front for carrying strollers and prams, my husband shot a picture story from our hotel room on the main square. The big red bus is loading; a distraught mother, carrying a young baby in her arms and wheeling a toddler in a perambulator, looks around helplessly, obviously wondering how she will board the bus; a well-dressed businessman comes up to her and says a few words; she smiles; he lifts the toddler out of the perambulator and sets him on the bus step; then the man hooks the pram to the front of the bus; everyone climbs aboard and the bus roars off. All this with the very British-looking background of Christchurch Cathedral, vehicles moving to the left, and uniformed schoolboys in straw hats guiding their cycles through the park.

A bridge overlooking Istanbul's Golden Horn harbor was the vantage point for another picture story. An old man in a rowboat that's tied to the bridge is frying fish over a charcoal brazier. As soon as the fish is brown a blue-smocked helper puts it on a piece of bread and passes it to an eager bystander, who hands his money over the bridge rail, then moves on. The next customer pushes himself into position, the helper puts another fish on bread, and the old man continues to turn the browning fish in his pan.

Whenever you see action that's a story in itself, hasten to focus. Keep on the lookout for those picture stories—many publications use them. Some are always open to picture stories, while others consider only those that are outstanding in both subject interest and technical quality. There's usually no set number of pictures required—however many it takes to tell the story.

A *sequence* uses several pictures, too. It can feature something occurring in stages, but is accompanied by explanatory copy; the pictures themselves do not have to carry the entire story. For instance: When you're packing for your trip, first you place the shoes and the toiletries bag in the suitcase; then you put in the underwear and nightclothes; on top you lay the dress clothes, spread out over the suitcase; then you fold them so they fit in; then you shut the lid and, voilá, the next scene shows you carrying the case to the airport. Or a *sequence* might be an evening at a nightclub. First scene shows the headwaiter escorting your party to the table; next picture shows you ordering dinner; then comes the nightclub act; you and your friends applaud; then you lean back smiling; then reach forward to toast with your brandy snifters.

If you witness something like the divers at La Quebrada in Acapulco, try to take the full sequence—the diver blessing himself at the shrine; descending the steps that have been cut into the cliff; mounting the starter platform; making the starter dive; scrambling up the steep cliff to the top of La Quebrada; and then the flaming torches illuminating his arc through the air; his sixty-mile-an-hour splashdown into the rock-girded cove, and finally his head emerging from the churning water, his arm upraised in a victory gesture.

A *juxtaposition* usually consists of two contrasting scenes. A picture of a Europe-bound Girl Scout troop as high school seniors and a picture of the same girls as second-grade Brownies beginning their plans for the trip would be a juxtaposition. So would a photo showing a scene in Chicago today placed next to one of the same area immediately after the 1871 fire.

For these juxtapositions you and your camera would have to have been present after the 1871 fire and when the Girl Scouts were in second grade, or know someplace to obtain a picture taken at the time.

To present a juxtaposition of a rural Finnish lake in summer and in winter, you'd have to make two trips there or work in tandem with a friend. Such a juxtaposition would be easy to do, though, illustrating some of the features of your home area. But the shot of the Acapulco diver standing on the cliff, juxtaposed with one of him in the water, raising his arm in the victory salute, would *not* make a good twosome—the action in between, the *real* story, would be lacking. Captions for juxtapositions are especially important. Be sure to make the meaning of the two pictures clear to your reader.

The *stopper* is a one-shot situation. This picture is used to draw the reader's attention to the story, so it needs to be vivid and dramatic: the mountain fortress of Sigiriya rising from the plains; the parachute ride at Knott's Berry Farm; tourists viewing Montreal's Old Town from a horse-drawn carriage; the dramatic architecture of Funchal's new casino on the island of Madeira, framed by mountains and sea; two canoeists exploring a river that's flecked with ice floes and bounded by snow-covered banks; a dramatic silhouette of Rio's seven-hundred-ton statue, Christ the Redeemer, atop Corcovado mountain—all are *stoppers*. But the parachute ride is taken from an unusual angle, the canoe appears against an extraordinary background, the wheels of the horse-drawn carriage are distorted to emphasize a focal point of the picture—otherwise these situations would surely be clichés. Once the reader's attention has been captured, he'll learn from the writer's copy what the stopper is all about, so it doesn't have to tell a story all by itself—just hint strongly that an interesting story accompanies it. If you examine the pictures in print advertising, you'll find they're usually stoppers.

Drop-ins can consist of any number of shots, or possibly just one. They are what we often think of as illustrations—something strongly tied to the text, used by the editor to emphasize a certain aspect of the article, as well as to break up large blocks of type and create an attractive layout. Usually they are captioned with explanatory material.

Almost anything can be a drop-in. For instance, to accompany an article on Australia's Barrier Reef I sent six photographs: only two people in sight on the vast beach of Hayman Island, with the hotel and mountains in background; adults and children fossicking on the reef at low tide; the launch, with people aboard, leaving for the outer reef; the underwater observatory, with its huge viewing windows, on Hook Island; Hayman's gaily painted train that transports guests on this island where no cars are allowed; and the Hayman Island airport, with a helicopter about to land. The magazine used the beach scene as a stopper (at the top of the center-spread story), and the launch ride and the underwater observatory pictures as drop-ins.

On a story about the *Wasa* I sent eight photographs: the ship as it looks today; the ship inside the museum building; the ship in a cradle of cables on its concrete pontoon in 1961; the ship during salvage operations; the museum building from the outside; the Swedish coat of arms from the sterncastle; the gigantic lion figurehead; and the brazier that once graced the captain's table. The editor selected the ship today, the ship in cables, the coat of arms, the museum building, and the brazier as drop-ins.

Occasionally I have only one photograph to illustrate a story—so I send it.

The most important thing to remember is, if the picture intrigues you, it will probably intrigue somebody else. Film is comparatively cheap, so if in doubt, shoot.

Can You Make It Look Real?

When you know ahead of time what you want, make a storyboard or a shooting script. Use an index card for each picture you intend to take, rough-sketching on it what you want the picture to show. For a "set piece," jot down all pertinent data: time of day, models, location, camera angle, clothes, props, etc.

Don't hesitate to use props that will enhance the meaning of your picture. Whether it's a parasol for a Japanese girl walking beneath the blossoming cherry trees or an ornamental lifebuoy chaperoning a shipboard buffet, if that's the prop that makes the picture, get it. I once illustrated a California garden article on a tight deadline; as a set piece, the only possible illustrations were of the the garden. But nothing was blooming at that time of year. Even citrus was out of season. I had no choice: I scooted to the grocery store and bought a couple dozen oranges, which we tied to the orange trees. I'm not in favor of faking as a general rule, but in this case it was necessary and the scene came out looking more like California than California, itself.

What if the prop is there, but you can't get it in your viewfinder? Sometimes both the subject and the background are important. Yet if you picture a man against twenty feet of metal, who's to know that's an airplane behind him? Or is it the Empire State Building, or the Eiffel Tower? On the other hand, if you shoot him in front of a recognizable airplane half a football field away, he'll be a skinny black stick. The solution is to back off until the background object exactly fills the viewfinder. Then bring the subject forward until his head and shoulders fill about one-third of the frame. Focus on him, letting the background fall slightly out of focus, and you'll have your picture.

Can You Compose in the Viewfinder?

Although this chapter is not intended as a course in elementary photography, you'll find reminders of some basics we should keep in mind.   If you have a single-lens reflex camera, your finished print will reflect exactly what your eye sees in the viewfinder. Too many photographers don't really see what's in that viewfinder. Is your finger or camera strap in the way? Is a telephone pole growing out of somebody's head? Is your horizon line in the dead center of the picture, thereby ruining it? Are there a dozen distracting centers of interest?

If you were to draw a ticktacktoe grid on your viewing screen you'd find your best pictures would have the center of interest at one of the four points where those imaginary lines cross—either one-third down from the top or one-third up from the bottom and either one-third in from the left or one-third in from the right. Many pictures are confusing because the viewer's eye doesn't know what to center on. Of course, the less irrelevant material in your photograph, the more the focal point stands out.

Try framing your subject with a tree branch, an arch, a wall, to give it depth, keeping the frame at least five feet from the camera. Consciously look for a natural frame, such as the man playing bongo drums between the upraised arms of his fellow musicians, or the little girl's smiling face framed by the two dogs she's roughhousing with, or the woman walking between two tall buildings.

Experiment with silhouettes, especially those instantly recognizable, like the man with the sombrero or the woman with the baby in the backpack. To take a silhouette you need heavy shadows on the camera side of the subject, against a bright background. A figure standing in a doorway against the sunny outdoors or in the open, outlined against the sky, make good silhouettes. Adjust the exposure for the bright-light area of the picture, and print (or have printed) for the lighter ar-

eas, too, so the main subject remains poorly lighted and underex-
posed.

Learn to *see* what makes a picture. A natural line should lead into
it—a pathway, a freeway cloverleaf, the movement of the waves, the
placement of the objects. The viewer's eye moves, naturally, toward
the center of interest, so any action shown should lead *into* the picture,
not out of it. The repetition of forms gives unity; so learn to use the
lines you see through your viewfinder to express your sense of significance. Look for rhythms—patterns of shape, length, angle, curve, direction, or interval that strengthen your composition and tie the elements together to present a unified picture for your reader. If what you
see isn't exactly what you want to convey, move a few steps in one direction or another, shoot from lower down or higher up, adjust the
scene until it *is* the one you want.

Learn which camera techniques enable you to concentrate on the
center of interest and blur the background, and learn which filters will
help you differentiate, on your print, the dirty white sails from the pale
blue sky. Use reflections whenever you can—the snow-capped mountain in the outside rearview mirror of the camper, your houseboat in
the unrippled lake, the kids jumping into the puddle that reflects
them.

And one last "should": If you see some dramatic episode about to
unfold, and you have only two frames left on your roll, you should—
you *must*—change your film *now*. Film, as we've said, is comparatively cheap. Don't waste an opportunity to take an outstanding picture by
changing rolls in the middle of the action.

By "dramatic episode" I mean something you're able to foresee and
that you're sure is worth more than two frames: the herd of elephants
lumbering across the horizon out of camera range, as your safari bus
approaches them; the opening set of the Davis Cup; the kibbutz kin-
dergartners about to present a biblical vignette for the visitors.

Can You Shoot on the Move?

Yes, it *is* possible to shoot a usable picture from a moving vehicle.
We sold and published a picture my husband took through a fast-moving car's dirty window of a boy on a fast-moving bicycle in the midst of
heavy traffic just at dusk. Technically the picture leaves much to be
desired. But the subject matter redeems it. (The boy had draped over
his shoulder a live lamb he was taking home for his family's celebration of a Muslim holiday.) So don't think "why bother," just because
there's motion or there's traffic or it's getting dark. If the subject matter
is interesting, take the picture anyway, on the move or not.

Your best on-the-move photographs will result when you're sitting
in the front seat taking pictures through the windshield of a car or bus
but you can shoot through the side window, too. Try to sit on the shady
side of the car, bus, or plane, to avoid reflections on the glass, and don't
use a polarizing filter, which reacts poorly with Plexiglas windows
and creates a bizarre effect. Take scenes in the middle distance, preferably those you're moving toward or away from, and pan to hold the

object in position if necessary. Hold the camera close to the window, but make sure that neither it nor any part of your body is touching the vehicle frame—the vibration will blur your picture. On a heeling sailboat, however, you'll have to brace yourself.

Protect your equipment as much as possible, to lengthen its trouble-free life and insure high-quality pictures. To minimize the effects of vibration on your camera in a plane, train, or bus, put it on the seat, if possible, preferably secured with a seat belt. In a car, place it on the floor behind the front seat, on the side opposite from the exhaust. Avoid, as much as you can, the ravages of dust, sand, and sea spray.

If your camera jams or something else seems wrong, don't force it—you may do irreparable damage. Instead, find the nearest expert and let him take it apart. However, telling the difference between an expert and an "expert" is not always easy. Two unhappy experiences, one mine, one a friend's, resulted from trying to sneak a thirty-eighth picture out of a thirty-six exposure roll (you can practically always sneak thirty-seven) in a foreign country. When I took the jammed camera into a nearby camera shop, the "expert" opened it in the darkroom, removed the film, and handed the camera back to me. I didn't discover until several hours and two hundred miles later that he had neglected to put back a small but important part, without which the camera would not work. It took three days to find a replacement. My friend's "expert" also opened the jammed camera and removed the film in the darkroom. He ran to the front of the shop triumphantly clutching the thirty-seven (thirty-eight?) exposed negatives, crying, "See! I got them out!"

Anyway, try to find an expert. And don't push for thirty-eight!

Can You Picture the People?

Most good pictures are better pictures with people in them. Sometimes the people are mainly there to show scale—how infinitesimal is the human being looking up at the enormous statues of Ramses II at Abu Simbel, or the gigantic Daibutsu (each of Buddha's eyes is three feet long) in Kamakura.

When we say there should be people in the picture, we mean local people—not tourists. A photograph of the Plaka, with a dozen Athenians sipping ouzo at a taverna, is charming. A photograph of the Acropolis, with a dozen gaping American tourists, is not. If you want to shoot the Acropolis try to wait until the tourists leave.

How the people in your pictures look, how they're dressed and coiffed, can be very important in relation to the markets you're aiming for. Would you use the same models to illustrate an article for *Car and Driver* as you'd use for *Town and Country*? If the photo's okay for *Ms.*, does that mean it'll work for *Business Week*?

When a single human being is the focal point of the picture, ideally he or she will look at ease, will not be staring into the camera, and will be actively engaged in some pursuit typical of the locale and his lifestyle.

Group shots are trickier. The more people there are, the more difficult it is to photograph everybody in an unselfconscious and flattering pose and retain the picture's interest. When my oldest daughter's Girl Scout troop left for Europe, the local newspaper sent a photographer to the leader's home. We set up some attractive photos, the girls all clustered around a globe or a map, looking at it and laughing and talking in a natural way. At the airport the airline photographer also took their picture. He lined them up in front of an Exit sign that had a No Smoking sign beneath it. The twelve girls and their two leaders are pictured in a stiff double row, twenty-eight black-shod feet, twenty-eight white-gloved hands, and fourteen mouths saying "cheese." (I was never able to use *that* picture!)

Watch out for distractions in the background. Don't frame your picture with a No Smoking sign. If a boy in a red jacket is flying a kite behind the statue you must shoot, wait until he leaves. Otherwise, nobody will look at your statue.

If you want to unobtrusively take pictures of strangers in the street, consider using a telephoto lens with a right-angle attachment. With it, you seem to be aiming at the church straight ahead while all the time you're photographing the funny old lady reading tea leaves, who's way off to your right, and suitably unaware of your interest.

Or you may want simply to ask permission to take the picture. For a close-up, that's only good manners. And people will usually welcome the photographer who wants to take home an image of them, if you establish rapport, making them feel you're a friend who wants to share their activity rather than a foreigner who's ridiculing them.

Except at the farthest travel frontiers, people are accustomed to photographers, and tolerate them, at least. We've always been amused by a friend who bought a miniature camera for his trip because he "didn't want to look like a tourist." This friend is six feet four, blond and blue-eyed, and the country he visited was Japan. In addition to the fact that he could hardly conceal his foreignness, no people in the world are more camera-happy than the Japanese. Everywhere you go in Japan, there are dozens of tourists, *and* dozens of Japanese, snapping away.

We've felt welcome as photographers in most countries. On many occasions we've taken a picture of a person or a landmark, only to have other people rush up, begging to be photographed also.

Sometimes locals expect you to pay them for posing. It's rumored that the old man and woman in coolie outfits who position themselves at a popular tourist stop near Hong Kong's Chinese border have earned enough to send three sons through college in England. If the deal is made ahead of time, that's fine, but sometimes you'll snap the picture and *then* discover a row of outstretched palms. You'll want to be prepared at least with small change, chewing gum, instant photos, or other modest gifts. Sometimes, though, the gift for posing is refused. A group of us recently photographed some charming little Greek boys dressed in their national holiday costumes of the Evzone Guards. We had asked their mothers if we might take pictures, and then we asked their permission to give the children a few coins. They politely but firmly indicated "absolutely not."

When you take pictures for publication, do you need model releases? Let's take that up in the next section, as we discuss:

Can You Avoid Legal Problems?

Most of the legal problems surrounding photography can be solved with common sense. There seem to be two major areas involving the law. One is your pictures, the kind of rights you are selling and who is entitled to reproduce them. The other is the people in your pictures, and *their* rights.

If you can get a model release, get it. A lot of the time you don't really need one for a picture to be used for editorial purposes. But if that picture is to be used for advertising, a release is imperative. And "advertising" may refer to more situations than you'd expect. For instance, a magazine's cover is considered to be advertising, since it attempts to sell the publication. The entire magazine is advertising if it's a house organ or company publication, since its purpose is to promote.

Sometimes you can take a picture in such a way that a person's identity is not apparent. Journalist Sherman Grant says he does this whenever possible and when it is not, he insists on a release.

If, however, you have good travel pictures, with recognizable people in them, for which you have no releases, look for markets that don't require them. (Usually that information is included in the *Writer's Market* or *Photographer's Market* listing.) A Sunday supplement editor told me once that he never bothers with releases, except for the cover. "I've never had any trouble," he said. "Or at least, only once." It seems he ran some freelance photographs of the Hell's Angels on the beach at Santa Cruz; one of them showed a Hell's Angel eating a popsicle. Monday morning the cyclist—and his attorney—were in the publisher's office, protesting that the picture destroyed his image, that the photographer had had no right to take it nor the editor to publish it.

The photographer *did* have the right to take the picture, and the editor *did* have the right to publish it, because it was taken in a public place. The courts have held that it is not an invasion of privacy to take pictures in a public place, since the photographer is a stand-in for the public—photographing something any member of the public could see if he happened to be there at the time. If, however, you go to somebody's house under false pretenses and with a hidden camera take pictures of him eating leopard's paw soup with snail darter dumplings— that's an invasion of privacy. He'll probably sue you and he'll probably win.

The courts have also ruled that the subject cannot recover damages from the photographer or the publication for taking and using his picture without permission if the picture was newsworthy and was published in the spirit of communicating the news, or if the person is a public personality, who has thus renounced the right to privacy.

Suppose, for instance, you're the survivor of a plane crash. You take pictures of the dead and injured, and the picture is published in the local newspaper and in a weekly news magazine. That's all right. But publishing that picture two years later, simply for its sensationalism, is all wrong, and the people pictured might well have grounds for court action. Publishing the picture on the anniversary of the crash or as part of an air safety campaign might be debatable. It would be wise to check with your attorney before submitting.

Surely you will want to restrict your photographs to those that don't violate privacy or good taste. But in case you want to protect yourself with a model release, here's an example of one:

> In consideration of value received, receipt whereof is acknowledged, I hereby give (*name of firm or publication*) the absolute right and permission to copyright and/or publish, and/or re-sell photographic portraits or pictures of me, or in which I may be included, in whole or in part, for art, advertising, trade, or any other lawful purpose whatsoever.
>
> I hereby waive any right that I may have to inspect and/or approve the finished product of the advertising copy that may be used in connection therewith, or the use to which it may be applied.
>
> I hereby release, discharge, and agree to save (*name of firm or publication*) from any liability by virtue of any blurring, distortion, alteration, optical illusion or use in composite form, whether intentional or otherwise, that may occur or be produced in the taking of said pictures, or in any processing tending toward the completion of the finished product.

Date   Model

Witness   Address

This is an example of the "ultimate" model release, and simpler wording might be equally satisfactory, and less intimidating, when you're trying to get a layman to sign. The main thing is to have the subject indicate he knows you're taking his picture, and he's willing for you to use it any way you want, without any (further) compensation to him. If the subject is a minor, be sure the release is signed by a parent.

Some countries prohibit the photographing of military installations, airports, harbors, or other strategic or sensitive areas, and it's not only good manners but solid common sense to observe the restrictions they outline.

Now let's talk about *your* rights, as a photographer. While we haven't room to discuss the subject of copyright, for either photography or writing, in any detail, keep in mind that the writer and the photographer *do* have rights, and should protect them. Putting the copyright symbol and the year next to your name on the photograph and on the caption sheet protects you to some extent. For absolute protection of your photographic rights, register your pictures with the copyright office in Washington, D.C. Since the ten-dollars-per-picture fee soon adds up, either register a number of photos as a collection, or group a number of them together and take a picture of the group, copyrighting that single photo. If your pictures are published in an uncopyrighted medium (e.g., most newspapers) before you register them with the copyright office, be sure the medium prints the copyright notice alongside the picture.

For up-to-date information on the copyright law, write:

Copyright Office
Library of Congress
Washington DC 20559

Request special circulars relating to photography, as well as a copy of the revised statutes. Ask to be put on their mailing list—you'll receive a steady stream of material about every nuance of copyright. Also, see *Law and the Writer* published by Writer's Digest Books.

Usually you'll sell "one-time rights," which means the publication is entitled to use the picture only once, and you may sell it again and again. Definitively state what you're offering: Stamp your picture or caption sheet with "One-time editorial use in one issue only." As a general rule, with black and whites you keep the negative, and the print may or may not be returned after use; with transparencies, if you send the original for one-time use, it's usually returned. If you sell "all rights" or "exclusive rights" you should be paid several times the amount of "one-time rights," since you're relinquishing the picture's future value to you.

Whether you sell your photographs on assignment or on a freelance basis, be sure you and the buyer are in complete agreement, in advance, as to the rights offered, the price to be paid, the expenses covered, and any other possible sources of misunderstanding. Generally, I've found media people fair and decent, but it's always wise to have the terms spelled out. Occasionally a photographer will complain that a newspaper has run a picture of his without paying him. Newspapers receive so many free publicity shots that you have to make it very clear that what you're sending is for sale, not a giveaway. In addition to indicating on the pictures and captions what rights you're offering, attach a note that says something like, "I'll call you in a few days to see if you'll be using the pictures or will be returning them, so I can submit them elsewhere."

Standard prices suggested for pictures used in various situations have been compiled by the Society of Photographers in Communications, 60 E. 42nd St., New York NY 10017. This organization publishes an annual *Guide to Business Practices in Photography*, with suggested minimum rates, and some publications do adhere to these rates; some even pay much more for top-quality work. However, many publications pay less. Check *Writer's Market* or *Photographer's Market* for current prices paid by individual photography buyers.

What Equipment Do You Need?

Practically all publications accept 35mm photography today, and most travel writer-photographers agree that the 35mm camera (especially the single-lens reflex, which permits you to see in the viewfinder the exact image you're taking) is the most satisfactory for their needs. With over a dozen major manufacturers, each producing several camera types, the range of sizes, prices, advantages, and disadvantages is too great to discuss here. (Philip N. Douglis considers the most popular brands in detail in the 1980 *Writer's Yearbook*.) The main thing to remember is: If you're buying a new camera, get as much information as you can before deciding, and select a model that's best for the kind of work you'll be doing—action shots, portraits, heavy-duty work, wilderness photography, whatever. Be sure to get a camera that feels comfortable to your hands and to your eyes. (To your glasses, too, if you wear them.)

Ideally, you'd travel with three identical camera bodies, plus three interchangeable lenses of different focal lengths, with black-and-white film in one camera, daylight color in another, and faster color in the third. Add to this an instant-processing camera for friend-making pictures to give away, and you'd be well prepared. But for most of us, all this would be too costly and too cumbersome, so you'll have to decide for yourself what's an acceptable compromise. If you're traveling alone, a 35mm camera with a zoom lens, plus a small Instamatic-type backup camera, might be all you can comfortably manage.

As you probably know, the "normal" 50mm or 55mm lens sees everything approximately the way the human eye does. To produce more interesting pictures you need a wide-angle lens (which lets you take a picture of the whole room after you can't back up any farther), and a telephoto lens (which moves you right up to your subject). The right-angle attachment for the telephoto is a handy accessory. A zoom lens offers many different focal lengths, and it's convenient to carry one lens instead of several. Sometimes, though, zoom lenses can be heavy, slow, expensive, and hard to focus, so select carefully.

If you're thinking of buying a camera or other equipment overseas, check out the exact model you want and jot down the hometown price, so you can see if you're really getting a bargain. Even if you are, remember, you'll be losing your chance to try out the new equipment at home and to shoot a couple of trial rolls of film. If you buy a new camera before you leave home, be sure you're thoroughly familiar with it before you start on your trip. New camera or old, check all the batteries and replace them if there's any doubt about their lifespan. A pencil eraser cleans batteries and terminals, or you can clean the batteries and battery compartment with a cotton swab dampened with alcohol. Clean the other parts of the camera with lens tissue and a camel's-hair brush.

If you buy a strobe to light your indoor shots and possibly provide additional light for outdoor pictures, be sure to get one large enough for your purposes, and be careful not to burn it out while recharging on uncongenial current. A flashgun and flashbulbs are a good backup, in case the strobe fails. However, in situations where flash is not permitted or you have to pay extra to use it, you can usually take a time exposure with available light.

A time exposure requires a firm resting place for the camera—a table, a balcony rail, a windowsill. If no steady surface is available, you'll wish you'd brought your tripod. But large, sturdy tripods are a nuisance to carry, and small ones are often rickety and unreliable. There are several substitutes such as: a shirt-pocket size platform with an elevating screw; a vise that threads into the camera and clamps to a firm surface; and a cloth bag filled with beans or Styrofoam that can be placed on a fencepost or in a tree crotch, and the camera then placed on it. My husband has even developed a method of taking time exposures without auxiliary equipment. He braces the camera on my shoulder, its strap around his neck. He adjusts and focuses, holding the camera with both hands. As he pulls the cable release we each take a deep breath and hold perfectly still until the exposure is completed. It took a little practice for us to perfect this maneuver. All these methods, of course, work best when you use the camera's automatic timer or a cable release to prevent jarring the shutter.

One of the most important pieces of photo equipment you'll carry is your notebook. You'll write down not only the opening and closing scene of each roll, and identification for any other sites you may have trouble remembering, but you'll also mark the exposure, time, light, distance, what the light meter said, what you actually did, and any other mechanical factors involved in taking the picture. That's the best way to learn what to do next time.

Whatever photographic gear you decide on, don't pack it in a fancy camera bag. That advertises the fact that you're carrying expensive equipment. Since at some point it'll probably be left in a car trunk or hotel room, vulnerable to theft, most professional photographers choose something as unlike a camera bag as possible—an airlines bag or a shabby tote with several zipper pockets—anything that holds gear safely and blends inconspicuously.

Keep careful records on whatever equipment and supplies you buy, and follow professional advice when it comes to deducting or depreciating it. Such photographic expenses as film, developing, darkroom supplies, reference books, photography-related phone calls, and materials for filing and sending pictures are, of course, deductible. More substantial equipment must usually be depreciated. For darkroom deductions or conventional expense deductions you need professional advice. Be sure to keep all records that show you're attempting to market photographs. (See next chapter for more on tax deductions.)

What about Film?

As we've said, take along enough. Color or black and white? That depends. While only a few publications, like *National Geographic*, reproduce nothing but color, many use color *and* black and white, and quite a few restrict their coverage to black and white. Most of the latter, however, still use color on the cover, and more and more newspaper travel sections are turning to color, at least for the lead story.

When working in color, *take slides, not prints.* Why? Because publications nearly always use slides, not prints, for color reproduction. Slides (call them transparencies when you're writing to an editor) cost about a third less, and can be duplicated or copied in color or black-and-white prints.

While color photographs are more desirable when the hues of the landscape, the clothing, the marketplace dominate the picture, black and white is best where contrast, texture, and tone are important, such as a flight of birds against a winter sky, or the silhouette of a snow-laden evergreen.

Try not to take too many different kinds of film. Keep each type in a different-color plastic bag, exposed film in a bag of still another color. Before going through airport security, either encase all film in protective lead foil or put your plastic bags on the counter and ask for inspection by hand.

Will most of your travel shots be indoors, at churches and museums, or outdoors, at horse races and regattas? Will more of them be at midnight or at noon? It's impossible to take along the ideal film for each situation, so you'll have to make compromises, sometimes by adding filters. Kodachrome 64 gives rich color to daylight slides, and Ektachrome 400 does well with less light. When there's barely any light, change the ASA to 800, then buy a special processing envelope, ESP, and the Ektachrome will be "push" processed, giving you the same amount of additional light as an extra f-stop on your camera.

For black-and-white pictures, Plus-X or Tri-X are good all-around films. In some cameras you can change film type in mid-roll, sometimes losing a frame or two, sometimes not. Use a changing bag, or follow the manufacturer's directions very carefully, and gently roll the film backward and, later, forward, on the spool. Whatever kind of film you use, you'll doubtless want thirty-six-exposure rolls for traveling. But take along a twenty-exposure to use the last day. Then shoot it and have it developed right away—don't leave it sitting in the camera, where it deteriorates if you don't take pictures for a while.

When you're buying film, be sure the date on the box gives you enough time to use it. Whether to have film processed while you're traveling, send it home, send it to a processing lab at home, or keep it with you throughout the trip, depends on climatic conditions, reliability of mail service, how long you'll be gone, and a number of other factors. Remember that the price of film bought overseas usually includes processing, which may be done at any US processing plant, but the mailer can be used only for the film with which it was packed.

Some travel writer-photographers are still following George Zimbel's recipe for "Cooked Film." Be sure you aren't one of them!

Take one roll of color film, place in camera, expose in bright summer sun. After exposure, place film and camera in automobile glove compartment, and heat for three hours. (If you don't have an automobile, try putting camera on blanket in sun, or on top shelf of hot closet.)

After film is thoroughly heated, take it to your film processor and have it developed. If you follow this recipe, your finished photographs should have an overall hue called *ghastly green*. Sometimes, if you are lucky, you may even get *brackish brown*, accompanied by disintegration of the image. This recipe is used by thousands of photographers and the results are guaranteed.

Can You Beat the Weather?

Need I say it? *Always* keep your camera and film out of the sun! In hot weather keep the film wrapped in foil or store it in an insulated bag. If mailing a roll of film, never deposit it in an outside mailbox.

Avoid shooting in the middle of the day in warm climates. You'll get better pictures before ten or after three. When changing film, if you don't have a changing bag, try to find a shady spot to avoid sunstreaks on the film. You can even use your own body to shade the changing operation.

If you'll be a long time in the tropics, you'll need to take special precautions against moisture. Buy silica gel. Read Kodak's booklets No. E30, *Storage and Care of Kodak Color Film*; No. C24, *Notes on Tropical Photography*; and No. AC17, *Photographing Your Trips Abroad*, for expert advice on handling photography under extreme weather conditions.

In cold weather moisture is a worry, too. Keep the camera under your coat as much as possible, pamper it with sportsmen's hand warmers, and tie a plastic garbage bag around it, after you've sucked all the air out of the bag. This way, whatever condensation forms after you bring the cold camera into a warm room will form on the outside of the bag, not the camera. Protect all your equipment from snow. Load and unload outdoors in the cold, though. The film gets tacky if loaded in a warm room and then taken out. Cold always makes film more brittle, so be especially careful in advancing or rewinding. If you're going to a below-zero climate have your camera professionally winterized first.

Rainy climates shouldn't deter you from picture taking. If you don't want to invest in an underwater camera or underwater housing for your camera, buy inexpensive special umbrellas and raincoats for the camera, as well as the photographer.

Sometimes the rainy-day, foggy-day, misty-day pictures are the best ones.

Where Do You Sell Your Photographs?

Mainly you'll sell the photographs you send to accompany your article. But sometimes the pictures will be so outstanding you'll want to think first in terms of selling *them*, accompanied by subsidiary written material. Naturally you'll check *Writer's Market* and *Photographer's Market* for likely targets.

Don't overlook the many publications that feature special photography showcases for their readers. *Friends* magazine, for instance, which is sent to Chevrolet owners and their families, runs such a showcase every month. Send your best pictures (either color or black and white) and they'll send you cash for each one they accept. They'll publish it when they have a group it fits into. They've used such themes as "Stop the Action" (hang gliders, a hot air balloon, air boats, and a motorcyclist), "Night Portraits" (Broadway in Los Angeles, the Canadian Parliament building, Chicago's skyline, and the fountain of a Florida hotel), "Chevy Owners Think Vacation" (Mount Rushmore, Lost Lake near Mount Hood, a dock at Nova Scotia, and the illuminated Capitol in Washington), and "Man Made Beauty" (a Japanese restaurant in Copenhagen, San Simeon's outdoor pool, St. Xavier Mission in Arizona, an arch in Guadalajara, and windmills in the Netherlands).

Many other company publications, trade journals, newspapers, travel magazines, and others have similar arrangements, or sponsor photography contests.

As you become more and more expert, a new marketing possibility opens up. Practically every magazine occasionally runs some kind of feature on how to take good travel pictures. You can be the one to sell them that feature.

Before deciding to undertake your own processing, consider carefully the cost of equipment and materials and the amount of time you'll be spending in the darkroom. At least wait to set up your darkroom until you're thoroughly familiar with *taking* pictures, so you won't be wondering whether any errors you see are from the photographing or the processing. Developing and printing color pictures requires significantly greater skill and a significantly greater outlay for darkroom equipment than developing and printing black and whites, so many photographers end up with a darkroom for black-and-white work, and send their color work out.

If you decide not to do your own darkroom work, do give some thought to patronizing a custom lab. Somewhat more expensive, but often worth it, the custom lab follows your processing specifications, and treats each picture individually. It can correct under- or overexposed film, right a crooked horizon, and perform other miracles.

Worried about the lab losing your exposed film? Make the first shot on each roll a sheet of paper with your name and address, so there's no way it can be misplaced. I have never done this, however, and of the thousands of rolls of film I've had processed, not a single one has ever gone astray. Do, though, be sure to write the roll number on your receipt or on the address label the processor will use. When you arrive home with a hundred-odd rolls of film, it's difficult to try to determine, "Is that Lake Michigan or Lake Superior?" And a year later, if you haven't labeled the pictures, you may wonder if it's Lake Tahoe.

How Do You Send Your Pictures?

How do you send your photographs to the editor? As safely but inexpensively as possible.

On black-and-whites, first have the film developed and a contact sheet or proof sheet made. This 8½x11 sheet shows positives the same size as your negatives. An editor will look at it with a magnifying glass and let you know which pictures he wants enlarged. This way, when you're paying for full-size prints, you know, at least, that somebody is going to buy them. If two or three of the pictures are irresistibly appealing, however, have them printed to send along with the contact sheet. Most publications specify 8x10 black and whites, although often they'll also consider 5x7s, which cost about a third less. Usually editors prefer glossy finish. Double-weight paper withstands more mailings, and presents itself more assertively. Be sure your prints are clean and don't have too many previous editorial crop marks in the margin.

Remember that photographic paper is a fragile item, the image upon it even more fragile. Do not write on the back of prints with sharp pens or pencils; do not fasten them with paper clips; protect them from sharp objects.

Usually you'll keep the negatives, and you'll notch the ones from which salable pictures have been printed, perhaps double-notching when it's sold and triple-notching when it's published. You'll handle them carefully and store them carefully. If you must send both negatives and prints, never send them in the same envelope, or even from the same mailbox on the same day.

With transparencies, the publication will indicate the smallest acceptable size, usually 35mm. If you've taken several pictures of the same scene, you won't need duplicates. If not, perhaps you'll want to send duplicates instead of originals, if it's on speculation. I usually send a large selection of duplicates and extra shots for the editor to choose from—similar to sending a proof sheet. However, I group them and caption them, and send only those that are of good quality and related to the text. Editors are not enamored of travel writers who send along boxes of uncaptioned, unsorted transparencies with a note saying "take what you want." Editors expect you to have some idea of what illustrations would be suitable.

On the other hand, they don't like to have the writer-photographer plan the layout for them, so I only gently suggest possible photo spreads. After the editor has made a decision about which pictures he wants, I send the originals for color separation.

Transparencies can be sent in several ways. If you use the box in which they came from the processor, check with the post office to see if it's large enough for their regulations. If not, put it in a larger box or big envelope. Transparencies can also be enclosed in plastic sleeves and taped to a sheet of typing paper, if there aren't too many of them. For a large number, especially on assignment, check with the editor about submitting them in a slide projector tray, all ready for viewing. I feel the best method of sending between twelve and a hundred transparencies is in a slotted acetate sheet, available at camera shops. They hold twenty transparencies safely and can be placed over a light table for scrutiny.

Clean your transparencies before sending them—buy a can of air to blow away the dust—and take every precaution to protect them from fingerprints, scratches, ink, glue, dust, etc. Never send glass-mounted slides—the risk of breakage is too great. If it's a very special transparency, have an internegative made. This is an expensive proposition, but it insures the possibility of making new transparencies (not duplicates) forever, with no impairment of color.

Send your photographs, either color or black-and-white, like a sandwich filling, between two layers of corrugated cardboard, which you can either buy at a stationery store or cut from grocery cartons. Or you can buy a regular photo mailer—a kraft envelope with two boards—at a camera shop. Ribs of one of the sheets of cardboard should be vertical, the other horizontal, for greatest protection. A few transparencies in plastic sleeves or black-and-white prints can be set into corners cut from old envelopes, attached to the cardboard. Secure the sandwich with rubber bands. For a large number of photographs, use a box or a fiberboard mailing case.

If you value your photographs—and you should—you'll take great care to pack and send them safely and speedily. Stamp the outer envelope *Photos—Do Not Bend*, and discuss with your postman the place he will leave returned envelopes, so he won't try to squeeze them into the mail slot. You will, of course, include an SASE with your photographs. You can send the photographs parcel post or with a manuscript at the special fourth-class rate. I wouldn't recommend it, however. For best results, send both manuscript and illustrations first class. If there's need for special speed, consider special delivery or express mail or one of the alternatives to the Postal Service. When sending negatives or original transparencies be sure to register, certify, or insure them, preferably with return receipt requested.

When sending photographs overseas, mark them *Press Photos: No Value.* Otherwise, your editor at the other end will have to pay duty on them—and he may not wish to. (If he refuses, the pictures will be returned to you by surface mail, which takes months.) Sometimes, when air mailing overseas, it's cheaper to separate the manuscript from the photographs. Always inquire about up-to-the-minute mailing rates and regulations.

What Goes in the Captions?

It is not enough to send a picture to an editor—that picture has to be carefully captioned. (You may sometimes hear it called a "legend" or a "cutline.")

The most important part of the caption is your name and address, which should be on every picture you send, whether it's your own or bought or borrowed from someone else. The credit line—the name of the person to be credited for taking the picture—should be included in each caption, too. For transparencies, the easiest way to do this is to write the name on some small stickers and affix one to each cardboard frame. Write a number on the frame also. This can be your regular file number, or a special sequence for this submission only. In either case, each number corresponds to one on the accompanying caption sheet, also identified by your name and address, which tells what is in each picture.

For black and whites, there are several ways of identifying with captions, but your name and address should be on the back of each picture, written very, very gently in light-colored felt pen or rubber-stamped or stickered. The prints can be numbered, with the captions appearing on an accompanying sheet, as with transparencies, or the caption can be attached to the print itself. There are three schools of thought about how to attach them. Some photographers like to type the caption on a small piece of thin paper and rubber-cement or tape it to the back of the picture itself. Both other methods involve typing the caption on a full-size sheet of paper and attaching it so it folds over the print, thus protecting the front of it. Some photographers like the type facing the image, readable when pulled down, while others prefer the type facing out, immediately readable. Either way, put your name on the caption sheet, as well as on the picture. Any of these methods is acceptable unless an editor expresses a preference.

It's also important to identify any people recognizable in your picture. Of course, you will have taken down their names, *spelled correctly*, at the time of the photographing, and this identification must be included, as well as the name of the place where the picture was taken.

What *else* should you say in the caption? The first thing to do is study the captions in the publication you're dealing with. Do they use bare-bones identification, or is the caption a direct quotation from the text? Do they introduce subject matter that is not covered in the text, or do they use mere labels? Do they include lengthy chunks of information, or is the photograph integrated into the text in such a manner that it has no caption at all? In some cases you merely need to provide the reporter's who, what, when, where, why, and how to identify the picture.

Some publications, on the other hand, prefer rather literary captions with supplementary material. For such captions, don't say, "These are sheep." Instead, pick something that is not obvious to the observer and is not covered in the text. Something like:

A flock of fat-tailed sheep, especially prized in the Middle East, graze on the slopes of Mount Atzmon, near the northern Israeli village of Tarshiha. The fat around the sheep's tails is used in baking special delicacies. The tail can weigh as much as thirty to thirty-five pounds; the shepherd must attach a special cart to the sheep's body to support the tail, which would otherwise impede the animal's mobility so severely that it couldn't graze.

It needn't be a literary masterpiece, but give the editor all the information he might possibly need. If you think of an especially charming line, send it along. But send the Five Ws information, too—in case the editor wants it.

How Do You Get Pictures, if You Don't Have Any?

If you don't have pictures to illustrate the travel article you're writing, don't give up—use somebody else's. There are hundreds of sources of travel photographs. Some will supply them at no charge; with others there may be a small fee for printing the pictures, and possibly an additional fee for reproduction. When the photograph is reproduced for an educational purpose, the reproduction fee is often reduced or waived. Promise the source that you'll ask for photo credit, which is about all you can promise.

These few pages only touch the tip of the iceberg as far as photo sources go. They include sample suggestions, but you'll find additional listings in *Photographer's Market*, *Writer's Market*, and *The Writer's Resource Guide*, all published by Writer's Digest Books, 9933 Alliance Rd., Cincinnati OH 45242; *Photography Marketplace*, *Stock Photo and Assignment Source Book*, *Literary Market Place*, all published by R.R. Bowker, 1180 Avenue of the Americas, New York NY 10036; *Picture Sources*, published by Special Libraries Association, 235 Park Ave. South, New York NY 10003; *Directory of Professional Photography*, published by Professional Photographers of America, 1090 Executive Way, Des Plaines IL 60018; and *Guide to the Special Collections of Prints and Photographs in the Library of Congress, Image of America, Early Photographs, Pictorial America*, all available from Superintendent of Documents, US Government Printing Office, Washington, DC 20540.

One writer, working on an article advising travelers not to forget their medical kits, garnered six outstanding photographs from six different pharmaceutical houses; another, writing about a visit to Stockholm when it rained every day, received a dozen sunny-day pictures from the Scandinavian tourist office; still another writer, preparing a nostalgic travel piece on passenger ships, was able to use three photos from the San Francisco Maritime Museum.

Here are some hints for finding what's where:

The US Government. The National Archives, Still Picture Branch, and the Library of Congress, Prints and Photographs Division, house vast collections of pictures, with entries from Mathew Brady's Civil War coverage to the present. Catalogs of these collections can be obtained from the Government Printing Office; permission to use pictures is granted for a small print fee.

The United States Armed Forces has a huge collection of free prints—ask local public information officers or write the Office of Information at the Pentagon. All government departments have photo libraries. These are just a few of the agencies housing large numbers of usable pictures: the US Forest Service, the National Parks Service, the US Fish and Wildlife Service, the US Children's Bureau, the Center for Atmospheric Research.

Foreign sources. The United Nations, as well as foreign government bureaus, has an extensive file of photographs. Travel agencies, hotels, and sight-seeing attractions, as well as airlines and railroads, are glad to have you use their pictures.

Tourist bureaus never charge for photographs—they *want* you to call attention to their attractions—so you're likely to get good results if you ask them for pictures.

State and city archives. State historical archives, charitable organizations, public libraries, museums, zoos, and church headquarters often have fine collections of photographs. They'll sell you a print for a small sum. Local chambers of commerce are good sources, too.

A random sampling includes the American Friends Service Committee, the Bancroft Library at the University of California, Chicago's Field Museum of Natural History, the National Recreation Association, the Red Cross, the Southern California Visitors Bureau, and Philadelphia's Office of the City Representative.

Commercial archives. The Bettman Archive, Brown Brothers, and Culver Pictures, all in New York City, have huge photo collections, with subject indexes available. You can buy practically anything from one of them.

News sources. Sources for news pictures, both historical and current, include:

United Press International
Commercial Library Division
220 E. 42nd St.
New York NY 10017

Wide World Photos
Associated Press Pictures
50 Rockefeller Plaza
New York NY 10020

The New York Times
229 W. 43rd St.
New York NY 10018

Also, check your local newspaper morgue, which may have pictures for sale.

Industry. The Corning Museum of Glass, in Corning, New York, has the most comprehensive photo library in the world on the subject of glass. In New York City, AT&T lists, in a free catalog, pictures that show aspects of telephonic communication. Shell Oil can supply photographs of camping, fishing, vacations, and outdoor recreation. Westinghouse Electric in Pittsburgh has a photo library related to science and industry, and Wells Fargo Bank in San Franciso offers illustrations for many areas of the Pacific Coast.

If any of these sources are near to you, it's best, of course, to visit in person and inspect the collection. Call first for an appointment. If you have to inquire by mail, allow plenty of time. Identify what you want as specifically as you can, and ask for a photocopy of the picture if in doubt.

Keep in mind several other sources of photographs, too. If your subject appears in a recent *Reader's Guide to Periodical Literature* or other magazine directory, see if the listing says "il.," indicating illustrations. If so, try either the magazine itself or the photographer for outtakes—pictures taken at the same time which weren't used. Newspapers and book publishers are often sources for outtakes, also.

Public relations agencies and PR representatives for practically all organizations are always ready to help you with pictures, and a note in Betty Yarmon's *Party Line* (Chapter 2) is sure to bring results.

Be selective, though. *Free* or *cheap* isn't necessarily *good.* When choosing photographs to accompany your travel articles, apply the same standards of selection as you would to your own work.

Other possible sources of illustrations are picture-taking friends, if you can manage to neither sever the friendly relationship nor settle for artistic duds. But if you have a friend who takes good travel pictures, you may find exactly what you need—and start your friend off on a new career.

If the story is a local one, where the newspaper sends a photographer, see if you can arrange with him for extra prints. Consider, also, the possibility of having a high school or college photography student work with you on local stories. Clarify the financial arrangements in advance, and hand him a shooting script.

The most expensive way to find photographs, but still a satisfactory one in certain situations, is through photo agencies. Some agencies deal with clients (you) and photographers (maybe you some other time) on an assignment basis; you tell them what you want and they find somebody to get it for you—at a price. Other agencies keep huge files of stock photos, paying the photographer when the picture is sold. Tell them what you want and they'll try to find the picture for you in their stock. Some of them have catalogs, and there are various "on approval" arrangements. There are hundreds of photo agencies, some specializing in black and white, some in color, some oriented to special subject matter or certain types of pictures, others more general. Study their listings in *Photographer's Market*, if you think this might be the answer to your present needs.

The most satisfactory solution, of course, is to learn to take your own photographs—to learn to say with pictures, as well as with words, exactly what you have in mind. But if this isn't possible, don't give up— you can still accompany your article with photographs provided by others.

Photography is increasingly important to the travel writer, so don't forget the vitality of visualization. Explore the medium of photography. Experiment. Experience. Enrich your travels and your life.

Rancho de Taos church, New Mexico

16

Freebies and Tax Deductions—Yes or No?

hen people hear I'm a travel writer, they always ask two questions. The first is, "How about the freebies? You say freelance travel writers get to see the interesting and the offbeat. Do they get to see it free?"

Then comes the second question—"How about your income tax? Can you take all those trips as tax deductions?" The only possible answer to both questions is, "It depends." Circumstances vary from trip to trip, from year to year, from day to day. Yes, being a travel writer generates some trip advantages and some tax advantages. No, it doesn't create a payless paradise of pure pleasure.

With freebies, it depends on *who* is offering *what* and *why*, as well as *where* and *when*. And, most of all, it depends on *how obligated* you become.

As your name gets known in travel circles, offers of hospitality may come your way—from the Christmas cocktail party to the all-expense world tour. We all know, though, that hospitality often carries at least an implied obligation. Since my opinion is not for sale, I never want to feel committed to praise something that might turn out to be unpraiseworthy.

We've spoken before of the travel writer's great responsibility—how readers count on finding a destination as you describe it. Sometimes readers pay out thousands of dollars and weeks of time to take a trip on your say-so. Sometimes it's the adventure of a lifetime for them—a honeymoon, a retirement celebration, a return to the roots of their ancestors, or a place they've always longed to see. Are you going to advise Hotel A instead of Hotel B because you sincerely believe A is in a

Los Angeles City Hall by night

more convenient location, gives faster service, has more cheerful employees, and provides a better value for the money? Or are you going to advise A because the manager invited you to spend a weekend as his guest? If the weekend was super, was it because your registration card was marked "VIP," or is Hotel A a regular provider of super weekends? It's your duty to find that out. And it's your duty to make it clear that you, as a person of integrity, do not wish to be obligated for the hospitality you accept.

Usually when you're invited on some kind of press junket there's no mention of the story you might write when you return. But everybody knows what you're there for. Your hosts want you to have a good time, and of course they want you to report favorably on their facilities. However, more and more travel writers are speaking out candidly, regardless of who picks up the tab for the trip.

Bruce Lee, for instance, begins a story this way for the Palo Alto *Times* and the Redwood City *Tribune*, of which he is city editor:

> . . . England . . . is at its loveliest in the spring. Flowers bloom in window boxes and in London's parks, and the grass is green in the countryside. And if this is England at its best, I'd hate to see it at its worst.

He writes about British Airways inaugurating daily nonstop service, San Francisco to London, and inviting a dozen journalists as guests. He goes on to say that the first month found planes less than half full, then adds, tongue in cheek, "Business must be booming this month. Two prospective travelers . . . tried unsuccessfully for two days to call BA on its toll-free number."

He continues disparaging his hosts and their country, detailing Britain's "inflated prices" on hotels, gasoline, restaurant meals, and even June cherries at $5.40 a pound. He calls crossing a London street "an adventure" since "the American pedestrian invariably looks the wrong way for approaching traffic." Although more charitable toward the hospitality of the English countryside, he concludes that "London can be fun if you don't mind crowds, high prices, usually poor weather, and don't tire easily."

Other well-traveled writers second the right to criticize a gift trip. A former president of the Society of American Travel Writers insists that acceptance of a free flight doesn't mean the writer is being "bought." "The airlines do not try to buy favorable publicity," he says. "They simply want to expose their services and their destinations to writers' eyes."

Sponsored trips and press junkets can be rewarding for the travel writer in many ways. You not only get to see the most interesting facets of wherever it is you're junketing, as well as being wined and dined to the nth degree, but you meet other travel writers, and the shop talk's always valuable.

Freebies of various kinds can put you behind the scenes. Usually plane fare is the hardest complimentary segment to secure. As Willard W. Marsh, Pan Am's Director of Public Communications, explains, Civil Aeronautics Board and International Air Transport Association regulations prohibit free transportation in exchange for publicity services, and media people can be invited only when the airline inaugurates a new service, adds a new destination, or introduces a new type of equipment. "The only other way," says Marsh, "is when the writer has a specific invitation from a country's government tourist organization. Then we sometimes provide the air trip." He admits that invitations of this type are hard to come by, and usually involve a written commitment from a media editor assigning the writer to a story on that destination.

Sometimes if you buy your own plane ticket, other parts of your trip will be hosted or sold to you at discounted prices. It depends. One of my own favorite types of hospitality is when somebody invites me to be a guest *after* I've written enthusiastically about a place I've paid to get to and simply loved. Then I already know what it's like and I'm sure I'll enjoy it. The public-relations people for the chamber of commerce, hotel, attraction, or whatever already know the way I write, and apparently like it. But if I encounter something unpraiseworthy on the second trip, I don't hesitate to point it out to my readers.

Many jobs related to travel writing, such as teaching resort writing classes or editing a resort newspaper, are not exactly freebies, since you're expected to work in payment for your vacation, but they provide interesting interludes in a travel writer's life. Port lecturers, enrichment lecturers, or tour leaders work hard, but sometimes find their jobs seem more like play than work. At home or abroad, there are more travel-writing-related positions than you may think.

Because my husband and I often collaborate in writing, photographing, and lecturing, we often accept—or decline—freebies together. Sometimes we've regretted accepting hospitality, because the thing our hosts wanted us to do was less interesting than what we had planned.

In one place, which I'm purposely leaving vague, we were invited to tour a cultural center, watch the entertainment, then stay for dinner and the evening show. It was a three-hour drive from our hotel. Since the invitation said noon, I thought it began with lunch. My mistake. But there was no mistake about it being noon. The midday sun fried us during the two hours we sat on bleachers in the open, watching some worse than mediocre folk dancing.

We spent another two hours listening to the church that owns the cultural center patting itself on the back. Everyone assured us that the dinner would be lovely and the evening show outstanding, but we never stayed to find out. When we left at four, mumbling hurriedly invented excuses, handing back to the PR people some forty dollars worth of unused tickets, we were hungry, thirsty, hot, tired, bored, and disgusted. Mainly I was disgusted with myself for not finding out more about the program in advance. If the dinner and the evening show were the big thing, why didn't we spend the morning and early after-noon in beachfront research, departing for the cultural center around three? We didn't because our hosts insisted on showing us *everything*.

Sometimes it wasn't the host's fault that we wasted our time. For in-stance, a famous US resort, where the hotels, restaurants, and sightsee-ing attractions all belong to a tourist organization, invited us to visit. Unfortunately, the only time we could work it in was the two days that the officers of the association were out of town, at a national tourism meeting. They assigned their "best guide" to take us around in her car and show us everything. However, when the "best guide" came to pick us up, she said her car wasn't working well, and she would sit in the back seat of our car and direct us. For some reason, perhaps because she was accustomed to driving herself or guiding on a bus, she kept getting us lost, and we drove up and down, back and forth, over the bumpiest back roads imaginable. We saw nothing very interesting, and most of what we heard was the story of her life, also not very inter-esting.

All the sight-seeing attractions we'd read about and asked to see were, it seemed, either "closed for repairs," "closed this day every week," "too far away," or "not worth the trouble"—or else we got lost looking for them or arrived after they had closed.

Another time, the director of tourism of a large foreign city with whom we had corresponded was moving his office the week we were in his city. Harried and hassled, he told his secretary, still at the old office, to "take good care of us." She asked if we wanted to browse through the photo files and see if there was anything we could use. The "files" were a dozen cardboard cartons, stacked for the movers in ran-dom order—months of "browsing." We explained that we wanted to go sight-seeing and take our own pictures, and here was this letter the director had written saying he would provide a car, driver, and guide for us. Somehow the car, the driver, and the guide never materialized. We paid for our own sight-seeing and took our own pictures.

You soon learn to regard freebies in the same light as entertainment you're paying for. Ask yourself, "Is this going to be worth the time I'll have to spend on it?" Sometimes it isn't.

We were in Cairo, for instance, with an alumni group tour for which we'd paid full price. We'd been told before leaving California that an international airline would take care of our transportation to complete an assignment at our next destination. The airline's Cairo representa-tive would firm up the plans. Unfortunately, the appointment with the Cairo representative was at the time our group was scheduled to see the Papyrus Museum, one of the most interesting sight-seeing oppor-tunities in Egypt.

But our sacrifice of the museum visit was useless. The representa-tive explained that during the weeks since we'd left California the air-line had decided to discontinue its service between Cairo and our next destination, and the last plane had flown there yesterday.

We have several travel writing friends who've also had free trans-

portation arrangements fall apart at the last minute, but whose com-
mitments necessitated continuing the trip anyway—at full fare. Other
friends have told us how they've missed the concert or the ball game
because their well-meaning hosts took a wrong freeway turn or misun-
derstood the starting time, which reminded us of the time our host
drove us on a three-hour trip to the winery, only to arrive after the tast-
ing was over and the winery was closed.

We've discovered that it never pays to adjust your plans in hopes of
securing something for nothing. As one experienced travel writer says,
"Nothing is ever *really* free."

City guidebook writer Martin Fischhoff feels differently, however.
He says bluntly that he lives on free meals. He defends this practice by
assuming there's no way the restaurant can change its menu or do anything unusual to impress the guidebook or travel writer, even after he
has identified himself. Therefore, according to Fischhoff, the reviewer's
er's critical judgment cannot be impaired. He has found free meals
easy to come by—except for one restaurant where the manager told
him frankly that he had masqueraded as a guidebook writer for a year
in New York to feed himself.

Tom Gannon, another tour-book author, takes a contrary view,
pointing out that the writer's function is to encounter the travel experience exactly as a reader would, without preferential treatment of any
kind. He feels that the acceptance of free meals makes a difference. It is
an untypical, and therefore unreliable, experience.

My own philosophy follows a line somewhere between these two. I
feel it absolutely essential for the travel writer to keep in mind, "For
whom am I working?" The freelance writer's obligation is to the reader. And while it is possible to do a terrific public-relations job of glor-
ifying a travel attraction, and also possible to perform an excellent
journalism job of evaluating it from the reader's viewpoint, you can
never do both jobs on the same story at the same time. Presumably,
even your public-relations job would be based on truth, but it would
concentrate on presenting the most attractive side of your client's
business. As a journalist, you compare this client against that client
(mentally, at least) to give your reader the best possible advice. You are
always representing *somebody*, and you must be clear yourself, and
clarify for your readers, which *somebody* you represent on a particular
story.

While the freelance travel writer has some responsibility to the attraction—to not, for instance, get off a careless and undeserved witti-
cism about a restaurant serving barbecued horsemeat or sauteed kitten
that harms the restaurant's business—his real responsibility is to his
reader.

Such publications as the *New York Times* travel section feel so
strongly that the travel writer cannot serve several masters at the same
time that they warn potential contributors:

Our authors must be personally familiar with their subjects.

More important, they must be entirely free to praise or criticize. Under no circumstances will we publish an article that grows out of a trip paid for by airlines, hotels, or any other organizations with an interest, direct or indirect, in the subject being written about.

To protect your reader, never let yourself, as a communicator, be used. In sensitive countries we've sometimes had the feeling that our popularity as guests was due to our host government's desire to present a favorable image to the North American public. If you mix politics with travel writing, listen carefully to all sides, then evaluate the facts; but don't become a mouthpiece for any self-serving faction.

Most national and international writers' organizations espouse specific rules and guidelines about freebies. For example, the Society of American Travel Writers, a professional association of writers, photographers, editors, broadcasters, and public relations representatives, feels that its purpose is to serve the traveling public by providing "complete, accurate, and interesting information on travel destinations, facilities, and services." The Society believes that "travel is a bridge between peoples," and its earnest desire is "to make and keep travel a quality experience for everyone."

Concerned with possible abuses, the Society "supports the limited and intelligent use of assistance from government travel departments, carriers, and others involved in the travel field. Reduced fares and trade discounts should be approved for bonafide travel writers to make such travel practical." The Society capitalizes the following guideline for its members:

Free or reduced-rate transportation and other travel expenses must be offered and accepted only with the mutual understanding that reportorial research is involved and any resultant story will be reported with the same standards of journalistic accuracy as that of comparable reportage and criticism in theater, business and finance, music, sports, and other news sections that provide the public with helpful information.

P.E.N., an international association of poets, playwrights, essayists, editors, and novelists, stresses the need for freedom of expression throughout the world, but points out that:

. . . since freedom implies voluntary restraint, members pledge themselves to oppose such evils of a free press as mendacious publication, deliberate falsehood, and distortion of facts for political and personal ends.

The Outdoor Writers Association of America is especially concerned about members accepting courtesy discounts on manufactured goods, and indicates that while discounts are common, ethical conduct precludes any stipulation that a favorable review be given in return.

The Society of Professional Journalists, Sigma Delta Chi, spells out its code of ethics still more firmly:

> Journalists must be free of obligation to any interest other than the public's right to know the truth.

All of these professional organizations, as well as many others, are listed in *Writer's Market*, where you can find out about their goals and requirements for membership. As you become more professional in your writing and selling, you will probably want to join an appropriate writers' organization. Membership can be helpful, and you'll abide by the codes and guidelines of your organization.

Even more important, you'll want to abide by *your own* code of ethics. Surely you have enough common sense to know the difference between right and wrong, and enough gumption to proceed accordingly. Accept free hospitality? Perhaps—if you're positive your host isn't attaching any strings to it, and you're convinced that you, yourself, would never be influenced to favor the most hospitable attractions in the travel industry.

Hosted trips and press junkets sometimes offer valuable behind-the-scenes experiences. That's the best part—the opportunity to see nontourist places and meet nontourist people. I often enjoy the hospitality I accept. But I've learned to accept *only* if the arrangements fit in with my own writing plans and I'm satisfied that the invitation is not a compromising one.

Tax Deductions

You can see that the answer to questions about what the travel writer enjoys free is, "It depends."

That's also the answer to the often-asked questions about what kinds of tax deductions the travel writer can take.

The best advice I can give you is—Go to an expert and follow *his* advice. Have him set up your books properly in the first place, then follow through according to the plan.

An East Coast tax attorney says a travel writer can save himself a lot of money and aggravation at examination time if he keeps an accurate diary of expenditures, accompanied by receipts, with a description of the purpose for which the expenditure was made, speedometer readings before and after auto trips, and other pertinent information.

"But most of those who come to me have *already* made a mess," he laments. "Please remind your readers that the IRS requires a receipt for any deducted expense over twenty-five dollars. In order to tie down travel and entertainment deductions, the taxpayer must substantiate the amount, the time and place, the business purpose, and the business relationship of any person or persons being entertained. So tell travel writers to keep good expense records."

While the IRS will permit you to deduct all reasonable costs, backed up by receipted bills, for a trip you clearly took to obtain a story, provided you sold the story and the sale price was greater than the expenses involved, most tax problems don't fit into such neat categories.

Can you take off the price of the trip if you've written the story but haven't sold it yet?

Can you take off any part of a four-thousand dollar, twenty-two-day trip during which you did research for travel writing, and now you've sold a fifty-dollar story that took you two hours of those twenty-two days to research?

What about the story you've just sold from the trip you took three years ago?

Can both spouses deduct an eight-thousand-dollar trip because one of them writes the story and the other takes the photos for the package that produces five hundred dollars in income?

Can both spouses take off the trip if one writes and photographs and the other provides secretarial assistance? Or can the one who is doing the writing deduct normal secretarial expenses paid to the other one, and the secretary then deduct the trip as a necessary expense to earn the secretarial money?

Can you take off food expenses on a weekend camping trip that results in a sale, even though you would have eaten that same food at home? How about restaurant meals? Do you deduct or depreciate your new typewriter? Your filing cabinet? Your telephoto lens? Your postal scale?

Can you take off on your income tax for all the books you buy, regardless of subject? All your film and developing costs? How about your car? A room in your house? Somebody to clean that room? Your basic telephone bill? Membership in writers' organizations? Membership in travel organizations? Membership in the country club, where you meet a lot of people in the travel industry?

These are some of the questions you'll have to ask your expert.

A senior tax consultant for one of the Big Eight accounting firms says that deductibility of travel and entertainment expenses requires that the expenditure be ordinary and necessary in the operation of the taxpayer's business and directly related to or associated with the business, as well as properly documented. He explains that in order to satisfy the "directly related to" test, the taxpayer must expect to derive income or some other specific business benefit (other than goodwill) and demonstrate that active conduct of business was the primary purpose of the activity.

While indicating that expenditures for entertainment at theaters, nightclubs, or sporting events generally will not satisfy the "directly related to" test (unless the writer specializes in reviewing theater, nightclubs, or sports), he admonishes travel writers to remember that "it is extremely difficult to justify a business discussion taking place in a distracting surrounding such as a nightclub." However, "the taxpayer may still be able to claim a deduction if he can prove the event was associated with his business, since business-related activity took place immediately before or after the nightclub rendezvous."

This talk of tax deductions may trigger other questions in your mind. Now perhaps you're wondering whether you can take a deduction for travel expenses only if *all* your income is derived from travel writing. Or *most of it*, at least. Can you show a tax *loss* from your travel writing business?

A CPA explains that if an activity is not engaged in for a profit, no income tax deduction attributable to the activity will be allowed. "An activity is presumed to be entered into for a profit if profits result in two out of five years," he says. "If this requirement is not satisfied, then the activity will be considered a hobby. In that case, losses will only be deductible to the extent of the income."

In other words, if you make a million dollars in a real-estate transaction, you can't reduce your tax liability by calling yourself a travel writer and deducting your expenses from an around-the-world trip, if the trip itself doesn't result in travel writing profits. Or at least you probably can't do it unless your travel writing business shows a profit two years out of five.

Again, the wise freelancer keeps good records. I was appalled to discover students sending queries without retaining carbons, and to discover them discarding rejection slips. They were astonished to learn that this negative correspondence might have value. Whether you paper your living room walls or keep them in a file, query carbons and rejection slips may tip the scales in your favor when it comes to convincing IRS that you're trying to make travel writing a business, not a hobby.

So you can see how the answer to the second question, "How much of your travel can you deduct on your income tax?" is also, "It depends."

The variables are many. There are no easy answers to these questions of freebies and tax deductions. There are no foolproof guidelines, either. But careful thought, plus astute selection of a tax expert, will show you how you can, with honor, enjoy some of the fringe benefits of the travel writing profession.

17

Around the World or Around the Corner: Your Role as a Travel Writer

 hen Arnold Toynbee called creative use of leisure the "mainspring of civilization," he must have had travel writers in mind. As leisure time increases for people of every age and occupation, travel often becomes the principal leisure time activity, and you, the travel writer, often help determine the quality of this leisure. Will your readers rush to meet adventure, discovering the half-hidden peaks and uncharted beaches you told them existed? Will they hurry to experience the Penguin Parade, the Mardi Gras, the cog railroad ride, the Rhine cruise you promised would delight them? Will they linger longer at the ancient amphitheater, inspect the farthest picture gallery, wait patiently in the safari bus, because you suggested they might find more to see?

It's gratifying, isn't it, to enrich the lives of others as well as your own. It's frightening, too. This power carries with it an awesome responsibility. Whether you're digging in the library stacks or sharing a day in the life of an Ozark schoolboy, you'll be careful to interpret the facts with perceptiveness and integrity.

You'll be careful, too, to keep in close touch with what your audience wants to read.

I recently asked a large cross-section of people what kind of travel articles they liked to read. The group ranged in age from nineteen to ninety, male and female; varied in occupation, interests, educational level, and financial circumstances; and included frequent travelers, infrequent travelers, eager travelers, reluctant travelers, former travelers, and future travelers. Two major threads seemed to emerge:

1. People want advice, facts, knowledge of how to do it. "Guides for

Great Lakes beach scene

the green traveler like me," said one. "Realistic details and warnings about pitfalls," said another. "How to save money"; "The basics— where to stay and eat, what to see"; "A knowledgeable traveler who tells the bad as well as the good—no babbling on about gorgeous scenery when the mosquitoes are big as bumblebees!"

2. People want to hear about people. "I like stories that humanize the traveler and the people he meets"; "I want to know the things that are unique about a place and its people, and also the things that are the same as at home"; "Tell me about the offbeat, inexpensive trips that pay off in opportunities to meet the locals." Others preferred "a story that gives tantalizing tastes of many areas and the people who live there"; "stories about the people in faraway places—I like to know about them, even if I never get to see them," and "travel articles that make me feel as though I'm *there.*"

When we think about it, we realize that most of the travel articles we consider good focus on people: those who will be doing the traveling or the people they will see on their trip. Touring monuments is fine— as long as a human being is doing the touring.

By now you know that the travel article with plus value doesn't begin with rolling a sheet into the typewriter. It begins with the barest glimmer of an idea that you might some day be going to some place.

The preparations, we know, include seeking advance information from many sources and planning ahead for on-trip research, photography, sight-seeing—knowing what to take along and whether to accept special privileges. Your pre-trip market study helps you plan itineraries for your stories. Ahead-of-travel query letters not only sell your article before you write it, but also help you define what you want to achieve.

Keeping in mind "What will my reader want to know?" you'll observe, assimilate, and distill. You'll find that all aspects of your research reinforce one another. But don't worry if you want to write about a trip that you took before you'd read the suggestions in this book. These suggestions make it easier, but many of the things you've probably done anyway. Though you've omitted some of the steps, you can still write a travel article. And you should. But you'll have to work harder. Before your next trip, you'll begin at the beginning.

You'll discover that much of what we call "research" doesn't really *feel* like research. As you explore the ambiance of the place, traverse its hidden byways, and talk informally to local people, it may seem less like work than fun. (But remember to note accurately the travel details and record any possible income tax deductions.)

You'll begin your quest for plus value by reading what others have written. Is there a writer in the world who doesn't love to read? Years ago I felt guilty every time I read for an hour—until I heard a very successful writer say, "If you have eight hours a day for writing, spend four hours reading, and if you can only spare two hours a day for writing, spend one of those hours reading." Read for information, for style, for marketing knowledge, for pleasure. Read enough to get different opinions, so you'll be able to digest them, and then start off with a fresh approach of your own.

Even more important than reading is thinking. Discuss with yourself what insights you expect to bring home from the trip. Remember, your mission is more than counting cats in Zanzibar.

Prepare yourself for constant change. The travel writer soon finds that the most permanent aspect of travel is change. Prices soar, routes change, hotels open and close. There are detours to accommodate the building of newer, straighter, wider roads; and military barriers to accommodate the take-over by new political forces. There'll be new restrictions and new restraints.

Many places I've loved cannot be visited just now. But there's another, happier side to this situation. Of the six or seven passports I've had, the present one is the first without prohibitions. All the others prevented me from traveling to one country or another. I would mourn my exclusion from Hungary, only to have my next passport say nothing about Hungary, but restrict travel to Cuba. The fact that a US citizen can now go everywhere, at least as far as his passport is concerned, is a hopeful sign.

As technology breeds the kind of changes that may one day have us careening from New York to Los Angeles by underground commuter train in fifty-four minutes, the travel writer needs increasing amounts of discipline—*self*-discipline. As the world grows smaller, its attractions multiply. We're increasingly tempted by the cajoleries of travel: the lures of sun, sand, and surf; the enticements of music and dancing; the persuasions of the champagne-and-caviar circuit. How nice a travel writer's life could be—without the writing. As a journalism professor once told me, "There aren't many people out there who like to write, but the world is full of people who would like to have written." Travel writers who succeed do so because they remember what they're there for and aren't distracted by beguilements.

As is often the case in the arts, amateurs don't have the same status as those who have made the effort, withstood the temptations, and mastered the skills to become professionals. But even if you remain an amateur, cultivate the professional attitude. After all, the real journey is within.

Don't be like my neighbor who, after being housebound all winter with sniffles and sinuses and several small children, accompanied me on an errand. "Anything," she said, "to get out of the house!"

"You really should get out more," I told her. "How about a hobby?"

"Well—I signed up for an adult ed art class."

"Great!" I exclaimed, as we drove through spring-green hills punctuated with blossoming apricot trees. Near the ivy-covered dorms of a rural university, canoeing couples courted on a palm-fringed lake, fresh-faced first graders alighted from the yellow school bus, and storybook farm buildings dotted patchwork fields of newborn crops.

"Yes," she replied. "I bought the paint and the canvas and made myself a smock. But I can't seem to get started."

"Why? What's the matter?"

"I just can't think of anything to paint."

Yes, the real journey is within.

If you're moving toward realizing your potential as a travel writer, it's reassuring to know that great opportunity exists. Not only is travel an ever-growing industry, but so is writing. With about 65,000 periodicals published in English, 35,000 of them in the United States, and over 600,000 books published each year, nearly 50,000 in the United States, and with 85 percent of the material being nonfiction, your travel article has a very good chance of finding a home somewhere.

However, this is not a profession for the thin-skinned. Every time you address that query letter, every time you put your manuscript in its big brown envelope, you're putting *yourself* in the public stocks. Is it good enough? Will they like it? Did I tell it the best way it could be told? All these thoughts buzz around in your head. Your mood as you stick stamps on the return envelope may vary from inadequacy (they'll probably send it back right away!) to belligerence (this is clearly a waste of stamps—they'll never use this envelope, because they're sure to keep my story!).

Writing is a public profession. You reveal so much of yourself. You may be writing about somebody quite different in a setting far away, but there's always a great deal of *you* in the story. Your secrets, your mistakes are there for the world to see. This is not a profession for one who takes each rejection slip as an indication of total failure or as a personal insult. And it's not for one who quails at criticism or takes it out on others when the writing goes badly. I once heard another writer say, "I didn't consider myself a professional when I started getting paid for my writing. That came the first time I didn't cry over a rejection slip."

Nobody likes to see the postman pull from his bag the brown envelope that signals rejection. But even that can give a warm glow, as you learn to read between the lines that say, "Not quite good enough— maybe next time" or "Sorry, we have something similar on file. Try us again." There's always "again" and "next time," always the hope that if you keep plugging and do your best, sending it out to market after market on your itinerary, using your salesman's skills, your manuscript *will* find a home.

To avoid postpartum depression, when you send something off, be sure you're already at work on your *next* travel story.

Remember, a travel writer has no neon sign, no skyscraper, no inventory. His capital assets are what he has seen and heard, smelled, touched, learned, and loved. And while they might not provide collateral, nobody can steal them, tax them, or appropriate them in any way.

If you feel that, even with strict attention to business, your work compares unfavorably with the professional travel articles you read, don't be discouraged. Everybody has to start *someplace*. Study and learn as much as you can, attend writing classes, find a capable mentor to help you, and listen carefully to professional criticisms and suggestions. There is only one thing that's required—that you do your very best each time. Don't continually compare your efforts to someone else's (although that can have advantages in a valid learning situation), but measure yourself against yourself. Are you the best travel writer *you* can possibly be? Are you a better travel writer today than you were six months ago? Where will you be six months from now?

Stretching, I hope. At the second meeting of a small graduate class, I asked each student to hand me a note indicating whether the material being covered was too simple, too complex, or about right. Replies were evenly divided between "a little too complex" and "about right." But one young woman put it especially well. "I'm stretching!" she wrote. "But it feels wonderful!"

It does feel wonderful. Stretch to the best that's in you. *Reach* for your best, and beyond. Reach for the opportunity to write for higher quality markets, and to write higher quality material. Do your best and then do better. Remember, you can only take from an experience what you bring to it. It is absolutely impossible to write beautifully if you have nothing whatever to say.

As a good travel writer you'll find gratification in creating something that didn't exist before. You'll find satisfaction in knowing you have written something others will read. You'll find pride in noticing the improvement in your own work, and pleasure in the interesting ideas, interesting information, and interesting individuals you will encounter.

You may have to make some sacrifices to accomplish this—give up the cajoleries and the beguilements. But you'll never be bored, you'll never be lonely.

If this is what you want to do, and you have faith in yourself, you can do it. If you have a message you want to impart, and enthusiasms you want to convey, you can do it.

If you believe you can be a travel writer, you can be one.

Keep your reporter's notebook handy, and your tape recorder and camera, too. Put business cards in your pocket and big brown envelopes in your suitcase, and when the first charter trip leaves for the moon, you'll be ready.

The Twelve Most Popular Types of Travel Articles

These are the most popular types of travel articles. Their patterns interlock and overlap, and often more than one pattern is distinguishable in a published piece. But thinking in terms of one or another of these popular patterns provides a helpful framework when you're planning or looking for a story.

PERSONAL EXPERIENCE

The personal experience travel article is the one only *you* could write, describing some adventure you've hand, mundane or unique, usually from the first-person viewpoint, with you as the star. Although it would seem to be the easiest kind of travel article to write, a good personal experience story is difficult to do, because of the temptation to tell *all*.

Each of us, of course, feels that *any* happening *we* experience is spellbinding. So, confident that the rest of the world will be fascinated, we tell the reader more than he cares to know:

> Today Maggie and I got up and brushed our teeth. We called room service for our breakfast. The waiter was late bringing it. He said he was sorry. The orange juice was in a tiny glass—only half the size of the glass we get at home.
> We went downstairs in the elevator and waited for Nick, our guide.

The reader doesn't want a blow-by-blow account of *your* trip. What he wants is to see your trip through his eyes, enjoying the highlights and putting *himself* in the hero's role.

The old-fashioned devices of diary style and letter style were originally intended to make the reader fool as though he were looking through the keyhole, getting exciting insights into esoteric goings-on. But the goings-on most people report are neither esoteric nor exciting.

Far better than a blow-by-blow, day-by-day account of a trip is a highlighted account, showing some of the good, some of the bad, some of the commonplace, some of the unusual, in an order other than chronological.

One of the differences between a publishable personal experience piece and a "Me and Joe," which all editors say they *don't* want, is in the choice of details. A publishable piece includes many details, but they are all relevant, all connected to the main theme, all interesting. A "Me and Joe" is a personal experience story in which the details are profuse, but irrelevant and uninteresting to the reader.

Again, we must overcome the inclination to tell everything exactly the way it happened. One of my students wrote a charming story about her adventures as a guest at various Japanese inns. She couldn't sell it. Her shots were too scattered: there were too many names and places; too many hot baths and low-table meals; too many helpful, giggling maids at too many delightful inns. "But," she insisted, "that's the way it really *happened!*" I finally persuaded her to have all the anecdotes and experiences occur at one mythical inn with one composite maid, with the time-and-place framework holding the story together. She sold the revised piece immediately.

I never recommend the slightest deviation from the truth where the details are important. If the hotel charges $38.95, don't round it off to $40.00. If the service is terrible, don't dignify it as "mediocre." But where precise details are of no consequence, the travel writer must learn to use the fiction writer's techniques in moving the facts around to express the truth more clearly and more interestingly.

The fiction writer creates plot through a combination of personal experience and applied imagination. The travel writer creates plot largely from personal experience; but the *selection* of material used, its *arrangement*, the *order* in which it is presented, and the *emphasis* accorded each facet—*that's* what makes the story.

People often reveal more than they mean to in writing their travel experiences, and sometimes the personality they reveal is unattractive. The whiners complain, "Why wasn't I told it would turn cool," or "everybody's always trying to cheat me—the sight-seeing tour was interesting enough, but it wasn't worth the price." Their personal experience stories seem to be litanies of personal grievances. Everybody, it seems, is out to trick them, insult them, and lead them astray. By all means, tell it like it is. Warn readers to bring sweaters or eschew the sight-seeing tour. But don't *whine* about it.

Some personal experiences are *very* personal. For instance, there currently seems to be an epidemic of women-traveling-alone stories that are more a guide to the mind and personality of the traveler than to the geographic area covered. Sometimes the tour is interesting; sometimes not so very.

Don't be too grim when relating your experiences. The most mind-boggling catastrophe often seems humorous when the dust has settled. So try to inject some fun for your reader into dead ends and disasters. And don't tell too much. Stop when you come to the end. If you don't have a long story, tell a short one.

In all successful personal experience stories the main focus is not on the author but somewhere else.

Among the most successful personal experience stories are those that tell the reader how he, too, can savor this experience. In these stories the "you" is strongly implied and the "I" small—so the writer is never the star.

Pat Mellegers addresses a common problem in "Traveling With Kids: It Doesn't Have to Be a Hassle." Her newspaper story promises, "Parents can avoid . . . pitfalls with . . . creative planning." After explaining that her family of four, including two young children, took a ten-day, eight-state, 3,500 mile car trip and "came back still on good terms with one another," she describes some of the steps taken, implying that if you, the reader, are as clever as she is, your personal experience will have the same happy results.

Often it's this universality and familiarity that makes the personal experience worth writing. The experience was the author's, but it could be anybody's. The once-in-a-lifetime personal experience story, on the other hand, gives an enticing glimpse of faraway places and a taste of adventure that the armchair traveler can identify with in a roundabout way. The unique experience—mountain climbing in Nepal, sailing solo across the Atlantic, even being at the critical place at the critical time as a war explodes into reality—doesn't necessarily invite the audience to participate by following the writer's example. But when deftly done, this most fiction-like personal experience technique draws the reader into the story and keeps him breathlessly awaiting development.

One of the masters of the once-in-a-lifetime personal experience story is Thor Heyerdahl, whose lifetime has encompassed many.

As Heyerdahl sailed across the Pacific on the raft *Kon-Tiki*, he wrote:

> Sometimes . . . we went out in the rubber boat to look at ourselves by night. Coal-black seas towered up on all sides and a glittering myriad of tropical stars drew a faint reflection from plankton in the water. The world was simple—stars in the darkness. Whether it was 1947 B.C. or A.D. suddenly became of no significance. We lived, and that we felt with alert intensity. . . .Time and evolution somehow ceased to exist; all that was real and that mattered were the same today as they had always been and would always be.

Although Heyerdahl's *experiences* are unique, the *emotions* he depicts are universal. The strong, precise language puts the reader aboard the rubber boat or the pile of balsa logs.

When you read Heyerdahl, creating an exciting story from true personal experience seems compellingly possible, doesn't it? The plus value of his writing lies in his ability to *show*, so that one man's personal experience becomes an adventure for all of us.

Advice

Some of the most popular articles you can shape from personal experiences are those that offer advice. I have advised, both humorously and seriously, how to get the most mileage from your travel dollar and the most pleasure from your vacation, how to select a sight-seeing program and a traveling companion, and many other travel-related "how-tos." Most of the themes have sprung from those notebook entries headed "Things I've Done Wrong."

At the Mount Kenya Safari Club, for instance, when I offered my husband a taste of my fish appetizer, he said, "Just cut me a tiny corner."

I started to cut the square in half.

"No," he said sharply. "I *told* you—only a small corner."

I pushed the plate toward him. "Here—take what you want."

He shoved it back. "Just cut me a corner!"

I burst into tears.

Did you ever hear such a ridiculous quarrel? Back in our room, still seething in silence, I began to write an article. I thought of other spats we'd had while traveling, and of friends' arguments with spouses—in the Paris taxicab over who took too long in the bathroom and that's why we're late; in the New England rental car over who misread the map and that's why we're lost; in the Cairo airport over who wanted to buy that camel saddle in the first place and that's why we're paying all this overweight. What is it that makes ordinarily congenial couples so touchy when they travel, I wondered. The article answers that question and suggests various ways couples can foresee friction and either avoid it or cope with it constructively. At the end I explain about the eye infection, the jammed camera, the shortchanging, the springless safari bus, the lack of sleep, the paucity of game—it wasn't the fish appetizer, it was *everything!*

Often an unpleasant travel experience turns out to be not so unpleasant after all, once enough time has passed so you can laugh about the experience—and convert it into helpful advice for others.

Evelyn Preston did just that after a disastrous auto trip to Yosemite. She warns that mountain vacationers are often so enthralled by woods and waterfalls that they forget the possibility of being stranded with "a volcanic radiator, stripped gears, or fading brakes." Her own experience with brakes giving out as she careened to a stop at the valley junction, smoke streaming from the front wheels, points up the importance of having your car thoroughly checked before you start off.

A "Things I've Done Wrong" notebook is an invaluable source of ideas for advice articles. Be sure to log all the information that you'll need to write your article.

"Things I've Done Right" can expand into advice articles, too, so jot down the details for future use.

When you think in terms of advice articles, be sure to select a relevant theme, and then show the reader how that theme applies to him.

Some themes are repeated again and again. Money—the saving of it or the spending of it—is always popular. Even articles with themes not explicitly connected to dollars and cents advise readers to consider in advance the amount of vacation money they'll have to spend, or remind them that car trouble at a resort can lead to expensive extended reservations or a rental car to transport them home.

Implicit in most money articles is the thought that the reader not only wants to *save* money while traveling, he wants to *spend* the money he has to buy the things that mean most to him.

A travel advice article could take a hard look at the romantic prose of travel brochures or could deal with finding travel situations with the *best* of something—whether it's weather, food, accommodations, friendliness of the locals, nightclub acts, or ruins.

On a more downbeat note—but still much needed and extremely useful—are the many advice articles that concentrate on the reader's comfort and safety: the least tiring arrangements; the best ways to protect yourself from injury while traveling; the steps to take if you are injured or ill. Health advice runs the full gamut, from learning CPR to staying alert with in-car exercises to snacking on grow-as-you-go alfalfa sprouts.

You can help your readers prepare for their trips with wise words on the selection of luggage; guides to unraveling the mysteries of airfares; suggestions for the care of elderly relatives left behind. You can advise them on such post-trip matters as what to take off on their income tax and how to present an interesting slide show.

Travel advice can be general, or it can be directed to a special group: how retired couples can find quiet motel rooms; how to pack for a convention; how to stock a boat with a month's equipment and supplies; "Ideas for Easy Trailering"; "How to Care for Your Camera While Traveling"; "How to Protect Your Oil Pan in Baja."

Slant for your specific audience. The readers of *Mother Earth News* won't look for the same advice as the readers of *Modern Maturity*. "What to Do with the Children on the Rainiest Day of Your Vacation" won't appeal to the same audience as "Ordering Wine with Assurance at a Three-Star Restaurant."

Even when you're talking about money, it's necessary to know your readers; the words "expensive" and "inexpensive" are subject to a whole range of interpretation. Naturally, the travel advice article sometimes grades into the how-to-do-it or the self-help article, which is fine. What it should *not* become is a sermon. Take great care not to sound preachy to your readers.

Be gentle and tactful; never make your reader feel foolish for not already knowing what you're telling him.

Present your information in a friendly, straightforward manner, and talk *with* the reader, not *at* him. Make sure he understands that you, too, are stupid sometimes, and often share his shortcomings. On the other hand, don't make yourself seem like such a bungler that he loses confidence in your advice. A sort of "before and after" technique ("I used to do this wrong, because I didn't know any better, but since I learned the right way I want to share it with you") is best.

The responsibility of the advice-giver is tremendous. Remember, people are going to *act* on what you're telling them. That's why it's important to ask yourself whether your problem was a typical one, or a fluke. Will what you're advising work in the demographic group you're advising it for? It's always good to incorporate the experiences of others with your own. Quoting others gives your advice substance and credibility. Some subjects, such as income tax or health care, *demand* quotes from an expert. And if you, as a result of personal experiences, are yourself an expert, be sure to make it clear to the reader why you are qualified to give this advice.

I cannot emphasize enough the importance of updating your information before passing it along to others. One of my favorite travel tips used to be: Two people traveling together should occupy an aisle seat and a window seat, in hopes that, if the plane isn't completely full, nobody will sit between them. That's still good advice, except—most planes today have few three-abreast rows, most seats are preassigned, and few planes fly with empty seats. Another piece of outmoded advice: Check in early for best plane seat selection. Today, if seats are not preassigned the early arrivals in the discount section will be seated from back to front, leaving the choice forward seats to those who check in at the last minute. By the time you read this, the seating situation on airplanes may have undergone some revolutionary change that makes this whole paragraph obsolete. The travel writer must check and recheck to stay on top of the situation. The travel advice article can be tightly structured: "Ten Do's and Don't's for Winter Travel"; "The Pros and Cons of the Organized Cruise." Or it can employ a one-two-three format, often in the second person, where I, the writer, am telling you, the reader, to first visit your library, then your travel agent, then . . .

Although the theme of your travel advice article should be one that's of consuming interest to your readers, it need not be—it probably *cannot* be—a *new* theme. The same good ideas sell over and over again. "I was amazed," a librarian told me, "at not only selling a story of my first trip to Europe, but at the amount of favorable response it received. All I said were things like 'Wear comfortable shoes' and 'Take along a sweater'—things I thought everybody already knew."

Some advice is timeless.

Humor

The *travel* humor piece is usually forged from your own experiences, also. It amusingly relates something you've done or seen or heard or felt.

Ask any editor what he wants and he'll say more humor. Why then is humor so hard to sell? It's hard to sell because it's iffy—humorous *if* the editor thinks it's humorous. And often the editor doesn't know if what he thinks is humorous will be humorous to his readers. Because he doesn't trust his own judgment about what will make his readers laugh, he tends to decide conservatively.

Still, today's travel writer can sell amusing experiences, if he takes the trouble to analyze the ingredients of a good travel humor piece. He may find himself writing the kind of humor that leaves the reader with a wry smile rather than a belly laugh .

That wry smile comes forth in response to tales of human foibles, where the reader can easily identify with the blundering traveler who's forever making wrong moves. Usually the joke's on you, the writer. (One travel writer, however, says she stopped writing humor—she got tired of making herself out to be such a jerk all the time.)

Patricia Brooks is a "jerk" we feel a chuckle of sympathy for, especially when she talks about some of the "bargains" she's bought while traveling. She purchased a pair of huge, low-fired clay pots in Haiti for four dollars apiece. First, each pot required a custom-built mahogany case to insure its safe shipment; then there were the handling charges; then she found it necessary to hire a customs broker to retrieve her treasures from the jaws of the government. As she says, "At $4 the pots were a steal, at $14 a good buy, but at $40.50 apiece, they were a luxury I could have skipped."

An inside look at the writer's ineptitudes makes the reader feel superior.

However, hyperbole is often an element of humor. But, the exaggeration must be told within the bounds of logic. The reader should be able to say, even while he's laughing, "I know somebody like that," or 'That sounds exactly like me."

Gerald Nachman pokes fun at himself in "The Obsessive Sightseer:"

> It doesn't seem enough, somehow, just to go someplace, or even take a snapshot of it. If you don't go all the way to the top (or, in certain cases, the bottom or the end or the edge) and collapse, you think you haven't properly "done" it.
>
> There is the equally silly experience of going somewhere famous and not quite knowing what to do once you've arrived. . . . It took all day to get to Carthage and only about ten seconds to see it. . . . I felt very dumb walking around the ruins looking for more ruins to look at and trying to think of more telling comments to make than, "Well, well, so this is Carthage, eh?"

While travel humor is often born of an unpleasant personal experience, it doesn't usually spring directly from raw, unleashed fury or righteous indignation. You have to wait until you've calmed down a little before you're capable of making it humorous social commentary.

Bill Farmer writes amusingly of shipboard accommodations so terrible the passengers can say:

> Poor Aristotle Onassis. He probably had to walk to the steam bath and massage parlor on his yacht. Both were combined in my cabin. The air-conditioning had failed, bringing the temperature to an equatorial 100 degrees. Luckily, too, the drive shaft or a faulty piston rod the size of a telephone pole ran between my mattress and bedsprings to massage my travel-wearied spine all night. After four hours of wrestling with the washcloth someone had mistakenly used as a sheet.
> . . .

He's making a humorous protest over a serious complaint, and through humor drawing attention to the problem.

Art Buchwald deals in human conflict, a favorite form of travel humor. He's subtle, and yet not so subtle that any of his readers could miss the point. He attributes his knowledge of "Gamesmanship Aloft" to his friend Oscar Nimbleby, who taught him to always let women with children board the aircraft first, so they would select their seats and there would be no possibility of their sitting near him. Nimbleby has also solved the problem of walking miles to and from the departure gate. By assuming a limp and requesting for a skycap with a wheelchair, Nimbleby hasn't walked ten steps in any airport for four years. Is Buchwald exaggerating? Of course he is. Isn't that what humor's all about?

Nobody who travels with a family ever runs out of humorous incidents to relate. Take care, though—before you set up members of your family as laughingstocks or embarrass them, be sure they'll perceive the experience in the same spirit as you do.

Excellent travel advice camouflaged by humor is often the best vehicle for reaching your readers. Gerald Nachman makes the reader wonder, "*How* does he know *me!*" His "Fear of Packing" begins:

> After 25 years I still make the same mistakes in packing, only today I'm a lot faster at it. . . . "You never know" are the three most lethal words in a traveler's lexicon. . . . Maybe you'll spill shoe polish on your socks in Madrid and the stores will be shut for a big Spanish holiday? Suppose they don't sell Crest in Tokyo?

And then he gives you the kernel that counts:

> . . . It is only in the quiet of your bedroom at home that all of these silly exotic notions occur. On the trip itself, it never matters what you have on. . . .

The rigors of dealing with the complexities of modern life are intensified when you're traveling, and the humor inherent in the problem intensifies, too. Erma Bombeck is prepared to deal with the complexities in the best possible way—humorously.

It has always been a mystery, she says,

> how the Fates know which gate to send me to. When I am carrying a newspaper and my handbag and have two hours and a half to change planes, I am at Gate 2.
>
> However, when I am carrying my own luggage, a three-pound novel, hot rollers, an extra coat and live cactus for my hostess, and have 12 minutes to make a connection, my gate is still being built.

Often it's best to select a small but universal subject, rather than write superficially about a vast one. As Richard Armour says, "In humor, part of the fun is seeing something inconsequential developed by the ingenuity and imagination of the author. The very overdeveloped may lead to the absurdity which, properly handled, is basic in a great deal of humor."

One "inconsequential" subject for travel humor is the universal misunderstanding of language. "Inglish Spocken Here," for example, compiles signs from all over the world, like the one from the cathedral in Seville, where "It is forbidden to enter a woman, even a foreigner if dressed as a man"; or the Hong Kong dentist's sign "Teeth extracted by latest methodist"; or this one on a ship's cabin door regarding the "Helpsavering apparata in emergings behold many whistles! Associate the stringing aparata about the bosoms and meet behind, flee then to the indifferent lifesaveringshippen obediencing the instructs of the vessel." Why not become a collector of such gems?

Other humorists translate from English to English, as in "How to Savvy a Sign," which explains that

> A sign will inform you the next place down the road has a "Rustic Setting." This means the mosquitos are terrific and the parking lot is a morass of mud. Or the sign might say "Leisurely Dining." This does not mean your leisure but rather that of the cook, who has a hot cribbage game going with a salesman.

As Dorothy Parker says, everything is stacked against the humorist from the start, because anybody feels free to object, "I don't think that's funny." Still, with ingenuity and an indulgent attitude toward the frailties of human nature, the travel writer can make important points while entertaining his readers.

Art Buchwald does this and more in "The Tourist's Prayer."

> Heavenly Father, look down on us your humble, obedient tourist servants who are doomed to travel this earth, taking photographs, mailing postcards, buying souvenirs and walking around in drip-dry underwear. We beseech you, O Lord,

to see that our plane is not hijacked, our luggage is not lost and our overweight baggage goes unnoticed.

Give us this day divine guidance in our selection of hotels. We pray that the phones work, and that the operators speak our tongue, that there is no mail waiting from our children which would force us to cancel the rest of our trip.

Lead us to good, inexpensive restaurants where the wine is included in the price of the meal. Give us the wisdom to tip correctly in currencies we do not understand. Make the natives love us for what we are and not for what we can contribute to their worldly goods.

Grant us the strength to visit the museums, the cathedrals, the palaces, and if, perchance, we skip an historic monument to take a nap after lunch, have mercy on us for our flesh is weak.

Dear God, protect our wives from "bargains" they don't need or can't afford. Lead them not into temptation for they know not what they do.

Almighty Father, keep our husbands from looking at foreign women and comparing them to us. Save them from making fools of themselves in nightclubs. Above all, please do not forgive them their trespasses for they know exactly what they do.

And when our voyage is over, grant us the favor of finding someone who will look at our home movies and listen to our stories, so our lives as tourists will not have been in vain. This we ask you in the name of Conrad Hilton, Thomas Cook and the American Express. Amen.

TRAVEL ARTICLES FOR SPECIAL AUDIENCES

The Who

Travel articles for special audiences include the *who*, the *how* and the *what*. They are aimed at the reader who is interested in a particular kind of traveler, a particular kind of travel, or a particular kind of activity at the destination.

While it isn't absolutely necessary to be one of those people you're writing about, you do need to identify with them, as well as with the people you're writing for. The *who* travel article is a people-oriented piece, told in a straightforward manner.

You can tell a travel article is a *who* when the reason for the article's existence is that it centers around parents with school-age children or mothers traveling with young babies; penny-pinching students or retirees with more time than money; swinging singles or lonely widows; teenagers on initial solo trips or servicemen on leave, starry-eyed honeymooners or couples celebrating their golden anniversary.

Most readers have many identities—a man may be a golfer, and also a father, a homeowner, a gardener, an employee, a stamp collector, an accountant, a Nebraskan, a son, a Methodist, a Rotarian, and a winner of the Irish Sweepstakes. But if you're talking to him about the links at St. Andrew's, you're addressing him in his role as a golfer, and that becomes the organizing principle of your story.

When the people in your article share one of your reader's roles, that reader will care about their travels. So you have to ask yourself, "Who is doing the traveling?" and then, "Who is the interested reader?"

Bride's and *Modern Bride* emphasize, predictably, honeymoon locales. Is Virginia what the newlywed couple has in mind?

There is no better place to start a new life together than on a mountain. Looking down from your aerie over the landscape spread below, you can examine the life you've lived up to now, and the vastly different life you've just begun.

There are no lovelier mountains for such beginnings than the Blue Ridge Mountains of Virginia.

While Virginia is a pleasant destination for non-honeymooners as well, and many aspects of trips there could be emphasized, this particular story is written about and for people *who* are going on a honeymoon.

Chronologically speaking, the next traveler after the honeymooner is the young parent. Such publications as *American Baby, Baby Talk, Expecting,* and *Parents* magazine occasionally publish "Baby Takes a Trip" articles, especially in late spring. One successful story about seven-month-old Susan is a highly structured piece, with subheads pointing the way to "The Five Minute Preparation Bonanza," "The Right Kind of Car Bed," "Setting Up Happy Naptimes," "Keeping Baby Happy and Quiet in a Restaurant," and other essential information. Remember, the *who* is not Susan, but her parents.

"Camping with Your Toddler" is highly structured, too, with instructions for "Packing," "Meal Planning," and "Setting Up Camp."

Any parent should be able to write a *who*. Whether your travel experiences with children involve an hour's trip to the beach or a year's sabbatical around the world, whether you camped or cruised or visited relatives, your adventures with your children can be made into something other parents would like to read. Remember, though, to focus on only what will interest *others*.

A *Parents* magazine story on teenage travel abroad describes in detail the various opportunities, but the article is not really addressed to teenagers—it's addressed to their parents, who will be selecting and paying for the arrangements.

You don't *have* to be a member of the *who* group you're writing for, but sometimes it helps. The seventy-four-year-old grandmother who writes in *Modern Maturity* about her "Adventure in the Galapagos" uses her kinship with *Modern Maturity*'s readers to good advantage in communicating her excitement to them. It's not just a trip to the Galapagos, it's one grandmother's dream come true, by dint of moonlight jobs and help from her children.

Often the *who* is related to the reader's vocation, for vocation often influences vacation. A story about a jeweler studying the Crown Jewels at the Tower of London or a tennis player studying the opposition from the stands at Wimbleton has vocation as the focal point. If you're an architect, like San Francisco's Bruce Beebe, you also might want to visit, as he did, Stonehenge; the Masjid-i-Jami in Isfahan, Iran; Katsura Palace in Kyoto, Japan; Angkor Wat, Cambodia; and Chandigarh, India. What ties together these diverse destinations is the *who*—the architect who selected them as the world's most interesting architectural sites.

Trends naturally affect the *who* of travel—whether it's the promoter drumming up trade in China or the woman who travels on business. Keeping abreast of trends is part of the travel writer's responsibility.

Sometimes it's the avocation that determines the *who*. When *Flower and Garden* published an article about Yorktown, Pennsylvania, it was, understandably, "Yorktown—a Gardener's View." This article appeals to anyone knowledgeable about gardens and/or about history; the way the two are woven together makes it doubly interesting.

Do you have a hobby that you travel with? Could you become the *who* and write about it? Or can you visualize a reader whose hobby makes him the *who* of your story?

Sometimes special circumstances determine the *who*'s identity. For example, the *who* should be black in a story for *Ebony*, which publishes "achievement and human interest stories about, or of concern to black readers."

Other special circumstances make the experiences of a particular *who* especially interesting to a particular reader. *Travel & Leisure*'s article "The Bespectacled Voyager" was written by an optometrist. Using a question-and-answer format, he supplies information to such queries as "How can I make on-the-spot repairs? Is it safe to have contacts duplicated in other countries?"

A more seriously handicapped traveler, is featured in *Light Magazine*, published by the Braille Institute of America. Stories of special trips made by Institute members are often published in the magazine. A group of teens and young adults found the textures aboard the *Queen Mary*—wood, bronze, and cast iron—different from those they're more familiar with in today's world.

Other handicapped travelers often write their stories as personal experiences. While the *who* is the handicapped person, whose impairment makes special arrangements necessary, the story, if written well enough, will appeal to many readers.

You won't always travel under unusual circumstances, but you can find a *who* if you look for one.

The How

In *how* stories, the method of transportation is the most important feature. The function of the story is to outline the conveyance's distinctive features and add helpful ancillary information. Whether it's water, wings, or wheels, you, the writer, must communicate to your readers the excitement of that particular means of "getting there." After all, as they say, that's half the fun. Water, the primal element, is enjoying a resurgence of popularity as a medium for getting from here to there, and travelers' choices of waterborne vehicles grow ever more varied.

Jean Kerr prefers an ocean liner. "Being on ship," she says, "is something like being pregnant. You can sit there and do absolutely nothing . . . and have the nicest sense that you are accomplishing something. I mean, you're getting there." A "Mini-Cruise Guide" in *Trailer Boats*, a magazine for people who hitch their boats to cars, begins:

> Nestled in the rolling Illinois farmland, less than an hour to the northwest of Chicago, lies the picturesque Chain o' Lakes. This chain, made up of ten interconnecting lakes, has the Fox River flowing right through it and offers boaters more than one hundred miles of boating pleasure.

The story continues:

> Launch facilities are far too numerous to list, so let's just say that no matter where you are on the Chain, a ramp is nearby.
> Fishing just below the dam is excellent, as it is at many spots along the way. Now and then a tiny riverfront bar pops into view, cradled softly in its picnic grove of oaks.

Canoe, the official publication of the American Canoe Association, assumes, not surprisingly, that its readers are already interested in getting wherever they're going in a canoe. Its articles tell of good rivers for paddling, good equipment to consider, good strokes for getting there. One of the best articles I've ever read is Marilyn Doan's "Kids 'n' Canoes," which gives the reader everything he ever wanted to know about safety measures, traveling with children, and "the acid test of any trip—the kind of memories brought home."

David and Lyn Hancock profiled an offbeat style of water travel for the readers of *Motor Boating & Sailing* in "Adventure by Inflatable." *Adventure*, singular, may be the wrong term, since the Hancocks not only live for months at a time in a thirteen-foot inflatable dinghy "packed to the pontoon with all our requirements for living and working," but cruise in their rubber inflatable along the rugged Alaska-British Columbia shoreline. As David is a wildlife biologist, the Hancocks often carry as passengers a mountain lion, a seal, or a racoon; eagles, falcons, or sea birds. While much of the article deals with the Hancocks' adventures in camping with this arkful, the inflatable boat remains their constant (and often their only) link with the outside world, and its importance as a *how*-to-get-there figures prominently in the story.

If wings are your *how*, you'll find plenty of opportunities to tell readers all about it. Richard Joseph, for instance, gave *Esquire* readers an overall view of air travel in the South Pacific, with a discussion of schedules and prices enlivened by a description of Fiji as "the center of a southwestern Pacific region that's just about ripe and yours for the basking."

Wingless, but still airborne, and the epitome of adventure, is the ten-story-high hot-air balloon that takes you on an African safari, as described by Bert Keating in *Réalités*. Lions, giraffes, warthogs, dik-diks, elephants, buffaloes, ostriches, rhinoceroses—"all the drama of an East African sunrise passed 500 feet below our feet. . . ."

When it comes to wheels, the standard passenger car isn't the only *how* on the road. Roberta McDow's "Van Touring Central America" in *Van Life and Family Trucking* is the tale of a nine-month trip she and her husband took in a Dodge Maxivan. Any kind of a recreational vehicle is a good bet. Jack Seville remembers a corny couplet:

> The only difference between men and boys
> Is the price they pay for their toys.

as he heads for an RV rally, which he described for *Saturday Evening Post* readers in "Wagonmasters of the 20th Century." Dorothy Clendenin chronicled an antique car tour from Montreal to Tijuana in *Road and Track*.

When you consider the current glut of articles advising us of destinations we can explore on one tank of gas, it's refreshing to see an occasional story about modes of transport that don't need any gas at all.

Aloft, which passengers find in National Airlines seat pockets, featured "Provence á la Cart," about gypsy carts and horses that can be rented to tour some of the most spectacular scenery in France. *Modern Maturity* gave its readers "Covered Wagon Adventure," wherein modern-day travelers, aged six to eighty-four, romp through Kansas in Stetsons and calico sunbonnets aboard authentic prairie schooners.

Two-wheeled travel seems to grow more popular every day. As *Motorland* says, "One of the best ways to sight-see is by bicycle, and the energy you use is your own." A story it published gave six bike routes in northern California, which take in the forts of San Francisco, Point Reys, the Livermore Valley, and the Gold Country.

A bike story can be even more ambitious in scope. In "Across Canada on Two Wheels," Mandy Joslin tells *Ms.* readers that each of her knees had to flex 4,250,000 times to get her and her bicycle from Vancouver to Newfoundland on the Trans-Canada Highway. Her many adventures during her three-month journey are vividly rendered, with her *how* providing the focus.

Even more unusual was a fourteen-year-old boy's wheeled navigation of the Great Wall of China—by *skateboard!* In an interview with a reporter, he called it "a bumpy experience."

Riding the rails is a big *how*. A newspaper travel story about Scandinavian trains begins:

> Americans who remember train travel might agree that the clikety-clack of the wheel on the rail is a pleasant inducement to sleep.
> But for passengers riding the rails in Denmark, Norway or Sweden, each click is an invitation to see another distinctive view: of fairytale villages, Arctic tundra, awesome fjords, towering mountains, great forests, glittering lakes.

The *how* is what's holding together the scenic diversity of the story.

The readers of *Modern Maturity*, being of retirement age and up, are probably more interested in trains than any other reading audience. Most of them remember the "clickety clack," and would be delighted to be able to take such a trip now.

For some travelers the only way to go is by animal-back. An article in *Aramco World* deals with Jordan's Camel Caravans, an organization that specializes in introducing western visitors to a camel-back view of Lawrence of Arabia's desert. William Tracey, author of the article, describes the second day with the Caravan:

> The next morning saw us "making friends with our camels" as the brochure explains it, a process that involves adjusting the foam rubber cushions beneath the woven saddle bags, stretching one leg across the kneeling camel's back and hanging on frantically as the mount lurches to its feet grumbling and protesting. Once up, however, riding a walking camel is as easy as sitting in a rocking chair. Unfortunately the chair keeps rocking and rocking and rocking.

Muleback is another possibility. Landt and Lisl Dennis describe a "Swiss Mule Safari" in *Travel/Holiday*.

> Getting in shape for a recent Swiss mule safari we jogged to the ramp of the

plane that flew us from New York to Geneva, did isometrics on the train to Sion where the expedition is headquartered, and practiced calisthenics at the railroad station as the group assembled. But still our muscles let out a loud holler soon after we scaled our first 45 degree stretch of verticle Alp. Neither of us had yet climbed aboard Nero, our four legged escort. We led him instead. Mules were for the others, we thought. We found out differently.

When you begin to think *how-to-get-there*, dozens of ways present themselves. Some are exotic, some not so. But the best, most universal means of transportation, always available, always useful, is on your own two feet. "A Walking Tour of Honolulu," "A Walking Tour of San Francisco," "A Walking Tour of Denver"—such articles are appearing with increasing frequency. They're designed for the normally sedentary traveler who wants to explore the sights in a good-sized city.

Perhaps, though, you'd like to write an article addressed to more serious hikers, describing wilderness areas that can only be reached afoot. Maybe you have in mind something like the *Sunset* article about Olympic National Park, titled "Walking—the Only Way to Go." Wonderful! Many readers would welcome your description of an off-the-beaten-track hike.

Whether it's on your own two feet or via pogo stick, cable car, or magic carpet, your transportation introduces your reader to a vital element of any trip—the *how*.

The What

Active travelers are interested in *what* they'll be doing on their trips, and they like to read about the variety of activities at their travel destinations. And whatever type travel activity you, yourself, prefer, you'll find readers interested in it.

Practically every traveler cares about the *what* of accommodations—eating and sleeping. Regular readers of such food and drink publications as *Bon Appétit* and *Gourmet* naturally expect to have their taste buds titillated, whether or not they're planning to visit the Hôtel de France in Auch or Ernie's in San Francisco; but even "meat and potatoes" people are lured by references to sophisticated dining when the locale is on their intinerary.

Most regional and city magazines carry special restaurant sections covering their areas, and some, like *New West*, go a step further with articles like "Dining Your Way through Vancouver's Chinatown." A health magazine, like *Bestways*, will review a restaurant that prepares its food "in the health tradition." Even the newspaper travel sections will sometimes run roundup restaurant reviews under such titles as "Dining Out in Milan." So if you think of eating as your reader's *what*, consider the target market first, before planning your story. But while you're on your trip be sure to jot down the details of memorable experiences.

Sleeping is a little different. Often the story deals with the ambience of a particular establishment, such as Frank Taylor's *Off Duty* article about the old Hotel del Coronado, which has been declared a national landmark. He not only describes the eight-foot chandelier and the brass elevator, but also reminds readers that it may have been here that Edward, Prince of Wales, first met Mrs. Simpson.

Sometimes sleeping and eating go together, as in a *House and Gardens* travel feature on finding cozy places for bed and breakfast in the English countryside.

Camping can be the *what*, as well as the roof over the head, the dining site, and possibly the means of transportation. Camping abroad stories proliferate—so much so that it's hard to sell one without a special angle. So *create* a special angle! Bill Thomas wrote an article for *Woodall's Trailer & RV Travel* on "Theme Camping" that tells about camps with special facilities for farming, cowpunching, exploring history, picking fruit, digging for artifacts, or panning for gold.

Often your readers will have a favorite activity they plan to pursue during their trips— the *what* they want to read about. Is it golf, tennis, skiing, fishing, or surfing? You can tell them where to find these activities and describe special festivities that may be connected.

For some travelers, the real *what* is in the shops. Information on what's available to buy is always popular, as is a recommendation of the best stores. Some notable shopping areas, such as the Virgin Islands, appear again and again in travel-oriented publications, with the writer telling the reader why the shopping is a bargain, what to look for, and what to do if you buy more than your customs quota. Even if your readers aren't shoppers, they'll be interested in features about offbeat purchasing.

For some readers the *what* will involve animals—San Diego's Wild Animal Suburb, a dude ranch in Arizona, or the Kissimmee, Florida, rodeo. Perhaps they know about these attractions already, and just seek specific details before planning a trip. Or they may be grateful to you for introducing them to a new vacation destination.

Part of the travel writer's function should be to introduce readers to enriching activities. For instance, Dorothy Loa McFadden says, "Nothing can hold your attention like watching something being made." She suggests that seeking out craftsmen—to watch, to photograph, to buy from—can lead to many happy traveling hours. "When you go to Europe," she says, "look for the places where you can see things made, of native materials and with designs which have often been handed down for generations." She goes on to describe some of the craft work that can be seen, telling her readers where to find it and how to arrange to watch the artisan at work.

Perhaps you'll introduce your readers to a hobby like gravestone rubbing, which was the subject of an excellent article in *Away*. The article gives a little of the art, poetry, and history of gravestones, lists the equipment and supplies needed for rubbing, and explains the details of the technique.

If your readers have a long-treasured hobby, perhaps you can help them to enrich it through their travels. Julia Child's *Travel & Leisure* article on "Mastering the Art of Choosing a French Cooking School" gives food for thought to those who are considering spending hundreds of dollars to watch the master chef in action. Her advice is helpful for those who intend to select a French cooking school and interesting even to those who do not.

Look for the *what* when you're traveling. Think about which ones would interest which readers. Whether it's an old reliable, like playing Ping-Pong; or a new skill, like racing down a cresta run, do think about *what* your reader, the active traveler, will do at his destination. Once you've defined him and transported him, write about activities he's likely to enjoy.

TRAVEL ARTICLES WITH EASY PEGS

The Roundup

Stories with natural pegs are easy travel stories. You can train yourself to find them anywhere.

The easiest and most familiar is the *roundup*. You've seen these in many magazines, and the possibilities are endless. It's often easy to ask twenty celebrities, say, about their favorite vacations. You probably don't even need twenty—five or six might do. It's even easier to interview one celebrity and ask him to name his favorite places for something or other, such as Lee Tyler did with Mike Roseto. She asked him to name his favorite golf courses, in terms of character, nearby accommodations, and surroundings, and a roundup of eight golfing areas resulted.

For a *roundup* the travel writer can take a group of whatever and convert it to a salable story—"The Covered Bridges of Indiana," "The Paradores of Spain" or "Burma Shave Signs I Have Loved."

Some publications seem to savor the *roundup*, even to seek it out. *Accent*, for instance, usually runs at least one *roundup*, in each issue, and they range from "Guarded Manners" (guards on duty at the Vatican, Prince Rainier's palace in Monaco, Buckingham Palace, and elsewhere) to "Odd Customs and Beliefs" (unusual religious ceremonies around the world).

Travel/Holiday uses a *roundup* in nearly every issue, and here the variety is astonishing. "Swiss Ski Resorts," "Britain's Stately Homes," and "Spain's Royal Palaces" may not seem so unusual, but how about "Aerospace Museums"—the many museums throughout the United States that document each step, from Kittyhawk to the moon, during the past eighty-odd years; or "The World in Mosaics"—from the floor of Diocletian's Bath in Rome to the steps of a Jain Temple in Calcutta.

Better Homes and Gardens runs frequent travel *roundups*, too. Is the reader interested in "America's Zingiest Zoos"—from Cincinnati to the Bronx, from St. Louis to San Diego? In "Indian Country Vacations" accomodations—"from the super de luxe to the primitive"—are mentioned, and the reader is told where to get additional information. Another issue features " 'Foreign' Vacations in the U.S.A.," rambling from Little Tokyo in Los Angeles to Holland, Michigan's Tulip Time Festival and San Antonio's Paseo del Rio.

Numbers lend themselves to *roundups*—"Seven Places You Won't See the Joneses This Summer" in *Apartment Ideas*; "Five Great Places to Get Away from It All" in *Medical Economics*; "Three RV Tours that Are High Roads to Adventure" in *Minnesota Motorist*, and "Ten Best Camping Trips in North America" in *Family Weekly*. Be sure you use the numbers instead of letting them use you. If there are only nine really outstanding nudist camps where your reader can reserve a holiday, don't include an inferior one to round the number off to ten.

Sometimes *roundups* cover a limited area—"Boston Markets" in *TWA Ambassador*, or "Tokyo's Coffeehouses" in *Travel & Leisure*. And sometimes the roundup traverses vast areas: "Sports Shrines for Hero Worshipers" in *Travel & Leisure* moves from Newport, Rhode Island, to Cooperstown, New York; on to Canton, Ohio; Springfield, Massachusetts; and Pinehurst, North Carolina. A *Rotarian* article gave a roundup of parks and monuments dedicated to peace, spread from Hiroshima, Japan, to the US-Canadian border; from a wooded savanna in West Africa, where the Benin, Niger, and Upper Volta rivers meet, to a memorial high in the Andes, on the Chilean-Argentinian border.

Roundups, like other travel articles, especially appeal to readers when they emphasize how to save money. Add the words "you" and "secret," and it's hard for the reader to resist looking to see what's offered. *Family Circle's* "Super Sunbelt Vacations Your Family Can Afford," is actually a roundup of six roundups, by six different authors. Throughout this entire *roundup*, the themes of "super" and "sun" and "saving money" promised in the overall title are emphasized.

Roundups that appeal to specific audiences are "Rocky Mountain Dude Ranches" in the *Continental Magazine*, "Some Far-out Vacation Ideas for Venturesome Spirits" in *Midwest Motorist*, "Getting Back to Good Old Mother Earth" in *Ban Club Digest*. Introducing the reader to things he can do himself, *Gentlemen's Quarterly* features "Games Europeans Play," a roundup of interesting keep-fit exercises, and *Gambling* tells "Where to Take a Gamble on Your Next Vacation," a roundup of foreign casinos.

Sometimes only two items are included in a roundup. A *Redbook* article on "Two Seductive Cities" links Santa Fe and San Francisco by more than their initials. If this is the year for your second honeymoon, says the author, you can find elegant hideaways, extraordinary scenery, sumptuous but inexpensive dining in both of these cities, and so many things to do you may even want to take the children along.

Sometimes you can create a roundup from parts of several previous travel articles by finding a common peg to tie the information together. And sometimes, if you don't create the roundup, the editor does. When I sent an article on Buena Park to *Off Duty* without querying, because I felt the article was so perfect for the market, the editor informed me that another writer was already researching California's theme parks but that he had cabled that writer to exclude Buena Park. When the article appeared in print, it included all that I had written, plus material on Disneyland and other theme parks by Hal Schell. The editor ran it all together as a roundup and gave us a joint byline, although Schell and I have never met.

The Historical Piece

When you're writing a *historical travel article* it's your job to bring the reader right to the scene of the action, so you have to make it read like fiction. You have to be sure, however, that your *facts* are not fictional but absolutely accurate. Your target audience determines how many of these facts there shall be and how learned the article's scope.

Another factor, of course, is how much space you have. While a *historical travel article* on Peru in *Américas* would not be as scholarly nor as finely tuned as one in the *Journal of Archaeology*, if it's the lead article it will be significant and in-depth. A twenty-three page well-illustrated article on "Mexico: A Story of Three Cultures" covers the geography and the cities and landscapes in considerable detail, dividing the country into northern, southern, and central sections. After explaining the constitution and government, the article moves on to culture and customs, folk arts, and literature. Under economic and social development it discusses labor, communities, housing, health, education, agriculture, gas, minerals, industry, electric power, banking and finance, foreign trade, communication, transportation, and tourism, so the article becomes a comprehensive overview. Its major focus, though, is Mexico's history, from pre-Columbian to the present. Although factual and accurate, the style is readable:

> Father Miguel Hidalgo y Costilla issued the now famous *grito de Dolores*, "Long live our lady of Guadalupe, down with bad government, death to the Spaniards!" His followers, an "army" of perhaps fifty thousand ill-clad men armed with bows and arrows, clubs, machetes, and a few guns, seized Guanajuato and nearby towns, and marched on Mexico City.

As is often the case in *historical* articles, the writer assumes a certain knowledge on the part of the reader, as, for instance, when he speaks of "now famous." This leaves two reasons for writing the historical travel article—to remind your reader and help him review the facts of history and to shed new light on an old story.

"The City that Died to Live," a *Reader's Digest* piece on Pompeii, does both. Although written long ago, its authors, Donald and Louise Peattie, did such an excellent job of bringing Pompeii to life, within the framework of historical accuracy, it could serve as a model for all travel writers who try similar types of articles. These are some of the devices that bring the reader on-scene, although nearly 1,900 years elapsed between the time Mt. Vesuvius erupted so disastrously and the time the story was written:

> The city of Pompeii basked among its silvery olive groves and dark umbrella pines. . . . The marble on suburban villas and on the temples in the heart of town glittered sumptuously as the sundial shadow crept toward the fated figure I *post meridiem*. The shopkeepers were closing their wooden shutters for the long Latin lunch hour. . . .
>
> A baker shoved 81 loaves into his oven and closed the iron door. In a wineshop a customer laid his money on the counter. Suddenly an earthquake convulsed the city.
>
> Thousands fled at once. These were the wise—and the wisest kept on traveling all that afternoon and night. Nothing else could have put them outside the circle of death that Vesuvius was inscribing around itself.

After telling about the various attempts at excavation and re-creation, the authors describe standing in Pompeii today:

> You step into a Pompeiian house like the House of the Golden Cupids. Its street wall windowless, such a home kept its smile for family and friends. All its rooms opened inward, around the *atrium*, a central patio where lay a pool fed by rain water from the sloping roofs. In that genial Pompeiian climate the family lived chiefly in the *atrium*; here the women sewed and chattered; here the doves swept down from the roof to drink at the pool. And here, or in the garden at the rear, children chased each other round the flower beds—the roses, narcissus and violets between low borders of box that today are carefully replanted there. It is the same old, old sunlight, falling on your hand today, that brushed the cheek of the young bride in the House of the Lovers. In its warmth you know that it is not the few hours of terror and the few moments of agony, so long ago, that matter here, but rather the six centuries of living from which survives the powerful and sacred sense of our common humanity.

Here we see ancient history brought to life in a popular magazine through the skill of the writing.

Some publications lean especially toward the *historical travel article*, so we expect to see in the *Iron Worker* an article on the restoration of Colonial Williamsburg, in *Early American Life* an article about "Savannah, a City Reclaimed," and in *National Motorist* an article about the copper mines of Jerome, Arizona. All of these stories combine the history with the present, telling the reader what he can see if he goes there today and what is the meaning of what he is seeing. Sometimes the focus is broader, such as "Camping with History—Zane Grey's Country" in *Camping Journal*.

As with all kinds of writing, the easiest way to make history come alive is to show the people.

When Fanny-Maude Evans wrote "Take Along a Hero or Heroine" for *Redbook*, she emphasized the value of doing your homework ahead of time and knowing the people who made the places memorable. She tells about Harriet Tubman silently leading three hundred slaves to freedom along Maryland's eastern shore; Sybil Ludington, a "teen-aged Paul Revere," who summoned New Yorkers to rebel against the British; and Sam Houston, who hated violence, yet "won one of the world's most decisive battles," and others.

Nostalgia, too, enters into the *historical travel article*. One writer who "first met Bill and Anna Wilkins at a flea market on Maryland's eastern shore" when they "had been dead for several years" took their scrapbook, stuffed with postcards and trip mementos, and followed in the footsteps of the trip to Florida they had taken forty-odd years before. He compares and contrasts the train ride, dinner in the diner, and the hotel. And then he *flies* home.

Finding a nostalgic or historical peg is easy, and usually pays off.

The Here and Now

In some ways the easiest travel article of all to write is the here and now. A *here and now* takes advantage of the fact that a locale— or a topic— is already in the forefront of readers' and editors' attention for some reason. Sometimes you can hang a basic story on a *here and now* peg by merely adding a sentence or two at the beginning and another sentence or two at the end. For example, a magazine article about Evora in the *Retired Officer Magazine* begins:

> Now that the political upsets in Portugal seem over, the country as a whole and the Algarve and Lisbon in particular are going to be prime tourist targets.

The article continues with the charms of Evora. Other times, you'll be inspired by the event itself to write the *here and now* so the peg will be integral. Look for news events, such as improved relations with a foreign country, like Cuba or China; the opening of an entire new area, like Cancun; the beginning of a new activity, like Atlantic City's gambling; wars, riots, strikes, and their ultimate resolutions; adventurers taking off from or landing at a particular place. But be sure to hurry when you're writing a story like this. A magazine's long lead time sometimes makes a newspaper travel section a better market for a current event.

The *end* of an era can be *here and now*, too. When our famous regional train whistled at its last grade crossing I wrote (and sold) a reminiscence, set near the end of World War II, involving my two-hundred pound father and four quart jars of dill pickles squeezed into an upper berth of that train.

Look for upcoming national or international expositions and events. An article on Newport, Rhode Island, in the *NRTA* [National Retired Teachers Association] *Journal* ties itself to the *here and now* with

> Whichever time period one chooses, Newport, R.I., is the place to be. Especially this year when the city will be host in September to Swedish, Australian and French contingents, all eager to compete for the world's greatest yachting prize . . . America's Cup.

Look for regional events to write about for regional publications: the county fair; the marble-shooting championship in the state capital; new attractions at the nearby theme park.

Can you make a *here and now* out of an anniversary? While the Pompeii story as history needed no other peg, a more recent *Reader's Digest* article was tied to the traveling exhibition, "Pompeii A.D. 79," which was drawing "record crowds" to view the three hundred artifacts recovered from the excavations; both the exhibit and the article were tied to the 1900th anniversary of the Vesuvius eruption.

Anniversaries of cityhood, statehood, or nationhood and upcoming commemorations of other civic occasions give you more time to plan ahead if you're familiar with or going to the area where these events are going to take place, and the tie-in is easy.

General trends, while not as mercurial as isolated news events, sometimes do change suddenly, so when you're writing about a trend, act quickly if you think a change is likely. Will there, for instance, continue to be a demand for stories on where you can go on one tank of gas? Sometimes you can *create* a trend, if you see something that links a group of isolated instances. For example, you take a train trip and meet two men and two women, each traveling alone on business; then you read a personal experience article written by a businessman about his travels by train; then a business friend tells you about taking the train to a convention. Is this, in fact, a trend? A little research may confirm your idea and give you a good *here and now*. Broad general trends likely to continue, such as women business travelers, women traveling alone, younger teenagers traveling farther, and people saving money by traveling close to home, may give you a little more working time.

Do you notice an overwhelming interest in adventure travel? That's a trend, isn't it? The trend toward more women business travelers has many facets to explore. *Mainliner*, United's in-flight, is changing its advertising thrust to attract the traveling woman executive who "doesn't want to be pampered, she just doesn't want to be ignored." Hotels are actively seeking the business of the woman business traveler with full-length mirrors, vaults for furs and jewelry, better security, and other services appropriate to the female executive.

Other trends that have led to recent successful stories: "new" gold hunters who have become hobby prospectors for the thrill of the hunt and, of course, the jigsaw puzzle of airfare deals.

Learn to watch the calendar and allow enough time (usually six to nine months, but check with the publication) to fit your story into seasons of the year and special holidays. Create "seasons" if you can, like "Now that the kids are back in school" or "Now that the wildflowers are in bloom."

Be aware of annual events such as: the International Balloon Festival in Albuquerque each October; the Calgary Stampede in the late summer; Aloha Week; Tulip Time in Holland, Michigan; fall colors; whale watching; the Great Raft Race, which is the Labor Day blowout in Tulsa, Oklahoma.

Seasons of the year make great travel stories. Spring: "New Season Show in the Smokies" (*Living Trends*); "Great Springtime Vacations Along the Gulf of Mexico" (*Better Homes and Gardens*); "Spring in the Delta" (*NorthNord*). Fall: "Share the Excitement of a Football Saturday" (*Michigan Living*); "A Rainbow of Fall Foliage Awaits the Camper Who Follows a Back-Country Trail" (*Points*); "Gather Autumn's Harvest Along New England's Roads" (*Away*). Winter: In addition to the usual paeans to the snow scene, the urgings to try winter sports, and the accounts of the preparations for Winter Carnival and Mardi Gras, there's *Woman's Day*'s advice to "Get Away for a Winter Weekend," *Travel/Holiday*'s report on "Cape Cod in Winter," and *Motorhome Life*'s recommendation to "Go Winter RVing."

The holidays are a gift to the travel writer. *Travel Life* had a wonderful three-way Christmas travel piece—all personal experiences: a caravan Christmas in Mexico; "Head Home for Christmas"; and "Camp the Holy Land at Christmas." "Christmas in Europe" and "Christmas Around the World" are perennial favorites, supplemented by stories that tell how Christmas is celebrated in individual countries. If you have any new ideas on Christmas travel, editors will welcome you.

Washington's Birthday, Valentine's Day, Halloween—all make good stories. Look for obscure holidays, too. Groundhog Day? Columbus Day? Benjamin Franklin's birthday? So start thinking six to nine months in advance: Now that the kids are back in school, Mom and Dad can treat themselves to a midweek holiday. Now that Christmas is over, let's consider Easter Week in Spain. Now that Thanksgiving approaches, why not plan a houseboat reunion for your family? Many travel writers keep a special calendar to remind them when to send off topical stories.

TRAVEL ARTICLES FOR ACTIVE AND ARMCHAIR TRAVELERS

Flavor Piece

Some travel articles appeal to armchair, as well as active, travelers. Whether your reader is looking forward to a trip or reminiscing about one traveled only in his daydreams, a *flavor* piece will take him on a journey. When done well, it makes him feel he's right there with you, experiencing the ear-shattering sounds and shoulder-shoving crowds of the bazaar; or the quiet and tranquility of watching, just the two of you, the sun setting beyond the gentle breakers.

The flavor piece is really a literary exercise; to write a good one you must be a good writer. Also, you have to feel strongly about the travel experience and be prepared to re-create that experience for your reader through emotion-evoking details.

Can you make your reader *see* the flavorful details?

Bill Thomas, in the *Elks Magazine*, shows his readers the Suwannee River:

> The Suwannee runs slowly and meanders, its black water feeling its way between soft white sand banks and rocky shores, choosing an uncertain path at times in the low cypress swamps that crowd close to each side. And along its path are great blue-water springs that emerge from the forest to flow sweet, cold and fresh. . . . The sandy bottoms of the springs, some of them 40 feet deep, are carpeted with watercress and other edible aquaplants. You can glide above them in water so crystal clear it's almost like flying.

He reproduces the *sounds* of the river, too:

> The rustle and swish of the lazy water is remindful of the pace of life here. . . . Feel the earthshaking rumble of logs drifting down to the mills and the chop and slap of the paddle wheel ghost boats. . . .

Bringing us back to the present, he writes of "great wading birds . . . squawking their displeasure."

He tells us so much about the "coffee-colored waters . . . trimmed on each side by a narrow ribbon of pure white sand," the "limestone strata sculptured into fantastic formations by erosion over the centuries" and "swirling patterns upon the dark surface of the water, broken only by the occasional roll of the great catfish," that we feel we are there with him—and Stephen Foster—gliding between the banks of the Suwannee. The flavor of the river is unmistakable.

John Updike's *New Yorker* article on Ethiopia takes us to the Addis Ababa Hilton, where you can see the cruciform swimming pool and the long white facade of the palace from upper-floor balconies. "In the other direction," says Updike, "there are acres of tin shacks, and a church on a hill like the nipple on a breast of dust."

He tells the reader what Ethiopia *feels* like, too:

> Emerging from the pool, which feels like layers of rapidly tearing silk, one shivers uncontrollably until dry, although the sun is brilliant and the sky diamond-pure. The land is high, and the air is not humid. One dries quickly.

And toward the end he tells us that the young American taking a picture sees through his viewfinder a scene "exactly like the sepia illustrations in his Sunday-school Bible."

Joan Didion imparts the flavor of Bogota to her readers:

I arrived in Bogotá on a day when the streets seemed bathed in high mist and thin brilliant light and in the amplified pop voice of Nelson Ned, a Brazilian dwarf whose records played in every disco storefront.

After viewing a mine that produces enough salt for all of South America and a cathedral carved into the mountain 450 feet below the surface, where 10,000 people can hear mass at the same time, she had lunch in a chilly dining room on the side of the salt mountain.

There were heavy draperies that gave off a faint muskiness when touched. There were white brocade tablecloths, carefully darned. For every stalk of blanched asparagus served, there appeared another battery of silverplated flatware and platters and *vinaigrette* sauceboats, and also another battery of "waiters"—little boys, 12 or 13 years old; dressed in tailcoats and white gloves and taught to serve as if this small inn on an Andean precipice were Vienna under the Hapsburgs.

I sat there for a long time. All around us the wind was sweeping the clouds off the Andes and across the savanna. Four hundred and fifty feet beneath us was the cathedral built of salt in the year 1954. One of the little boys in white gloves picked up an empty wine bottle from the table, fitted it precisely into a wine holder, and marched toward the kitchen holding it stiffly before him, glancing covertly at the marwtre d'howtel for approval. It seemed to me later that I had never before seen and would perhaps never again see the residuum of European custom so movingly and pointlessly observed.

As we can see, each of these flavor articles introduces the reader not only to the geographic area, but also the personality of the place and of the writer.

Gimmick

When you want to take your reader on a journey, consider the *gimmick*. The *gimmick* is a very narrow subject, or a specific facet of a larger topic, or a small topic treated in a special or unusual format. The *gimmick* is often a good travel story pattern, and an easy one to write, because it focuses so sharply.

The capsule sentence for the *gimmick* type of article usually falls into place easily. If you're taking your reader on a journey to the Kentucky Derby, the Grand Rapids Furniture Museum, or Seattle's Space Needle, your capsule sentence is limited by the objective of the story, so there are fewer choices and fewer bypaths down which the writer can accidentally wander.

Individual sights and events often make good *gimmicks* when you're traveling, so learn to look for them, recognize them, and create them.

Very small segments of the traveler's world can be turned into profitable *gimmicks*. For example, "Our New Sign Language"—a description of upcoming new highway symbols—appeared in *Motorland*; "Senet"—an ancient Egyptian game shown in the tomb paintings and billed as "King Tut's Favorite Game"—appeared in *Games*; and "Topkapi's Turkish Timepieces"—an outstanding collection of clocks and watches in Istanbul's Topkapi Palace appeared in *Aramco World*. These are all fragments of a subject.

Equally limited, although covering a bigger area, are subjects like "Wyatt Earp's Kind of Town (the ghost town of Bodie) from *Off Duty*; "Placer County Big Tree Grove" (a special race of giant sequoias) from *National Parks and Conservation Magazine*; "The Little Volcano that Couldn't" (about a resort hotel in El Salvador that was built so guests would have a good view of the volcano erupting, but the volcano hasn't erupted since the hotel was built and the hotel has had no guests) from *Signature*; and "Day Outside Amsterdam" (getting out in the country to Vreeland) from *Travel & Leisure*.

Often the *gimmick* is a single event, perhaps taking up only a brief amount of time during the trip. My sheep dog trial was like that. (Incidentally, by the time I completed all the research, the *New York Times* had a new editor who thought sheep dogs "not compelling enough.")

The most "gimmicky" kind of *gimmick* is the puzzle or quiz. You often see this sort of thing in in-flight magazines. There's the crossword puzzle with gems like "What to eat in Honolulu, 26 across" and "What to call your friend's father in Spain, 39 down." Sometimes you'll see a map of a confusing area like the Caribbean, with all the islands numbered, and the reader is supposed to guess which islands the numbers indicate. Or there'll be a questionnaire with a heading like "Are You a Graduate Globetrotter?" and questions like: "Where would you be calculating coinage if this is what you had in your pocket: drachma, yen, bolivar, schilling, or guilder?" or "Which country's airline would you be flying if you go: Aer Lingus, Sabena, Lufthansa, El-Al, or KLM?"

You've probably seen some gimmicky things like this, too—"Bermuda: From A to Z," with "A" for ale (they tell you which pubs to patronize) and "Z" for Zebra Crossing (the black and white striped pedestrian crosswalk). If you're clever at making up games and puzzles of this sort, don't hesitate to work out a travel theme and send it off.

Definitive Destination

For the *definitive destination* article you need to know *everything*. You have to anticipate the questions your reader is likely to whisper and answer them before they occur. Some destinations are easier to define than others, and some destinations demand a longer article than others. In any case, the article has to be information-packed and tightly structured, with sure transitions holding it together. And even though you're trying to tell everything, you'll still need to decide what to emphasize and what to skip over. You need a strong capsule sentence to define your message.

Trailer Life's article on Washington, DC, is a *destination* article. It begins:

> If you're an American, no matter where you live—Dubuque, Dallas, Minneapolis or Muleshoe—you have a second hometown. All of us do. That other repository for our loyalty and allegiance is our splendid national capital city, Washington, DC.

And it ends:

> . . . only Washington is every American's second hometown, and every visit is a happy homecoming.

And everything in between is related to that framework. The article tells the history of the building of Washington and describes the sights in considerable detail. It goes into the geography of the city and the attractions on its outskirts, like Mount Vernon; discusses musical and theatrical events; and tells the reader how to see the government in action. But because of the readership of this publication, the article says nothing about hotels or restaurants. It does mention that there are no campgrounds or RV parks within the city limits but tells where they can be found outside the city.

This emphasis on the parodoxes continues, with discussion of island politics and integration, culminating in this paragraph:

> Bermuda is a paradise, to be sure. But it is also a microcosm of all the problems attendant in our own country, not the model of integration so glibly propounded elsewhere. But because Bermuda *is* an island—a fragile, tiny, crowded island— there is no room for mistakes. Patriotism runs high, and both blacks and whites want what's best for Bermuda. If any country is apt to solve its problems reasonably and without violence, it's this little one sprawled in the sea.

> Above Bermuda, the kiskadees and longtails cast slender shadows across the sun. Below Bermuda, human forms slip in and out of decayed hulks and the ballast stones are all that's left of the holds of ancient ships. The British pour another cup of tea and the sun and the gold shine.

Although it could certainly be classed as a *destination* piece, a *Réalités* article on Petra deals with an even smaller segment of the world. Petra is, after all, only one small city. However, this article tells *everything* about it—the history, the people, the geography, who's digging where, and what's being done to keep the tourists from ruining the place.

The well-structured *destination* piece—"Auckland"—in *Pacific Travel News* tells about the geography of the city, its population, surrounding areas, volcanoes, water on all sides, shopping areas, climate, and transportation. And then come the subheads—"Hotels & Dining," "The Overview," "Museums," "Sightseeing by Car and Boat," "Sports & Events," "Shopping," and where to send for more information.

Still different, and more comprehensive in some ways, is *Geo's definitive destination* piece on Los Angeles. This is a type of piece that goes beyond mere detail in an attempt to actually grasp the *meaning* of a place. It expresses *its* theme by telling the reader the city's theme:

> Mobility is the theme of Los Angeles, not stasis, monuments, concern for the past (*which* past?). It is called a city: it is, in fact, an immense post-urban process, the tentative validation of a concept New York only hints at and neither Cleveland nor Des Moines dares to express. But L.A. is settled by refugees from New York, Cleveland and Des Moines, from the Dust Bowl and the South, from Heartland America. They are here for this. It is the first American experimental space colony on earth.

Exploring the city's meaning:

> In Los Angeles, just as the architecture sometimes seems a joke on history or nature—a hamburger stand shaped like a Japanese temple, a family dwelling like Hansel & Gretel's house—so people sometimes grow into shapes different from what they must be elsewhere.

He goes on comparing and contrasting:

> No other city offers a black, bubbling, surly stench as a major tourist attraction. Los Angeles presents the La Brea Tar Pits, the world's largest Ice Age fossil deposit, embedded in a lake of asphalt. The Indians used the tar to caulk their canoes; the white man used it for roofing. Now we visitors stand on a concrete observation platform. Below, there is water of a suspicious color, and slow, giant bubbles rhythmically explode at the surface, as if the ancient mammoths and tigers and camels were still breathing within eons accretion of tar.

And analyzing the ethnic components:

> That there are large black, Japanese, Chicano, Chinese and Russian communities that guard their ethnic purity is well-known. There are also extended families of those faithful to UFOs and Scientology, and you can listen to soft Scientological rock on an L. Ron Hubbard radio station. There are those who converse in tongues and those awaiting a call from mail-order prophets who bless cripples and change the tires on their wheelchairs.

Not exactly a travel piece perhaps, but definitely a *destination* piece. Herbert Gold, the author, ends by urging the reader to laugh along with him at a city with signs like this:

L.A. MINI SUPERETTE
Gas, Food, Tums
OPEN 24 HOURS A DAY
(Closed Midnight to 7 a.m.)

Index

Accuracy, 10, 37, 113-114, 125-126, 199, 205, 216-217, 240
Addresses, obtaining, 22, 36, 90, 127-128
Adjectives, 115, 191
Airlines, literature from, 30
Airport x-rays, 87, 89
Air travel, 81-82; and dental work, 79; fares, 236-237; luggage, 94-95; tickets, 73
Alcohol, and travel, 107-108
All rights, photographs, 221
Anecdotes, 125-127, 129, 139, 197, 199, 202, 204
Angles, subject matter, 139
Anthologies, 138
Apparel, travel, 74-76, 93-94
Appointments: interview, 198-205; with editors, 169-170
Assembly-line market research, 135-136
Assignments, 65, 137, 153, 154, 172, 176-178, 190; vs. on speculation, 176
Assignment sheet, 90
Atlases, 22, 28
Authors, as research sources, 40
Automobile clubs, material from, 20-21, 24
Automobile travel, 68, 75-76, 81

Background, photographing, 215
Back-of-the-book stories, 144-145
"Backyard" subject matter, 11
Blending, of articles, 141
"Blind" quotes, 204
Book rate, 89
Brochures: as resource material, 24-30; writing, 146-147
Business cards, 85

Cameras, 85-86, 216-217, 221-223, 225; attachments, 222-223; techniques, 216
Capsule sentence, 182, 189, 190
Captions, 212-214, 227-229
Cash, for travel, 76-77
Card catalog, library, 35
Checklist, for query letters, 172
Clarifications, 204
Clichés, photo, 211, 213
Clippings, 165-166
Company publications, 219
Composition, photo, 215-216
Condensations, 138
Conflict, in article, 186-187
Consulates, 106
Contact sheet, 226-227
Contests, 146, 226
Copyrighting, photos, 220-221
Copyright law, 137
Cover photos, 211, 219, 223
Credentials, professional, 85

Credibility, 204
Credit cards, 73, 76-77
Credits, photo, 228, 230
Cross indexing, 39-40
Crowds, 104-105
Currency, 76-77; converting, 92
Current events, 24, 88
Customs, local, 74-76, 101
Customs regulations, 94-95

Details, 113-116, 203
Diaries, trip, 87-88
Discounts: trade, 240-241; travel, 69, 237
Documents, travel, 73-74, 90, 92
"Down home" articles, 11
Drama, in articles, 188
Driving regulations, 76
Duty regulations, 94-95

Editors, 152-160, 163-178, 227
Embassies, 106
Emergency services, 80
Encyclopedias, 21-22, 39
Ending, article, 193-194
Entertainment, local, 104
Equipment, travel, 75, 91-92
Errors, 116, 118, 125-126
Events, special, 69-70, 72, 205-206; photographing, 216
Excerpts, 138
Exclusive rights, photos, 221
Expenses, 129-130, 159-160, 223, 241-243; paid, 241; postage, 152; and rejection slips, 175
Experts, 124, 126, 199, 206
Exposés, 112-113

Face-to-face interview, 198, 206
Facts, 115-116, 167, 187; from interviews, 205; kinds of, 39-40; recording, 113-114; updating, 126-127
Fares, reduced, 240
Featurettes, 140
Fillers, 140
Film, 86-87, 223-225; changing, 216; cost, 211; mailing, 89
Filters, photographic, 216, 224
First rights, 137-138
Flashbacks, 187-190
Flash equipment, 222-223
Focal point, photograph, 215, 217
Focus, article, 198
Food: articles, 134; local, 81, 101-103; ordering, 76-77
Foreigners, questions of, 82
Foreign Independent Travel, 64
Foreign languages, 7-8, 77-78, 88-89, 92, 105

Foreign markets, 142-144
Form queries, 172-173
Framing, of subjects in photographs, 215
Freebies, 235-241
Fuel shortages, 75-76

Getting lost, 105
Go-aheads, 137, 153, 154, 160, 169, 176-177, 198
Government publications, 38
Government research sources, 25-29
Groups, photographing, 217-218
Group travel, 64
Guidebooks: as resources, 18-21, 24, 26, 30-31, 37; writing, 147
Guides, 67-68, 88, 98-99; authors as, 23-24

Health, 78-81
Historical societies, 29
History, background guides, 19
Holding fee, 138
Holidays, 69-73
Home library, 16-31, 89
Hook, of article, 156, 185-190
House organs, 219

"Iceberg theory," 14
Identification, 73-74, 85
Immunization, 79, 92. See also Yellow card
In-flight magazines, 30, 134-135
In-room magazines, 30
Insurance, travel, 76
International Driving Permit, 75
Interviews, 197-206; appointments, 69-72; arranging, 105-106; focus, 202; foreign languages, 76-77; questionnaires, 126-130; small talk, 202; tape recording, 88; telephone, 205
Itinerary sheets, 135-137

Jet lag, 80-81

Kill fees, 138

Landmarks, 100, 211
Language, 190-191; usage, reference sources, 16-17
Legal aid, 80
Legal problems, and photographs, 219-221
Length, article, 159, 166, 182
Letterhead, 174
Librarians, 34-35, 106
Library research, 32-41; home reference material, 16-31, 89
Live research, 14-16, 124, 139
Local color, 101
Luggage, 94

Mail arrangements, 72-73
Mailing: to foreign markets, 143; lists, 130; on-trip, 107; photos, 226-228; supplies, 89-90
Manuscripts: held, 138; mailing, 89; submitting, 176-177
Maps, 24, 26-28, 36, 76, 91
Marketing itinerary, 43-44, 46-48
Marketing manuals, 163
Market research, 43-61, 133-147
Markets: association, 146; foreign, 142-144; juvenile, 147; kinds of, 48-61; outdoor, 102; simultaneous submissions, 137-138; stay-at-home, 146-147
"Mattering moment," 187, 189
Meals, 81; reviewing, 239
Medical services, 79-80
"Mentions," 113
Model releases, 219-220; sample, 220
Multiple sales, 138
Museum guidebooks, 24, 68

Name dropping, 100-101
Newsletters, travel, 145
Newspapers, 37; photographs, 221, 223; as research sources, 24-25; subject indexes, back issues, 35-36; supplements, 134; trip columns, 146
Notes, compiling, 125
Notetaking, 39-40, 88, 101, 114, 116, 118; at interviews, 201; and photography, 223

Off-season travel, 70-71
"Off-the-record," 204
One-time rights, 137, 221
Opening, article, 185-189
Outlines: queries, 173-174; selling, 138

Passports, 92, 247
Payment, 8-9, 47-48, 61, 138, 158; in copies, 20; foreign markets, 143; for photographs, 210, 221
People: local, 100-103; focus on, 246; in photographs, 217-218, 229
Periodicals, 37; local, 106; as research references, 24-25; subject indexes, 22, 40-41, 47
Permissions, in photography, 218-221; model releases, 218-220
Personality, and travel, 68-69
Photographs: black and white, 223-224, 226-227, 229; close-up, 211, 218; color, 223-224, 226; dated, 211; distance shots, 211; drop-ins, 214; juxtapositions, 213; payment for, 47; and queries, 160; reflections in, 216; silhouettes, 215; special events, 70; "stoppers," 213-214; taking, at interviews, 198

Photography, 209-232; reference material, 17-18
Picture sources, 230-232
Picture stories, 212
Place names, 100
Plus value, 8-10, 32, 114, 246-247
Postage costs, 89, 152
Praise, 113, 235
Press junkets, 113, 236, 241
Press release queries, 173
Pretrip queries, 172
Privacy, invasion of, 219-220
Processing, film, 224, 226
Progress reports, 177
Props, in photography, 214-215
Publications: government, 25-29; specialty, 22-23, 30-31
Public transportation, 99
Publishing industry, reference sources, 44-45

Qualifications, in queries, 156-157
Queries, 151-178; foreign markets, 143; keeping records of, 176; pretrip, 172; press release, 173; and taxes, 243; telephone, 169-170
Query letters, examples of, 134-135, 153, 155, 156, 157, 158, 159, 164, 165, 167, 168, 170, 171
Questionnaires, 126-130
Questions: asking strangers, 105-106; interview, 199-200, 203
Quotations, 39-40, 125, 126, 199-205

Reader, relationship with, 9-11, 18, 45, 46, 111-118, 125, 126, 130, 133, 181, 199-200, 203, 245-246
Reference books, 16-24, 37-38
Regional magazines, 134; as research sources, 24-25
Rejections, 163-164, 174-177
Rejection slips, 243, 248
Reprints, 138, 172
Research: amount, 168-169; and editors' suggestions, 154; and go-ahead, 176-177; importance of, 10; for interviews, 198-199; leftover, 135; live, 139; permissions, 71-72; pretrip, 12-25, 75; and queries, 157, 166-168; reusing, 137, 139, 141; sources, 121-130
Responsibility, 10, 235-236, 239-241, 245
Rewriting, 192
Rights: author's, 137; of interviewee, 205; photographer's 220-221; selling, 137-138
Roundups, 206-210

Sample copies, 45-46
Seasonal articles, 141
Seasonal travel, 70-71

Serializations, 138
Service, quality of, 112-113
Shooting scripts, 214
Show vs. tell, 191-192
Sidebars, 115-117, 190
Sight-seeing, 64-69, 88, 98-99, 105
Simultaneous submissions, 137-13 P
Slant, 181-182
Solo traveling, 65-66
Sources, verifications of, 167-168
Specificity, 9, 43, 127, 181, 199
Spinoffs, 140
Students: identifications, 73-74; travel, 20, 66-67
Style books, 16
Subject matter, 11; angles, 139; controversial, 199; offbeat, 133-134; vs. style, 166-167
Syndication, 138

Tape recorders, 87-88, 101, 114, 127, 200-202, 205
Tapes, mailing, 89
Taxes: deductions, 223, 241-243; and rejections, 175
Telephone: books, 22, 36; interviews, 205; proposals, 169-170; rates, 72
Timeliness, article, 166
Titles, article, 159, 194-195
Tour companies, 29-30
Tours, 68; English language, 24; kinds of, 66-68; town, 100; walking, 99-100; writers', 64-65
Transitions, 192-193
Translations, 138
Translators, 92, 106
Transparencies, 223-224, 227-229
Transportation, modes of, 99-100
Travel agents, 15, 63-64; manual for, 145-146
Travel companions, 65-66, 105
Traveler's checks, 73, 76-77
Travel industry, 10, 37, 247; trade journals, 61, 146
Travel literature, 90; mailing, 89
Travel markets, special, 145-146
Typewriters, 93

Universities, as research resource, 124
Updates, 140-141

Verification, of facts, 167-168
Viewpoint, article, 182-184
Visas, 92

Work for hire, 137
Writer's organizations, and freebies, 240-241

Yellow card, 79, 92

Photo Credits

The photographs in this book were converted to halftones using a mezzotint screen in order to create richer blacks and velvety tones. The mezzotint etching process of irregularly shaped dots was developed in seventeenth-century Holland primarily for the reproduction of paintings.

Page ii: courtesy Guam Visitors Bureau; page xiv: J.F. and L.P. Zobel; page 4: J.F. and L.P. Zobel; page 12: Michigan Travel Commission; page 32: Swiss National Tourist Office; page 42: German National Tourist Office; page 62: J.F. and L.P. Zobel; page 83: South African Tourist Corporation; page 84: Redwood Empire Association; page 96: South Carolina Department of Parks, Recreation, and Tourism; page 109: Malaysia Tourist Information Centre; page 110: British Tourist Authority; page 119: Swiss National Tourist Office; page 120: J.F. and L.P. Zobel; page 131: Canadian Government Office of Tourism; page 132: Las Vegas News Bureau; page 148: Heyward Associates, Incorporated; page 150: J.F. and L.P. Zobel; page 161: Tourism attaché in Los Angeles (Foreign Service of the Philippines); page 162: Illinois Department of Commerce and Community Affairs; page 179: Washington Area Convention and Visitors Bureau; page 180: Oklahoma Tourism and Recreation Department; page 196: J.F. and L.P. Zobel; page 208: Oklahoma City Convention and Tourism Center; page 233: New Mexico Travel Division; page 234: Greater Los Angeles Visitors and Convention Bureau; page 244: Michigan Travel Commission; page 250: Colorado State Division of Commerce and Development, Office of Tourism.

Postscript: Throughout this book I have used the pronoun *he* not to exclude women but to conform to rules of grammar.

—L.P.Z.